The Worlds of *Farscape*

CRITICAL EXPLORATIONS IN SCIENCE FICTION AND FANTASY
(a series edited by Donald E. Palumbo and C.W. Sullivan III)

1 *Worlds Apart? Dualism and Transgression in Contemporary Female Dystopias* (Dunja M. Mohr, 2005)

2 *Tolkien and Shakespeare: Essays on Shared Themes and Language* (ed. Janet Brennan Croft, 2007)

3 *Culture, Identities and Technology in the* Star Wars *Films: Essays on the Two Trilogies* (ed. Carl Silvio, Tony M. Vinci, 2007)

4 *The Influence of* Star Trek *on Television, Film and Culture* (ed. Lincoln Geraghty, 2008)

5 *Hugo Gernsback and the Century of Science Fiction* (Gary Westfahl, 2007)

6 *One Earth, One People: The Mythopoeic Fantasy Series of Ursula K. Le Guin, Lloyd Alexander, Madeleine L'Engle and Orson Scott Card* (Marek Oziewicz, 2008)

7 *The Evolution of Tolkien's Mythology: A Study of the History of Middle-earth* (Elizabeth A. Whittingham, 2008)

8 *H. Beam Piper: A Biography* (John F. Carr, 2008)

9 *Dreams and Nightmares: Science and Technology in Myth and Fiction* (Mordecai Roshwald, 2008)

10 Lilith *in a New Light: Essays on the George MacDonald Fantasy Novel* (ed. Lucas H. Harriman, 2008)

11 *Feminist Narrative and the Supernatural: The Function of Fantastic Devices in Seven Recent Novels* (Katherine J. Weese, 2008)

12 *The Science of Fiction and the Fiction of Science: Collected Essays on SF Storytelling and the Gnostic Imagination* (Frank McConnell, ed. Gary Westfahl, 2009)

13 *Kim Stanley Robinson Maps the Unimaginable: Critical Essays* (ed. William J. Burling, 2009)

14 *The Inter-Galactic Playground: A Critical Study of Children's and Teens' Science Fiction* (Farah Mendlesohn, 2009)

15 *Science Fiction from Québec: A Postcolonial Study* (Amy J. Ransom, 2009)

16 *Science Fiction and the Two Cultures: Essays on Bridging the Gap Between the Sciences and the Humanities* (ed. Gary Westfahl, George Slusser, 2009)

17 *Stephen R. Donaldson and the Modern Epic Vision: A Critical Study of the "Chronicles of Thomas Covenant" Novels* (Christine Barkley, 2009)

18 *Ursula K. Le Guin's Journey to Post-Feminism* (Amy M. Clarke, 2010)

19 *Portals of Power: Magical Agency and Transformation in Literary Fantasy* (Lori M. Campbell, 2010)

20 *The Animal Fable in Science Fiction and Fantasy* (Bruce Shaw, 2010)

21 *Illuminating* Torchwood: *Essays on Narrative, Character and Sexuality in the BBC Series* (ed. Andrew Ireland, 2010)

22 *Comics as a Nexus of Cultures: Essays on the Interplay of Media, Disciplines and International Perspectives* (ed. Mark Berninger, Jochen Ecke, Gideon Haberkorn, 2010)

23 *The Anatomy of Utopia: Narration, Estrangement and Ambiguity in More, Wells, Huxley and Clarke* (Károly Pintér, 2010)

24 *The Anticipation Novelists of 1950s French Science Fiction: Stepchildren of Voltaire* (Bradford Lyau, 2010)

25 *The* Twilight *Mystique: Critical Essays on the Novels and Films* (ed. Amy M. Clarke, Marijane Osborn, 2010)

26 *The Mythic Fantasy of Robert Holdstock: Critical Essays on the Fiction* (ed. Donald E. Morse, Kálmán Matolcsy, 2011)

27 *Science Fiction and the Prediction of the Future: Essays on Foresight and Fallacy* (ed. Gary Westfahl, Wong Kin Yuen, Amy Kit-sze Chan, 2011)

28 *Apocalypse in Australian Fiction and Film: A Critical Study* (Roslyn Weaver, 2011)

29 *British Science Fiction Film and Television: Critical Essays* (ed. Tobias Hochscherf, James Leggott, 2011)

30 *Cult Telefantasy Series: A Critical Analysis of* The Prisoner, Twin Peaks, The X-Files, Buffy the Vampire Slayer, Lost, Heroes, Doctor Who *and* Star Trek (Sue Short, 2011)

31 *The Postnational Fantasy: Essays on Postcolonialism, Cosmopolitics and Science Fiction* (ed. Masood Ashraf Raja, Jason W. Ellis and Swaralipi Nandi, 2011)

32 *Heinlein's Juvenile Novels: A Cultural Dictionary* (C.W. Sullivan III, 2011)

33 *Welsh Mythology and Folklore in Popular Culture: Essays on Adaptations in Literature, Film, Television and Digital Media* (ed. Audrey L. Becker and Kristin Noone, 2011)

34 *I See You: The Shifting Paradigms of James Cameron's* Avatar (Ellen Grabiner, 2012)

35 *Of Bread, Blood and* The Hunger Games: *Critical Essays on the Suzanne Collins Trilogy* (ed. Mary F. Pharr and Leisa A. Clark, 2012)

36 *The Sex Is Out of This World: Essays on the Carnal Side of Science Fiction* (ed. Sherry Ginn and Michael G. Cornelius, 2012)

37 *Lois McMaster Bujold: Essays on a Modern Master of Science Fiction and Fantasy* (ed. Janet Brennan Croft, 2013)

38 *Girls Transforming: Invisibility and Age-Shifting in Children's Fantasy Fiction Since the 1970s* (Sanna Lehtonen, 2013)

39 Doctor Who *in Time and Space: Essays on Themes, Characters, History and Fandom, 1963–2012* (ed. Gillian I. Leitch, 2013)

40 *The Worlds of* Farscape: *Essays on the Groundbreaking Television Series* (ed. Sherry Ginn, 2013)

The Worlds of *Farscape*

Essays on the Groundbreaking Television Series

Edited by SHERRY GINN

CRITICAL EXPLORATIONS IN SCIENCE FICTION AND FANTASY, 40
Donald E. Palumbo *and* C.W. Sullivan III, series editors

McFarland & Company, Inc., Publishers
Jefferson, North Carolina, and London

ALSO OF INTEREST AND FROM MCFARLAND
Power and Control in the Television Worlds of Joss Whedon (2012), by Sherry Ginn
The Sex Is Out of This World: Essays on the Carnal Side of Science Fiction (2012), edited by Sherry Ginn and Michael G. Cornelius

LIBRARY OF CONGRESS CATALOGUING-IN-PUBLICATION DATA

The worlds of Farscape : essays on the groundbreaking television series / edited by Sherry Ginn.
      p.   cm. — (Critical explorations in science fiction and fantasy ; 40)
[Donald E. Palumbo and C.W. Sullivan III, series editors]
Includes bibliographical references and index.

ISBN 978-0-7864-6790-7
softcover : acid free paper ∞

1. Farscape (Television program)   I. Ginn, Sherry, editor of compilation.
PN1992.77.F32W78 2013
791.45'72 — dc23   2013025861

BRITISH LIBRARY CATALOGUING DATA ARE AVAILABLE

© 2013 Sherry Ginn. All rights reserved

No part of this book may be reproduced or transmitted in any form or by any means, electronic or mechanical, including photocopying or recording, or by any information storage and retrieval system, without permission in writing from the publisher.

On the cover: Ben Browder as John Crichton and Claudia Black as Aeryn Sun in *Farscape* (SCI FI Channel/Photofest); background images Hemera/Thinkstock and iStockphoto/Thinkstock

Manufactured in the United States of America

McFarland & Company, Inc., Publishers
   Box 611, Jefferson, North Carolina 28640
   www.mcfarlandpub.com

This one is also for Larry
with all of my love

Table of Contents

Acknowledgments — xi

Introduction: Through the Wormhole and What Crichton Found There
   SHERRY GINN — 1

Farscape, the Impossible and the Accident
   J. P. TELOTTE — 11

War and Peace by Woody Allen or, How I Learned to Stop Worrying and Love the Wormhole Weapon
   ENSLEY F. GUFFEY — 22

Into the Uncharted Territories: Exploring the Nature of Evil
   ROBERT L. LIVELY — 40

The Emperor's New Farts: Socioeconomic Disenfranchisement and "Colonic Miasma"
   MICHAEL G. CORNELIUS — 55

'Scaping the Mythic Triad into Uncharted Territories: Hero, Antihero and Villain
   BILLIE JO MASON — 61

Friends, Enemies, Partners, Mates: Examining Relationships in the Uncharted Territories
   SHERRY GINN — 74

Joining the Conversation: Ben Browder Writes John Crichton
   JESSIE CARTY — 92

Friend ... Enemy ... Alien ... Ally: Female Community Aboard Moya
   SHERRY GINN — 104

Sentient Space: Moya as Homeplace
    MICHAEL G. CORNELIUS   123
Of Big Blue Butts and Bias: The Problem Body
    ELIZABETH LEIGH SCHERMAN   142
The Ballad of John and Aeryn
    SHERRY GINN   160
"Winona has been very reliable": Female Gendering of Weapons
    in Fiction and Fact
    ENSLEY F. GUFFEY   164
A Legendary Tale: Scapers and the Myth of Fan Power
    TANYA R. COCHRAN   168
Primal Scream — With Accompaniment
    JESSIE CARTY   185

Appendix A: Farscape *Character List*   191
Appendix B: Series Episode List   195
Appendix C: Farscape *Bibliography and Filmography*   199
About the Contributors   201
Index   203

Acknowledgments

I fell in love with *Farscape* from episode one, despite the atrocious theme song (thank heavens for a mute button). I know I presented a paper on the women of the series in 2002 (I can find that one still on my computer), but there were others prior to that time. An entire chapter (as well as parts of another) in my first book was devoted to *Farscape*. And I remember someone at a Popular Culture Association conference, or perhaps it was a PCA-South conference, telling me that she knew I would be talking about *Farscape*, which is why she had come to my presentation (she was right, I did). The idea of writing a book devoted to *Farscape* or editing a collection of essays on the series is something I thought about for quite some time and now it is finally happening, although I note that the publication of this book will coincide with the 10th anniversary of its last season (2003).

Despite its popularity among its core fan base and the myriad awards received by the cast and crew, *Farscape* was never able to realize the numbers needed to keep such an expensive program on air. Re-watching the series during the summer of 2012 brings the excitement and, I must admit, exasperation back. Taking notes on each episode of each season gave me dozens of ideas for more in-depth analysis. I am astounded at the lack of critical analysis of this series with its rich tapestry of characters who, although "alien," act all too human, serving as a lens through which to view the human condition. Is that not what the best science fiction does?

My thanks to everyone who submitted a proposal and who then prepared their essays for this collection. I also thank all of those people who discussed *Farscape* with me for the last dozen years or so as well as those who discussed the project with me over the course of the last couple of years. Special thanks to Donald E. Palumbo for being enthusiastic about a *Farscape* collection, even though the series has been off the air since 2003 (at least for first-run episodes). I also would like to extend warm thanks to Tanya R. Cochran, Michael G. Cornelius, and Jessie Carty for editorial help with various essays in the book. Unlike Noranti, I do not have a third eye and the sharp eyes of those three really helped me when I was second-guessing myself.

Rockne S. O'Bannon, David Kemper, and Brian Henson have tried to keep *Farscape* alive via the graphic novels, and I hope that they will be able to continue that endeavor (although the news is not good at this point in time). The cast and crew of *Farscape* were phenomenal and I continue to look out for projects in which Ben Browder (he is from my hometown, you know, and I keep searching my memory to determine if we've ever met) and the others engage. I have a conference in Australia in 2013 and am looking forward to visiting all of the locations used in filming the series while there.

This book is dedicated once again to my husband and partner, Larry Williamson. Words cannot express how I feel about this man or how grateful I am for all of his support. As I have said before, thanks for being my rock, for always being there. And thanks for not being too jealous of Crichton.

Introduction
Through the Wormhole and What Crichton Found There

SHERRY GINN

TV Guide called *Farscape* the best science fiction show (then) on the air and ranked it #4 on its list of "The 30 Top Cult Shows Ever." During its four-year run, it won three Saturn awards for "Best Syndicated/Cable Television Series" (in 2001, 2002, and 2003). Nominated four times for "Best Actor in a Television Series," Ben Browder (John Crichton) won the award in 2002, and its male and female actors garnered numerous "best" nominations during the series run. Produced by Jim Henson Productions and Hallmark Entertainment, *Farscape* combined human actors with puppets and spectacular visual effects in a storyline that combined action-adventure and romance and broke many of the so-called conventional rules of science fiction. This action-adventure-romance combination ensured that it would find both male and female fan support. Unlike the majority of science fiction programming, which is filmed in Hollywood, British Columbia, or the United Kingdom, *Farscape* was filmed in Australia. The two stars of the series, Ben Browder and Claudia Black, were American and Australian, respectively; and, the majority of the cast members were Australian or New Zealander as was much of the crew. By the end of the series, seven of the major characters were female—eight if you count the ship—and the majority of the production crew was also female (Kemper). The series aired in the U.S. on the Sci Fi Channel (now Syfy) from 1999 to 2003. The channel's decision to cancel the series at the end of its fourth season sent shock waves throughout the kingdom of Scapers, as fans are known. That intense campaign has achieved almost mythic status and is generally believed to have "forced" executives at the network to order a made-for-television miniseries entitled *Farscape: The Peacekeeper Wars* which premiered October 2004 (see Cochran, this collection).

Farscape broke many of the conventions of series television, such as filming on location in Australia using Australian actors and crew. Unknown in America many of these actors were very well known in Australia and New Zealand and cast and crew members reported their immense delight at the quality of the people who guest-starred on the series as well as those who wrote or directed episodes.[1] Aliens on the series were presented as just that — alien. However, as Booker points out, *Farscape* is very much like *Stargate SG1* as

> the discovery of the Stargate [and, on *Farscape*, the wormhole] allows contemporary humans (rather than humans of some distant future) to interact with advanced technology, making it easier for audiences to identify with the protagonists of the series. In addition, the fact that the characters ... come from the same cultural background as the audience facilitates the allusiveness of the series, which constantly refers to other works of 20th-century popular culture [178].

Indeed, the character John Crichton maintains a steady stream of pop culture references, which serve to link him to the home to which he desperately wishes to return, but which also serve to distinguish him from the beings that he now confronts on a daily basis. John Crichton is, after all, meant to serve as "us" — the audience. That is, Crichton serves as the window through which we observe the wonders and dangers of the universe beyond Earth and even on Earth as well. Ben Browder comments that Crichton is the proxy for the audience. According to Browder, Crichton "is actually a sci-fi geek. He is that generation that watched *Star Trek* and then wanted to be an astronaut."[2] However, as Jes Battis has noted, Crichton cannot be considered as representative of the audience. The audience is not white, male, middle-class, highly-educated, able-bodied, and heterosexual (*Investigating* 24–25).

Crichton is Alien to the beings that inhabit the section of the universe in which he is marooned; however, I contend that the other members of Moya's crew can also be considered alien (Ginn "Exploring"). Crichton's "humanness" and his penchant for spouting pop culture references make him stand out as alien; his crewmates aboard Moya are alien by virtue of the characteristics of their species as well as their actions prior to the events occurring on *Farscape*. For example, Zhaan is an anarchist and a murderer, whereas her species is spiritual and peaceful. D'Argo was accused of murdering his wife, and if he was not guilty of that offense, he was guilty to styling himself "Ka" or general in the Luxan army. Rygel is a deposed emperor, and his disgusting personal habits as well as his repulsive personality make one wonder if perhaps his subjects are not better off now that he is no longer on the throne. *Farscape*'s producers were determined that these species be as "alien" as possible and used various means for depicting those differences, not simply relying upon make-up or prosthetics. Given that the Jim Henson Company, famously known as the creators of the Muppets, helped produce *Farscape*, their contribution to the series was the creation of two of its major characters, Dominar

Rygel XVI and Pilot, as well as myriad other characters over the series' four-year run. Jan Johnson-Smith speculates that the use of

> animatronics/Muppets in a central role suggests a youngish audience for the series, but the frequent and blatant sexuality of its often-complex physics and grim narrative and a tendency to bondage/torture scenes suggests otherwise [161].

I contend that the "animatronics/Muppets" are a bridge to people who grew up watching *Sesame Street* and *The Muppet Show* and are aware of the production values of The Henson Company. But these people are now adults and the other aspects of the series mentioned by Johnson-Smith attract adult viewers. I would also argue that the series is not nearly as sexual as one might think (see my essay on relationships, this collection).

Production values on the series were so high that it was never apparent that these creatures were not humans in monster suits or CGI. *Farscape*'s aliens also deviated from the standard set by Gene Roddenberry of *Star Trek* fame, who had insisted all of his aliens be humanoid. Indeed, Executive Producer Brian Henson wanted a show that was primal and emotional, something that would provide a vision opposite to *Star Trek*.[3] Henson knew that he wanted something different, high-brow and literary, something special,[4] and several of the alien species encountered in *Farscape* were decidedly not humanoid (for example, the Scarrans and the Hynerians). The series was also very "female-friendly" with a large number of women both on and behind the screen (Kemper). Female characters of whatever species could engage in roles that were traditionally masculine, traditionally feminine, or neither (Battis "Farscape"; Ginn *Our Space*; Jowett). They could hold positions of power and authority in their worlds and frequently did. They could also be evil and dangerous and often were. And they were freely sexual.

Like *Babylon 5*, *Farscape*'s writers and producers conceived of multi-episode storylines with the major story arcs spanning the entire run of the series. The series' writers presented the characters' stories in a variety of ways, including flashforwards, flashbacks, time travel, dimensional shifts, differing points of view, all with a tongue-in-cheek satiric panache. Popular culture references were liberally scattered throughout the dialogue. This served to situate the main character, Commander John Crichton, as a human being with whom the audience could identify as well as contrast him with the beings he met. Whereas most science fiction series situate humans as the norm with some non-human being as the "other" to examine humanity through the lens of otherness (for example, Spock in *Star Trek*, Data in *Star Trek: The Next Generation*), *Farscape* situated the human as the other. An astronaut who was a theoretical physicist John Crichton was presented as a man lost, a man who did not have all of the answers, and a decidedly non-macho male, who nonetheless could be considered a hero on a quest (à la Joseph Campbell) as could the major female character, Officer Aeryn Sun. With several plot diversions along the way, series creator Rockne S. O'Bannon and Executive Producers David Kemper and Brian Henson conceived of the love story between the major characters from the beginning and allowed it to proceed, to its logical conclusion. However, they were not averse to letting the characters argue, fight, and part when necessary. The writers were also not averse to killing off major characters when the need arose, doing so several times over the course of the series.

Through the Wormhole

Astronaut John Crichton is a physicist who has developed a theory that involves "skipping" off the Earth's atmosphere as a means to counter Earth's gravity when launching vessels into space. On the day that he tests his theory, his module *Farscape 1* is propelled through a wormhole and shot through space. He exits the wormhole in the midst of a battle between a Peacekeeper (PK) battalion and a biomechanoid living ship of a species called Leviathan. The Leviathan ship, whose name is Moya, was herself a prisoner of the Peacekeepers. She is attempting to escape, crewed by three other prisoners: a Luxan warrior named Ka D'Argo, a Delvian priest named Pa'u Zotoh Zhaan, and the deposed Hynerian emperor, Dominar Rygel XVI.

The Peacekeepers are trying to recapture Moya and the escaped prisoners. Crichton's ship accidentally hits a PK prowler, killing the pilot, the brother of Captain Bialar Crais. Moya evades recapture using Crichton's theory to aid in "starbursting," a propulsion technique whereby the ship can jump across vast distances of space. Moya cannot starburst on her own because she wears a "control collar," a device used to pacify her and prevent escape. Officer Aeryn Sun is part of the prowler patrol attempting to recapture Moya. As Moya starbursts, Aeryn's prowler is sucked into the wake and she travels with the ship to its next destination. Crais vows revenge on Crichton and the first season revolves around the crew's attempts to escape from Crais and the bounty hunters who seek the reward Crais has offered for their recapture.

Crais will be a recurring character throughout three seasons of *Farscape*. The first season finds him disobeying orders and pursuing Crichton, even into the Uncharted Territories. Crais is determined to kill Crichton and avenge his brother's death. Eventually Crais will realize that the death was accidental, and he will become an unlikely ally for Crichton as Crichton attempts to elude the Sebacean-Scarran hybrid Scorpius, who is determined to acquire Crichton's knowledge of wormholes. Crais will "bond" with the hybrid spaceship Talyn, Moya's offspring, and together they will sacrifice themselves in an unsuccessful attempt to kill Scorpius ("Into the Lion's Den Part II: Wolf in Sheep's Clothing" 3.21).

Aeryn's capture by the crew of Moya leads to her irreversible contamination, the Peacekeeper's term for any Peacekeeper that comes in to too close contact with alien species: the penalty is exile or death, and most choose death. Aeryn however joins Moya's crew; we will learn that she is no ordinary Peacekeeper. The crew experiences many adventures, many life threatening, all dangerous. As noted, Season One episodes revolve around Moya's crew trying to protect Crichton from Captain Crais, who wishes to avenge his brother's death. Not completely selfless, the other crew members wish to evade recapture and return to their homes one day.

Although Moya's crew is bound together by their desire to escape the Peacekeepers and return home, they grow into a "family" over the course of the first season. Refreshingly this family contains no patriarch or matriarch, although Carlen Lavigne points out that Moya could be considered a mother figure, given that all of Moya's crew are reliant upon her home space, and Pilot, who controls Moya's functions, could be considered a father. There was some jockeying for position as Moya's captain following the escape and for some time afterwards, nevertheless each character brings his or her own strengths to the family. Decisions are made by consensus; however, during the first season decisions are always made in the interests of the child.

One of the most unique plotlines during the first season revolves around the ship's pregnancy, certainly the first time of which I am aware that a space ship bred. As noted, Leviathans are physically bonded to a pilot, who controls their internal functions and provides navigation, nevertheless they can breed. Moya, we learn, was part of a Peacekeeper experiment designed to create a hybrid, a Leviathan warship. Named Talyn after Aeryn's father, the hybrid ship is male and covered with weaponry. However, Talyn becomes increasingly unstable, eventually going insane. Talyn does not need a pilot since he is a hybrid; however, he does need a corporeal being to provide control functions and navigation, which a pilot would normally provide to a Leviathan. Talyn temporarily bonds with Aeryn, but is consumed with jealousy over her feelings for Crichton. Aeryn rejects Talyn after Talyn tries to kill Crichton. Crais and Talyn bond and leave the others to find their own destiny; however, they eventually return to Moya and sacrifice themselves to save Crichton and company.

At the end of Season One, Aeryn is badly wounded and needs treatment. Specifically she needs a graft of a piece of nerve tissue from a genetically compatible donor. Such a donor would probably be available only on a Gammak base, a top-secret military installation, which just happens to be close to their location. Obviously the crew would like to avoid such a base, since they are all wanted by the Peacekeepers for various reasons. But by this point in time,

Crichton is falling in love with Aeryn and will risk everything to find help for her. Scorpius, a half–Scarran, half–Sebacean hybrid, captures Crichton. Scorpius has developed a device that allows him to extract memories from neural tissue. Scorpius places Crichton in his Aurora chair and learns that Crichton possesses wormhole knowledge. Crichton escapes from Scorpius, but Seasons Two and Three revolve around Scorpius' quest to recapture Crichton and steal the wormhole knowledge from Crichton's brain. Scorpius uses a variety of techniques to steal that knowledge, even creating a clone of himself and implanting it into Crichton's brain. These tactics will cause Crichton to go mad slowly, so slowly that no one notices. Season Four shows Crichton and crew fighting back against those who would use the wormhole knowledge as a bargaining tool and a weapon; Crichton lets all know that he will detonate such a weapon of mass destruction in order to save his friends and family.

Scorpius is the result of the Scarran rape of a Sebacean woman (Peacekeeper is their job, their species is Sebacean — genetically similar to human). Scorpius wants the wormhole technology implanted in Crichton's brain by the Ancients so that he can exact revenge on the Scarrans for their rape of his mother, and hence his own birth, as well as their torture of him after birth. Crichton and crew realize that if Scorpius obtains the wormhole technology then he (and the Peacekeepers) will have a weapon of mass destruction and be able to rule the universe, eventually finding their way to Earth. Each member of Moya's crew, including Crichton, has one major goal and that is to return home, right old wrongs, and find peace. Crichton wants to return to Earth, and he wants to take Aeryn with him. Along the way, he will be forced to ally himself with Scorpius as he learns of Scorpius' desire to destroy the Scarrans.

As mentioned previously, John Crichton is meant to serve as "us"— the audience; he serves as the window through which we observe the wonders and dangers of the universe beyond Earth and even upon Earth as well. Yes, Crichton is truly an Alien in the part of the universe where he finds himself after his journey through the wormhole, and as Telotte notes, "that circumstance repeatedly motivates a fundamental examination of just what it means to be human" (26). No one in "known" space or in the Uncharted Territories has ever encountered *Homo sapiens* before. Crichton looks like a member of a species called Sebacean; however, it is quickly established that he cannot be Sebacean because his body contains bacteria unknown in this part of the universe. Moya's fellow prisoners are surprised when they discover that he does not have internal translator microbes, which are injected into all beings at birth in this part of space ("Premiere" 1.1). Imagine Crichton's problem: He looks like a member of a militaristic police force that frightens most beings to which it comes into contact. Hence Crichton is scary by virtue of his looks; to humans, he is a very attractive man. As he tries to survive in a hostile environment, he becomes increasingly hard and bitter, gradually descending into madness as the Scorpius clone worms its way into his psyche. He becomes increasingly dangerous to the alien species to which he comes in contact, and he earns — deservedly or not — a reputation for death and destruction, until finally he is willing to destroy everything in order to protect his friends, his lover and their child, and the knowledge of the location of Earth.

Beyond the Wormhole[5]

The *Farscape* Universe — Peacekeeper-controlled space, the Uncharted Territories, Tormented Space — we journeyed to and through them all, with Crichton and crew. Along the way we were thrilled and chilled, gladdened and saddened, furious and frantic, often at the same time, in the same episode. Executive Producer David Kemper's statement "On this show, I want to be afraid. I need to be unsettled"[6] was as true of the viewer as it was of those in charge of production. As one of the few people who has written about Farscape, Jes Battis notes that the series is considered "cult" because the fans "truly admit to loving [the] program" ("Transgressive" 78). And, if the 2012 Dragon*Con can serve as an illustration then Scapers do love the program still and are, at the very least, an enthusiastic and loyal group of people who miss it.

I for one do miss *Farscape* very much and am greatly surprised at the lack of critical attention and scholarship on the series. Hence, this collection, the purpose of which is to celebrate the series and examine concepts, characters, and themes that have not been studied previously. The collection, although not specifically divided this way, first presents essays that examine themes running throughout the series. Secondly, several characters from the series are discussed in detail. Several of the authors also contributed brief notes designed to discuss an aspect of the series that was particularly worthy of notice albeit in more concise form than usually found in a traditional academic essay. These essays, what I term inter-chapters, also address characters or themes of the series.

J. P. Telotte, who has written and presented on *Farscape* in other collections, here talks about the series in terms of its "accidental" origins and how the series resonates with its audience, many of whom discovered the series by accident. Ensley F. Guffey discusses how the Peacekeeper-Scarran conflict provides a mirror for examining the policies and rhetoric of the Cold War between the U.S. and the U.S.S.R. from the end of World War II until the fall of the Soviet Union. Robert L. Lively examines that same conflict, as well as various characters, through the lens of the Wisdom Tradition, which proposes that evil is the result of a lack of self-identity and self-knowledge.

Michael G. Cornelius, in his inter-chapter, shows that Dominar Rygel's tendency to fart when anxious and afraid serves to humanize him — which is especially important given that Rygel is a puppet with a half dozen or so people providing mobility, animation, vocals and more — to the other sentients traveling on Moya, noting that this biological process actually removes some of the mystique of his royal status and makes him no better — or worse — than anyone else aboard Moya. Billie Jo Mason follows Crichton, Crais and Scorpius on their mythic journey, à la Joseph Campbell, noting that each character vacillates between being a hero, an anti-hero, and a villain (yes, even Crichton). I examine the various emotional and sexual relationships that occur on the series, doing so through the lenses of the Triangular Theory of Love and the principles of evolutionary psychology. Poet Jessie Carty studies Ben Browder's foray into the writer's room via the two episodes he wrote for the series. Another of my essays describes the female characters of the series and how the six women who reside upon Moya over the course of the four seasons (Aeryn, Zhaan, Chiana, Jool, Noranti, and Sikozu) create a community, learning that they can rely upon each other to do what is necessary to survive. Michael G. Cornelius explores the living ship Moya's status as both a sentient being and a home place/space where other sentient beings reside. Elizabeth Leigh Scherman's essay examines the nature of disability and its presentation on *Farscape*, especially ways in which the series subverts the very idea of the concept through its presentation of characters such as Noranti and Traltixx, as well as how even Crichton can be considered as disabled in this part of the galaxy. In my inter-chapter I propose a theory of why it took Aeryn Sun so long to admit her feelings for John Crichton and begin a true relationship with him. Ensley F. Guffey discusses the tendency of male characters in historical fact as well as various fictional works to give their weapons female names in his inter-chapter. In the final full-length essay Tanya R. Cochran investigates the myth of the Scapers and their attempts to save *Farscape* from cancellation. The collection ends with Jessie Carty's application of a poet's perspective to the opening credits' voice-overs occurring throughout the series.

As Battis noted in his full-length examination of *Farscape*, there are myriad other analyses that need to be made with respect to this award-winning and ground-breaking series. Perhaps this collection will ignite a spark. I do so hope that the next treatment of the series will not be so long in coming.

Notes

1. Commentary by Rockne S. O'Bannon for the first season episode "Thank God It's Friday ... Again." In this commentary O'Bannon discusses the excitement of having Rowan Woods direct for *Farscape* as Woods is a very famous director in Australia.
2. Comment by Ben Browder, "SyFy Twentieth Anniversary Special," Broadcast on 10

December 2012. The section on *Farscape* occurs at about the twentieth minute into the two-hour special.

3. "In the Beginning: A Look Back with Brian Henson," Special Feature, *Farscape* Season One DVD. See Appendix C for a complete citation.

4. Comment by Brain Henson, "SyFy Twentieth Anniversary Special," Broadcast on 10 December 2012.

5. I have included a List of Characters and an Episode List in Appendices A and B, respectively. *Farscape*'s writers and producers created a lexicon of colorful phrases, character and place names, and so on for use in the series. I have not included those here. The companion guides (see Appendix C) as well as Jes Battis' book on *Farscape* (see below) can be consulted for those terms.

6. Interview with David Kemper, *Farscape: The Official Magazine*, number 2 (Sept./Oct. 2001).

Works Cited

Battis, Jes. "*Farscape*." *The Essential Cult TV Reader*. Ed. David Lavery. Louisville: University Press of Kentucky, 2010. 104–110. Print.

_____. *Investigating Farscape: Uncharted Territories of Sex and Science Fiction*. London: I. B. Tauris, 2007. Print.

_____. "Transgressive TV." *The Cult TV Book: From Star Trek to Dexter, New Approaches to TV Outside the Box*. Ed. Stacey Abbot. New York: Soft Skull Press, 2010. 77–83. Print.

Booker, M. Keith. *Science Fiction Television*. Westport, CT: Praeger, 2004. Print.

Campbell, Joseph. *The Hero with a Thousand Faces*, 3d ed. Novato: New World Library, 2008. Print.

Ginn, Sherry. "Exploring the Alien Other on *Farscape*: Human, Puppet, Costume, Cosmetic." *The Wider Worlds of Jim Henson: Essays on His Work and Legacy Beyond The Muppet Show and Sesame Street*. Eds. Jennifer C. Garlen and Anissa M. Graham. Jefferson, N.C.: McFarland, 2013. 228–240. Print.

_____. *Our Space, Our Place: Women in the Worlds of Science Fiction Television*. Lanham, MD: University Press of America, 2005. Print.

Johnson-Smith, Jan. *American Science Fiction TV: Star Trek, Stargate and Beyond*. Middletown, CT: Wesleyan University Press, 2005. Print.

Jowett, Lorna. "Representation: Exploring Issues of Sex, Gender, and Race in Cult Television." *The Cult TV Book: From Star Trek to Dexter, New Approaches to TV Outside the Box*. Ed. Stacey Abbot. New York: Soft Skull Press, 2010. 107–113. Print.

Kemper, David. "Ladies Rule!!!" *Farscape: The Official Magazine* 4 (Jan./Feb. 2002): 63–66. Print.

Lavigne, Carlen. "Space Opera: Melodrama, Feminism, and The Women of *Farscape*." *Femspec* 6.2 (2005): 54–64. Print.

Telotte, J. P. *The Essential Science Fiction Television Reader*. Lexington: University of Kentucky Press, 2008. Print.

"*TV Guide* Names the Top Cult Shows Ever." *TV Guide* 29 June 2007. Web. 23 May 2008.

Farscape, the Impossible and the Accident

J. P. TELOTTE

In an effort to explain the cult appeal of the science fiction series *Farscape*, Jes Battis opts for pointing to what he sees as its very "impossible" nature, as a show "too strange and vast to conceive of, too weird and idiosyncratic to make, and too outrageously wonderful to be canceled" ("*Farscape*" 104). Of course, we have to acknowledge that the series *was conceived* by Rockne O'Bannon and Brian Henson, *made*, at least for four years, and then, lamentably, *canceled*. But noting such obstinate facts avoids actually confronting the show's rather slippery status, its "too"-ness at which Battis points, and that, I would suggest, is paradoxically responsible for both its demise as a broadcast series and its continuing existence as a cult text. I would like to qualify that "impossible" description of *Farscape* from the vantage of what might seem like an equally difficult or dodgy descriptive turn of phrase, the *accident*, for I believe that vantage will allow us to better understand the series' appeal, while also framing *Farscape* as a particularly revealing example of how all effective cult texts function.

Rather than an "impossible" event, then, we might think of *Farscape* as a series that, in its conception, found its core narrative trajectory, and, in the course of its production and then its cancellation, gained much of its cult status from what might simply be described as an accident. The show recounts how astronaut John Crichton encounters and is sucked through a wormhole in space, and then finds himself, as he announces at the start of each episode (with slight variations over the course of the series' four full seasons), "lost in some distant part of the universe on a ship, a living ship, full of strange alien life forms." It is a compelling situation, one that not only offers almost infinite possibilities for the sort of adventures, discoveries, and dramatic encounters that drive much science fiction programming, but also establishes an urgent desire for communication and interaction, as he adds, "is there anybody out there who can hear me" and "help?" At the same time, this circumstance opens new models for self-discovery, for encounters with a suddenly estranged self. For Crichton, unlike the heroes of most science fiction narratives, here finds himself to be the alien creature, a homeless being who must constantly try to make a place for himself in what are described as the "Uncharted Territories" of the universe, even as he holds out a slim hope for reversing his course; for as he also episodically laments, he continues to be "just looking for a way home."

Of course, accidents are often integral to cult works, on television or in any other medium. As history shows, cult texts are not simply created by design, by following some tried generic formula. Rather, an element of chance, of the seemingly impossible, of the accidental — a working against the formulaic grain or against our expectations — often seems to underlie the connection of audience to text. For a television series and its audience, it may simply be a case of pushing the wrong buttons, thus accidentally landing the viewer — much like John Crichton — on an unexpected channel where he or she encounters equally unexpected yet intriguing "life forms." Perhaps the accident is one of surprise, at becoming comfortable and immersing oneself in what seems a very simple entertainment, a distraction from the everyday, only to find a voice there that speaks with an amazing eloquence or in a tone the viewer recognizes, suggesting that there are others "out there" who also speak the language of alien-ation — or of truth. Or it might be a case of a chance scene, line of dialogue, or a single image that evokes a better time or place, that accidentally signals, even if only momentarily, what we might think of as "a way home." What I want to suggest — and as I think those opening lines especially hint — is *Farscape* had from its very inception a fortuitous congruence between such cultish possibilities and parts of its narrative. Certainly, and rather paradoxically, its *formulaic* opening always forecast for viewers a *non-formulaic* potential: the sort of accidental situations, encounters, or paths that the best cult works consistently offer.

I base this notion of the cult-as-accident — of the accidental *discovery*, accidental *communication*, and accidental *path*—largely on the work of the cultural critics Paul Virilio and Sylvere Lotringer. Describing the sort of accidents that seem increasingly prevalent throughout our modern technological and thoroughly media-informed culture, one that is always speeding headlong into the future while disregarding the possible consequences of its speed (including surprise wormholes), they allow that accidents are simply inevitable, if often covered up or recast by the media as something else, something more familiar and less troubling. But they also argue that there is an important economy built into them, a payoff that accompanies any sense of failure or, in the case of a television series, one that never manages to reach a huge viewership. As they say, ultimately "the accident is positive" because "it reveals something important that we would not otherwise be able to perceive," in fact, "something absolutely necessary to knowledge" (63), perhaps even to our survival. Yet the payoff differs from one type of accident to another. For whereas an industrial accident, if properly reported and understood, might help us to avoid some catastrophic failure in the future, might keep us from repeating the same "mistake," an aesthetic "accident" like a television series or film could well prime us to replicate the same experience, that is, to engage in cult-like behavior that fulfills another sort of need. It might well enable us, like Crichton, to find our way in those "Uncharted Territories" of life and so discover "a way home"—which, I would offer, is the real payoff of the cult experience.

What I want to consider here, by way of helping us to understand this notion of cult status, is how a series like *Farscape* profitably evokes this sense of the accident. In some ways it is, after all, highly conventional, generically recalling the popular tradition of the space opera which, with its interplanetary settings, heroic figures, adventurous actions, and melodramatic situations, dominated the early and far-from-sophisticated science fiction television programming of the 1950s, typified by shows like *Captain Video* (1949–55), *Space Patrol* (1950–55), and *Tom Corbet, Space Cadet* (1950–55).[1] The trappings of that form, further developed and explored in series like *Star Trek* (1966–69), *Blake's 7* (1978–81), and *Buck Rogers in the 25th Century* (1979–81), have certainly become familiar and even predictable. However, *Farscape* also has much of the unconventional and unpredictable about it, as if it were seeking to overturn or "accident" our very expectations of the form. Its use of creations from Jim Henson's Creature Shop (notably Dominar Rygel XVI and Pilot); its elaborate visual effects, combining computer-generated imagery with its sophisticated puppetry; its creation of a *living* space ship, Moya, as a kind of central character (who, in the first season, even becomes pregnant and gives birth to a sentient warship); its repeated focus on — and depiction of— various alien sexual practices, seen especially with the characters D'Argo and Chiana; its emphasis on strong, even dominant female characters, like the Peacekeeper Aeryn Sun; and, its inversion of a key feature of most science fiction narratives, as the human finds himself the sole representative of his kind, surrounded by a bewildering array of other species, and thus the real alien here — these are all signature elements of the series and attractions that readily signal its difference from our normal experience of the space opera, as well as of most other science fiction television programming. While any one of these differences might well be enough to lure a cult audience, I would suggest that no one of them would satisfactorily explain the extent of *Farscape*'s following, one that would lead a mainstream publication like *TV Guide* to proclaim it in 2007 the fourth best "cult show ever."[2]

At least one element of the accident, though, does help to suggest the larger appeal of *Farscape* and begin to justify that cult attribution. It is the sense of what I have termed *accidental discovery* that operates on multiple levels here and parallels John Crichton's own sense of surprise at his situation. In his book-length analysis of the series, Jes Battis nicely captures some of this element of surprise, as he describes his own chance discovery of and original reaction to the show, particularly how he had encountered bits and pieces of the series, all of which initially struck him as "confusing and irredeemably silly" (*Investigating* Farscape 21). However, they also gradually drew his attention and led him to realize that what first bothered him was part of *Farscape*'s rather "innovative" approach to both televisual and science fiction narrative — its emphasis on multiple characters and multiple points of view, resulting in lines of action and of dialogue that reach across episodes and story arcs to gradually unfold in significance as viewers encountered additional characters and began to recognize and appreciate their complex relationships. Thus, while the "lost" astronaut — and only human in this mix — Crichton effectively represents the audience in the narrative, his point of view never dominates the narrative, and his sense of what is right or wrong never stands — for long — as the only rule. Rather, he, like the audience, is repeatedly surprised by new information, his perspective qualified by others as the larger narrative gradually unfolds. Thus, his comment to the rest of Moya's crew in the opening episode, "What is *wrong* with you people?," quickly forecasts what is "wrong" with him, as subsequent episodes underscore: that he is too troubled by difference, too quick to form judgments about situations in these "Uncharted Territories," too ready to see things only from his conventional, Earth-centric vantage, a vantage invariably challenged as episode builds upon episode to unveil a complex universe.

And certainly, the great variety of "strange alien life forms" that Crichton encounters on Moya and in the course of his efforts at trying to find "a way home" constantly underscores that sense of difference, while also challenging his — and our — conventional values. For not only is Crichton always encountering new species, both attractive to him (such as the Sebacean Aeryn or the Interion Jool) and repellant (most obviously the Sebacean-Scarran hybrid Scorpius), but he repeatedly finds his own secure identity radically challenged by these encounters. At the start of the episode "Out of Their Minds" (2.9), for example, Moya absorbs a blast from a Halosian ship that jolts the crew and, to their surprise and irritation, shifts their personalities into other bodies, so that Rygel's consciousness is transferred to Crichton's body, Aeryn's to Rygel's, Crichton's to Aeryn's, D'Argo's to Pilot's, Pilot's to Chiana's, and Chiana's to D'Argo's. The result is that each must, for a time, walk in another's shoes, live in another's body — and consequently, come to a better, if also somewhat uncomfortable, appreciation of their differences. An even more telling instance of this sort of challenge to subjectivity occurs in "My Three

Crichtons" (2.13) in which an alien probe strikes Moya, engulfs Crichton, and produces two genetic copies of him; one is an evolved version with advanced mental capabilities, and the other a prehistoric version with heightened sensory capacities. Even as members of the crew find themselves more attuned to one or the other versions of Crichton — causing him to wonder about his own acceptance in the group — John must come to recognize that both versions are, as he says, part of "what I am." And when confronted with the cold, unfeeling logic of his evolved self — a self willing to sacrifice either the throwback or the original Crichton to save himself and the ship — he ends the episode worried about what this "one possible genetic path," as D'Argo puts it, might mean for the future of humanity. It is a worry that speaks well of him and that, along with the less-evolved Crichton's willingness to sacrifice himself for the group, helps demonstrate to the others what humans are (or should be) really like — emotional, caring, even self-sacrificing.

Such accidental encounters with the alien other, even the alien *self*, and with difference thus consistently create challenging mirrors, both for Crichton and for the other members of Moya's crew. In another early episode that details an accidental replication of the crew members (this is, tellingly, a recurrent theme), "Exodus from Genesis" (1.3), the Delvian priest Zhaan sees Rygel painting a portrait of himself and, curious at the rather crude image he has produced, asks, "Is that how you see yourself?" Later, she redoes his "artwork," producing what she terms a "spirit painting," that is, a portrait that captures the true spirit of a person. In this case, it underscores a resemblance between Rygel and one of the most revered leaders of the Hynerian people, his ancestor Rygel the Great. More than just a kindness, Zhaan's effort provides an ideal for which Rygel might aim, while it also points up the series' ongoing effort at bringing characters more in line with their best possibilities, allowing them to grow. Through their encounters with difference, with other species and other characters who have dissimilar desires and motivations, the crew of Moya — themselves already accidentally thrown together in their efforts at escaping the Peacekeepers — are constantly challenged to consider how they see themselves, how others see them, and how they might, in effect, "touch up" their own images.

Another key cult feature of the series and of Crichton's character is a persistent media and cultural self-consciousness, as the show repeatedly refers to films, other television series, key events in American cultural history, and a broad array of pop culture icons, ranging from Albert Einstein to Marilyn Monroe and Ronald Reagan. In weaving this sort of web of cultural referentiality, the show effectively establishes a line of communication with an audience already situated in and saturated by such material, offering them an unusual perspective — for science fiction television — on the series' plot events, a sense of *accidental communication*. In such situations it is as if we had suddenly stumbled onto an unexpected dimension of the scene. As an example, we might consider the "Kansas" episode (4.12) wherein the hard-edged Peacekeeper warrior Aeryn sits down in front of an Earth television and, trying to learn the English alphabet, intently begins watching *Sesame Street*, which is, of course, populated by muppets produced by Jim Henson's Creature Workshop, like *Farscape*'s central characters Rygel and Pilot. And in the miniseries that concluded *Farscape*'s run, *The Peacekeeper Wars* (2004), a dream sequence offers a nearly shot-by-shot homage to the ending of *2001: A Space Odyssey* (1968) that not only serves to send up some of that film's ponderous seriousness, but also aligns the series' often-suggested concern with human development, even evolution (as noted in "My Three Crichtons"), with the larger science fiction tradition of such development. Such knowing references are a consistent source of humor in the series, help to establish its rather mixed tone, and point up its characteristic pop culture mode of address, even as they also point to the possibility of more serious intentions here.

In fact, those self-conscious references create the context for a more significant dimension of that address, another level of *communication* that we consistently encounter in Crichton's own peculiar dialogue. For it too is full of references to contemporary popular culture, especially movies and television, as we see when Crichton repeatedly refers to his nemesis Scorpius as "Harvey," after the character of the imaginary rabbit in the film *Harvey* (1950); when faced with the odd variety of life on Moya he observes, "Boy, was Spielberg ever wrong; *Close Encounters* my ass" ("Premiere" 1.1); or when he peppers his conversations with mentions of Cameron Diaz, Yuri Gagarin, *E.T.: The Extraterrestrial, Dr. Strangelove, Buffy the Vampire Slayer, Star Trek, The Wizard of Oz*, and even the poem "Casey at the Bat." M. Keith Booker suggests that such repeated allusions serve to produce "a sort of dramatic irony in that audiences will generally understand his references, while no one else on *Moya* has any idea what he is talking about" (163). However, while this sort of allusive dialogue is an important and recurring device, and even part of the series' cult attraction, it is not simply because of the passing sense of irony it invariably produces.

What we see in this persistently reflexive manner of speech is an interesting commentary on the nature of communication here and on Crichton himself. Of course, in the world of *Farscape* the *act* of communication is usually not itself a problem, thanks to the presence of "translator microbes" that effectively explain how different species can all seem to speak the same language, and that recall similar efforts at explaining such a narrative necessity in other series, most famously in *Doctor Who*'s reliance on his Tardis' translator function. But as Crichton demonstrates, that communication is often at odds—full of slips, confusion, and only partial understanding, as is dramatized when, in "Look at the Princess, Part I" (2.10), he finds himself accidentally caught in a situation where he is betrothed to a planet's hereditary ruler and slated to be frozen as a statue for 80 cycles simply because he agreed to kiss her (after a fight with Aeryn). Against such a backdrop Crichton's comments take on an added resonance, as they seem aimed both at himself and also *at us*. In fact, the impression is that we are *accidentally* overhearing someone's thoughts, as he talks to keep himself sane, or that we have by chance tuned in to a kind of message being sent out into the ether that only we can understand. As such, it recalls his introductory commentary wherein he wonders "is there anybody out there who can hear me?" Hearing Crichton, understanding him in ways that no one else in his strange environment can — knowing, for example, that when he imagines himself and Scorpius preparing to fight the Scarrans as the Crash Test Dummies from television safety ads, he sees little hope for survival — we become more than a typical television narrative's audience. We are effectively invited to share Crichton's complex situation, as he resolves to struggle even in the face of apparently impossible odds. His immersion in, yet ironic detachment from this strange universe, in fact, becomes evocative of our own cultural situation. This accidental recognition that others *do* speak the same language as we do, that we share certain touchstones and interpretations, thus becomes another crucial part of the cult-ural glue that binds audiences to the series.[3]

Yet perhaps the most important element in that cult pattern is *Farscape*'s development of what I have termed the *accidental path*. In his discussion of how cult films work, Bruce Kawin describes the encounter with such texts as always something of a chance encounter, an inadvertent intersection of paths, as if one were to go walking out "after midnight," "searching for the films that are searching for me" (25). What *Farscape* envisions is just that sort of "searching" but on a grand scale, literally across the universe by way of both the accidental and intentional use of wormholes. While participating as an astronaut in conventional space exploration, Crichton is thrown into an unknown part of space, what is constantly referred to as the "Uncharted Territories," and, as we have noted, he subsequently tries to discover a way of using wormholes to find "a way home." Yet at the same time, he is constantly being chased — by the character Scorpius, by Peacekeeper forces, by the Scarran empire — by all those who would use whatever knowledge of wormholes he has in his head, including that which has subsequently been implanted there by the Ancients (an interdimensional race of advanced beings), for military means, for purposes of destruction or conquest. Crichton, consequently, realizes that what he knows about wormholes represents both his only hope to ever reach home again *and* the primary obstacle preventing him from realizing that goal. It is the sort of paradoxical situation that allows for elaborate plot complexities, but also one that speaks to *Farscape*'s cult appeal, particularly its ability to bind up the sort of difficult choices and irrational situations that seem so much a part of the postmodern condition, while it also presents those choices and situations as escaping easy or convenient solutions. It is part of this characteristic that Jan Johnson-Smith observes when she describes what she finds to be the series' key attraction, its tendency for "stripping individual moments and events of narrow and short-term considerations, and replacing them with broader, more contextualized concerns" (165–66).

But the larger point of *Farscape*'s wormhole conceit is a very simple one, the notion that the accident *is* destiny here. Or as Crichton notes in the episode "Bad Timing" (4.22), "Sometimes things don't happen quite the way you imagine." Jes Battis notes how early on in the series Crichton's "primary concern is simply to return home. But over time his emotional attachments, as well as his political and ethical commitments, branch out considerably," and he links that shifting focus to the series' efforts at raising "all kinds of interesting questions about technology, masculinity, and nationhood" (*Investigating* Farscape 3). Wormhole "technology" thus becomes a key stand-in for various contemporary Earth technologies — rocketry, nuclear power, even the internal combustion engine — that start out as tools of knowledge, exploration, and development but open onto dangerous and destructive applications that we must culturally negotiate as they begin to take us places that we had never foreseen. That sort of branching out is, of course, the series' own demonstration of the point Crichton makes, and a further clue to its appeal, as it consistently transports us where we might not have imagined, to our own "Uncharted Territories," at least those that network television usually prefers not to explore.

Besides suggesting the rather unusual ambition or scope that has often been attributed to *Farscape*, then, that notion of a constant branching out also affords a different view of individual human direction, pointing up how seldom life follows a simple, plotted line, and rather how much is due to the chance occurrence, the unpredictable event. For example, as the series opens Crichton is helping to develop the "Farscape Project," an international high-velocity deep-space exploration mission, when that wormhole deposits him in the middle of a space battle. There he collides with another ship, causing it to crash and bringing the Peacekeeper Crais, brother of the pilot killed in the crash, to vow that he will capture and kill Crichton. His planned future as an astronaut, following in the path set out by his father, Jack Crichton, is thus completely sidetracked by a series of quite literal accidents that open up a completely new future, one in which getting home gives way to figuring out how to make himself at home in this newly complex, seemingly constantly changing reality that he now inhabits. In fact, given the possibilities of time and dimensional travel that Crichton discovers over the course of the series, infinite realities begin to seem possible, even infinite personal destinies. That fact is especially thrust home when, in the "Kansas" episode (4.12), he finds that his presence in the past has accidentally altered Earth history so that his father is scheduled to helm the doomed *Challenger* shuttle mission — and his death would invariably affect John's life as well. Having to "fix" the past just so that he can go on to an unpredictable future, Crichton begins to realize the very contingent nature of his life.

More to the point, over the course of the series he gradually comes to recognize that the very concepts of home, family, and even self are all similarly contingent and subject to change. Home, finally, is not necessarily the Earth but some place still "uncharted." His family is the one he is in the process of creating with his Sebacean mate Aeryn, the child she gives birth to in the middle of a firefight in *The Peacekeeper Wars* miniseries, and those "strange alien life forms" that have become his friends,[4] his support, even his saviors through all of his wanderings. What Crichton comes to realize is that his real task is becoming at peace with the sense of instability that this state of affairs brings, with the fact that destiny is not a carefully planned out scientific expedition like the Farscape Project on which he was working, but rather a constantly evolving set of paths that he must choose and/or to which he must adapt. If that sort of conception is challenging, if that view of human life as defined by accident demands a revisioning of our sense of human nature or of life's purpose, it is also a valuable challenge, one that again speaks directly to the show's cult appeal. For it reminds us not only of what might be found in that sort of "walking after midnight" that Kawin describes (25), but also of our own responsibility in the accident of destiny. Thus whereas Crichton, in the premier episode, tells his father, "I can't be your kind of hero," he is challenged over the course of the series and finally must commit himself to a most fundamental human task, one with which anyone can identify: finding out just what "kind of hero" he *can* be. Such a task, I would suggest, sits well with a cult audience, with viewers who are looking for something, even if they are not quite sure what.

But this point recalls that sense of compensation that, Virilio and Lotringer assure us, is typically part of the economy of our accident-prone culture, or as Edward Tenner has described such situations, one of the ways in which "disaster is paradoxically creative" (327). As Virilio and Lotringer offer, "the accident of art is the accident of knowledge" (109), and in a series like *Farscape* with its clearly artistic intentions knowledge finally is the real payoff. Over its course the series drives home a great variety of truths, including the strength and leadership of women, the value of diverse cultures, the wisdom of compassion, the worth of other ways of knowing. Yet it seems to afford such knowledge almost accidentally, since in a world bound by conventions and constrained by certain ways of seeing — such as those typically afforded by network television and its popular genres — this may well be the only way we might encounter, or be willing to accept, such different, potentially subversive concepts. In this context we might consider the point that Crichton makes, rather off-handedly, in the very first episode when Aeryn hesitates to join the other escapees on Moya, insisting that she must remain true to her Peacekeeper training which forbids her from having compassion for others, questioning commands, or resisting the aims of the Peacekeepers — in this key instance, simply helping her companions escape their pursuers. He insists, however, that she "can be more," that she can learn to be a better being. That she accepts that challenge forecasts the strength of character she will manifest throughout the series, but it also demonstrates one of the most important pieces of knowledge or messages we might find in a cult text, that of our abiding ability, despite all conditioning, to "escape" our own cultural bonds, not to do the *impossible*, but simply to "be" something better.

Finally, we might emphasize how this term "escape" seems to resonate tellingly with the series title and its cult appeal. For the title *Farscape* immediately suggests a text that is playing at extremes, affording a vision or horizon far beyond the normal range, if not of the *impossible* then certainly far beyond the boundaries typically set by our world and visualized in our mainstream texts. That sort of expanded vision only further underscores the series' cult potential, for as Kawin reminds us, the cult work is one that, by its very nature as a radically different sort of experience, usually situates itself at the margins of our culture, "a culture that eats and breathes and oils itself with compromise" (24), with the stuff of sameness, with the normative vision, in this case of conventional broadcast television. In contrast, *Farscape* as an unfolding text consistently suggests how we might look beyond that world, escape from that everyday realm to other possibilities. Through its group of "strange alien" types, thrown together by chance yet gradually transformed — *almost impossibly*, against their natures — into "friends," it visualizes various ways out, as it takes us into and helps us explore the "Uncharted Territories" of culture and of self.

Notes

1. For a detailed discussion of the early television space opera, see Wheeler Winston Dixon's essay "Tomorrowland TV: The Space Opera and Early Science Fiction Television."

2. *TV Guide* first compiled this listing in 2004, shortly after *Farscape* was canceled. That it would still rank the show as one of the top cult series in 2007 suggests its continuing importance. See "*TV Guide* Names the Top Cult Shows Ever."

3. Bruce Kawin suggests that this sort of effect is the real key to a cult work's satisfaction. As he offers, "what this sacred text gives its worshippers, and what they are grateful for, is a mirror. It tells them something they realize as the truth, something they have been waiting to hear and to have validated" (24).

4. In the series' later seasons, Crichton's introductory commentary adds a telling note, as he describes those "strange, alien life forms" on Moya as "my friends."

Works Cited

Battis, Jes. "*Farscape.*" *The Essential Cult TV Reader.* Ed. David Lavery. Lexington: University Press of Kentucky, 2010. 104–10. Print.

_____. *Investigating* Farscape: *Uncharted Territories of Sex and Science Fiction.* London: I. B. Tauris, 2007. Print.

Booker, M. Keith. *Science Fiction Television.* Westport, CT: Praeger, 2004. Print.

Dixon, Wheeler Winston. "Tomorrowland TV: The Space Opera and Early Science Fiction Television." *The Essential Science Fiction Television Reader.* Ed. J. P. Telotte. Lexington: University Press of Kentucky, 2008. 93–110. Print.

Johnson-Smith, Jan. *American Science Fiction TV*: Star Trek, Stargate, *and Beyond.* Middletown, CT: Wesleyan University Press, 2005. Print.

Kawin, Bruce. "After Midnight." *The Cult Film Experience: Beyond All Reason.* Ed. J. P. Telotte. Austin: University of Texas Press, 1991. 18–25. Print.

Tenner, Edward. *Why Things Bite Back: Technology and the Revenge of Unintended Consequences.* New York: Random House, 1996. Print.

"*TV Guide* Names the Top Cult Shows Ever." *TV Guide* 29 June 2007. www.tvguide.com/news/top-cult-shows/070629-071. Web. 23 May 2008.

Virilio, Paul, and Sylvere Lotringer. *The Accident of Art.* Trans. Michael Taormina. New York: Semiotext(e), 2005. Print.

War and Peace by Woody Allen or, How I Learned to Stop Worrying and Love the Wormhole Weapon

ENSLEY F. GUFFEY

"Wow. Battle looks completely different when you're in the middle of it than it does to the generals up on the hill!"—Woody Allen, *Love and Death*

Popular culture studies assume that any given cultural element is both product of and a reflection on the time period in which it was produced. This idea lies at the core of the so-called "*Popular Culture Formula*" which "states that the popularity of a given cultural element ... is directly proportional to the degree to which that element is reflective of audience beliefs and values" (Nachbar and Lause 5). With the advent of cable networks and niche programming, television became a means to refine such cultural inquiries by presenting scholars with cultural elements that were popular with smaller audiences and therefore provided a more nuanced view of a given time. For the historian, such windows into the recent cultural past allow a rare opportunity to gauge the reaction of the too-often historically silent majority of the population to the events of their time.

Nowhere is this more evident than in the representations of military and political policies and international arms races portrayed in the award-winning science fiction series *Farscape*. Originally conceived shortly after the fall of the Soviet Union and the end of the Cold War, *Farscape* entered production as the world entered a new phase of nuclear proliferation, terrorism, and militarization in the late 1990s. *Farscape* was able to ask important and often subversive questions concerning the nature of recent history and of the paths the world seemed to be taking into the future. Furthermore, the show's heavy reliance on cast and crew from Australia provided a small-power/everyman perspective on these questions — a perspective which was unique to American television of the time.

Farscape was, in part, an extended meditation on Cold War policies, arms races, ultimate weapons as a road to peace, and the recurrence of these themes in modern history. For John Crichton and the audience, the Peacekeepers and Scarran Imperium are in many ways respectively coded as the United States and the Soviet Union. By using human historical and cultural experience to interpret the institutional enmity between the Peacekeepers and Scarrans, *Farscape* fashions a lens which illuminates and questions the military-political practices of both these fictional empires, and of the very real nations and non-state organizations of 20th and 21st century Earth.

As with so much else in *Farscape*, the key to this perspective lies in the character of John Crichton. Series creator Rockne S. O'Bannon has stated that

> [Crichton] represents you or me or any member of the audience. He's seen all the same movies that we have and he's got all the same cultural references, but the poor guy's essentially dropped into a galaxy innumerable light years away. It gives us that wonderful, fascinating touchstone that we can all identify with [Bassom 28].

Furthermore, as Jes Battis points out, Crichton is specifically coded as an American astronaut who "is never unmoored from the ideological frameworks that compose the United States" (163). These points are vital to Crichton's interpretations of military-political structures he encounters in the wider galaxy.

As *Farscape* posits a fictional Earth differing only slightly from our own, Crichton would have grown up with a world which was, until 1991–92, divided by the Cold War into two armed camps around the United States and the Soviet Union. Jack Crichton's gift to John of a puzzle ring given to him by Yuri Gagarin[1] firmly places Crichton and his family in the world of the Cold War and the Space Race ("Premiere" 1.1). Crichton would also have seen the hoped-for "peace dividend" at the end of the Cold War disappear in the face of new arms races and new international military tensions. Throughout the mid and late 1990s, nuclear weapons technology became available to both nation states and terrorist organizations through black markets originating in former Soviet and Warsaw Pact states, and in 1998 Pakistan tested nuclear weapons, increasing tensions with its nuclear neighbor, India. This personal and global history is at the core of the way Crichton — and the audience — views galactic politics at the far end of the wormhole.

As they concern the Peacekeepers and Scarran Imperium, those politics have reached a point of tension just short of war when Crichton finds himself catapulted into their midst. In the Uncharted Territories, this hostility has already begun to erupt into open conflict in the form of skirmishes among the various forces deployed there by both sides ("Eat Me" 3.6). The two empires are also competing for political alliances and influence with various systems in the Uncharted Territories ("Look at the Princess, Parts I–III" 2.10–2.12), and both claim territory there, including sectors claimed where each disputes the other's title ("Bringing Home the Beacon" 4.16). As a result of these conflicting interests, which both see as leading inevitably to war, the Peacekeepers and Scarrans have embarked upon an arms race by which each seeks a decisive advantage over the other.

In between these two maneuvering superpowers are an unknown number of smaller polities, ranging from the Hynerian Empire and Luxan Territories to individual worlds like Sykar and Dam-Ba-Da, as well as billions of sentients, including Moya and her crew. In addition to his function as the viewpoint of the extradiegetic audience, Crichton also serves as the viewpoint and voice of these intradiegetic billions who live between and among the superpowers, and are all too often subject to their whims of policy. This is Cold War Earth writ large indeed, with Crichton and Company standing in for the "every-human" caught between the U.S. and U.S.S.R., *circa* 1945–1992.

The first superpower encountered by Crichton and the audience is the Peacekeepers ("Premiere" 1.1). From the outset, the Peacekeepers are portrayed as militaristic, hierarchical, totalitarian, and technologically far in advance of Earth. We quickly learn that the Peacekeepers are also slavers, forcing the Leviathan living ships to serve their ends by means of control collars. Much later, it is revealed that the Peacekeepers were originally human, taken from Earth around 25,000 B.C.E. by the Eidelons and altered to enforce and guard the peace negotiated by their benefactors (*Farscape: The Peacekeeper Wars* [*PKW*]). This leads to what is perhaps the single most important fact about the majority of Peacekeeper personnel: their human appearance. Indeed, outwardly they look just like Crichton, and us. The Peacekeepers are both familiar and alien at once, and there is nothing about their society that we do not recognize from one period of human history or another.

Based upon the Peacekeepers' totalitarian political structure, the apparent total subservience of Sebacean society and economics to the military state, as well as the Peacekeepers' prejudicial racial policies, Jes Battis has written that the Peacekeeper political-military system "bears more than a passing resemblance to German Nazism" (Battis 164). This reading is supported both within the diegesis ("Kansas" 4.12), and by remarks made by executive producer Brian Henson (Henson). As Battis is careful to point out, however, there are some problems with this coding.

Though presented from the outset as racial purists, the Peacekeepers apparently remain open to mixed species and non–Sebacean individuals who display unusual skills or talents, particularly in the Science Military. Scorpius himself is an example of this, as are Linfer and Strappa, two humanoid aliens acting as lead scientists on Scorpius' wormhole research project in Season Three. Commandant Mele-On Grayza has undergone implantation of an alien gland into her chest, and her grayish complexion differs significantly from that of other Sebaceans, indicating that she may be of mixed heritage, yet she has achieved high rank and considerable political power within the Peacekeeper hierarchy. Clearly Peacekeeper prejudices, while undeniably systemic, can be set aside if the potential gain is considered great enough. The Peacekeepers also show themselves willing to ally with other races, such as the Luxans, when such alliances will advance their agenda, and although undoubtedly racist, there is no evidence that the Peacekeepers have ever practiced a policy of genocide.

Finally, totalitarian systems are not exclusive to any one political philosophy. The growth of such systems is a risk faced by any nation engaged in massive arms production. As Joseph Maiolo points out in *Cry Havoc*, his groundbreaking reexamination of the worldwide arms race between 1931–1941 C.E., "the liberal democracies struggled with the problem of how to arm themselves against the threat of total war without succumbing to totalitarianism," because "no matter what type of regime or its military starting point, the [arms] race sent everyone down the same totalitarian track" (4). In the post–World War II world, Maiolo finds the same pressures at work in the United States:

> The mounting cost of the U.S. nuclear and conventional force build-ups against [the U.S.S.R.] revealed a real anxiety among some Americans of inadvertently erecting a "garrison state." Most prominent among them was President Eisenhower, who feared that the burden of an all-out armaments spree would crush a flourishing economy, and with it American liberties [403].

Bearing Peacekeeper history in mind, it is likely that the militarized totalitarian society that produced Officer Aeryn Sun is the result of literally millennia of sustained arms build-ups and war economies as the Peacekeepers struggled to fulfill the role given to them by the absent Eidelons. Taking into account the Peacekeepers' past reputation as upholders of "everything good" ("...Different Destinations" 3.5),[2] and their continued self-indoctrination as an organization that maintains order and harmony, the Peacekeepers begin to look less like Nazi Germany and more like Cold War America ("PK Tech Girl" 1.7).

This is particularly true when the United States is viewed through the lens of a small-power polity like Australia. The belief that after World War II Australia traded one set of imperial masters in Great Britain for another in the United States has "exerted a profound influence on media opinion and on popular and political leaders' attitudes" in Australia, and continues to pervade "much of the scholarly literature" on Australian policies during the Cold War (McLean 66). Although reliance on American protection against large power threats from the Soviet Union or China was an entirely rational policy on Australia's part,

> there is no reason to conclude that as a result of these developments Australians grew more pro–American in sentiment or more inclined culturally to be subservient to the United States... When all was said and done, Australians, for all their sense of affinity with America, regarded it as a foreign country, in a way that was not true of Britain [73].

This is not to say that Australians are particularly anti–American, or that they see the United States as some sort of warmongering international bad-guy, but in terms of the strong Australian influence on *Farscape* as a whole, this small power lens is essential to an understanding of the Peacekeepers. During World War II, the Cold War, and after, the United States projected military power in the Pacific largely through naval forces organized around large aircraft carriers with advanced command, control, and intelligence capabilities. The Peacekeepers project power over vast interstellar distances through fleet groups centered on enormous vessels called command carriers, usually escorted by an array of smaller craft ranging in size from single-seat fighters to capital vessels. Press images of heavily armed American military forces in fatigues, helmets, goggles, and masks are uncomfortably echoed in the faceless infantry troops of the Peacekeepers, and Peacekeeper Special Forces troops share a reputation for frightening and deadly efficiency with units like the U.S. Navy SEALs, Green Berets, Marine Force Recon, and U.S. Army Delta Force. The parallels between the two are readily apparent. Furthermore, "from the Australian point of view the peculiar status of the United States was that it was *neither completely alien nor completely familiar*" (McLean 74) [emphasis mine]. In a very real way Americans are to Australians as the Peacekeepers are to John Crichton: familiar yet often disturbingly other.

Crichton functions not merely as the point of view of *Farscape*'s largely American audience by virtue of being human, but also *specifically as an American*, as a conduit through which that audience experiences — at least in small part — the anxiety felt by Australia and other small powers when dealing with either Cold War superpower. Perhaps Crichton serves yet another purpose by allowing Australians to enjoy a bit of *schadenfreude* at America's expense, for no matter what he does throughout the series and mini-series his life is inextricably dominated by the policies and actions of the Scarrans and Peacekeepers, the superpowers which dominate *Farscape's* own interstellar cold war.

The Peacekeepers also resemble the Cold War United States in terms of racial policy. The United States ended racial chattel slavery in 1865, the last industrialized nation to do so. The armed forces were not racially integrated until 1949, while effective civil rights legislation was only passed in 1964, the Voting Rights Act in 1965, and African-Americans and other minorities continue to suffer overt and covert discrimination at the time of writing (2011–12). In addition, and unlike the Peacekeepers, the United States does possess a history of genocide from its treatment of Native Americans, and during World War II interned almost all resident Japanese-American men, women, and children for the duration of the war. For most of its history, the face of the United States, like that of the Peacekeepers, was white, and while the Peacekeepers appear to be more egalitarian in their treatment of genders than the United States, it is telling that the highest ranking female Peacekeeper in the series, Commandant Mele-On Grayza, has found it necessary to be surgically altered to give her an advantage over males, has had to use sex to advance her career, and is still out-ranked by at least two grades by Grand Chancellor Maryk, a white male.

The Scarran Imperium is a far more mysterious, and more menacing, polity than even the Peacekeepers. For most of the series, the Scarrans are seen as individual operatives engaged in semi-covert operations and intelligence gathering. They first appear in the three episode arc "Look at the Princess," where the Imperium's envoy to the Breakaway Colonies, Cargn, is attempting to manipulate the Colonies' royal succession in order to create a Scarran puppet state (2.10–2.12). Shortly thereafter, a Scarran operative abducts and interrogates Crichton in an attempt to determine why Scorpius is so interested in him ("Won't Get Fooled Again" 2.15). Later Crichton and D'Argo are menaced by a literal Scarran sleeper agent ("Season of Death" 3.1), and all of Moya's crew are threatened by yet another Scarran secret agent, Axikor, disguised as the leader of a band of Coreeshi bounty hunters ("I Shrink Therefore I Am" 4.8). Even when operating on a larger, more militant scale, as in "Infinite Possibilities: Parts I & II" (3.14–3.15), the Scarrans are careful to maintain a low profile and plausible deniability through the use of Charrid mercenaries and the mechanic Furlow until they believe they have achieved their goals.

Though Crichton manages one way or another to foil the Scarrans' nefarious schemes in each of these encounters, they nonetheless reveal that the Scarran Imperium possesses a well organized, highly efficient covert intelligence system. This system has infiltrated the Uncharted Territories deeply and widely enough to be able to take advantage of intelligence gathering opportunities as quickly as they occur. The network echoes that of the Soviet Committee for State Security, the notorious KGB, which *TIME Magazine* has called "the world's most effective intelligence gathering organization" (Kohan 6). The interrogation techniques used on Crichton are, given certain advances in technology, the same used by the KGB, namely "stimulants, hypnotics, and hallucinogenic agents" (Hilden).

Even the self-aggrandizing motives of Scarran agents like Cargn and Axikor resemble those of KGB operatives as described in an internal CIA memo:

> Personalities and the private connections of individual officers are often crucial to the success or failure of an operation — or a career. In many ways, the KGB is an organization made to order for the man who wants to claim all the glory for himself and put all the mistakes on the backs of his subordinates [Lambridge].

This structure also encourages competing power-blocks at upper levels such as those within the Scarran Hierarchy. There, powerful Scarrans like War Minister Ahkna seek to subvert the Imperium's intelligence resources to secure their own political advantage, much as Yuri Andropov and Vladimir Putin used the chairmanship of the KGB to further their political goals.

At the top of this often shadowy empire is the Emperor Staleek, who strides across the screen with the sartorial splendor of Sergei Eisenstein's *Ivan Grozny* and a brutal menace and cold intelligence worthy of Stalin himself. Always on guard against internal threats like Ahkna, Staleek is vitally concerned with achieving "power, acknowledgement of [his] personal intelligence, and to gain acceptance in the upper echelon of civilizations," goals which would have been familiar to Russian leaders from Peter the Great to Dmitri Medvedev (*PKW*). As S.M. Plokhy points out, when dealing with the Soviet Union,

> U.S. and British diplomatic services ... had a long tradition of treating cultural difference between the two sides as evidence of [the U.S.S.R.'s] inferiority ... it was customary to suggest that they displayed Oriental features, torn between extremes of humanity and cruelty. They presumably inclined towards tyranny, possessed a peasant mentality, were disorganized, and could work only in short bursts of frantic activity [64].

The Scarrans are viewed similarly. Scorpius/Harvey dismisses them without the *crystherium utilia* flowers as "simple, brutish creatures" ("We're So Screwed, Part III: 'La Bomba'" 4.21). Like the Soviets, the Scarrans are all too aware of this perception. As Staleek says, "at the peace table, we know how we're viewed: brutish, ignorant" (*PKW*). Such errors in judgment were to prove costly in both fact and fiction.

Like the Soviet Union, the Scarran Empire's apparently overwhelming strength protects a debilitating secret. For the Soviets the secret was a shrinking economy and industrial base which was unable to maintain both arms production and domestic growth, and finally incapable of doing either. For the Scarran Imperium it is the species' reliance on *crystherium utilia*, without which they apparently devolve, at least intellectually ("La Bomba"). Scarran territorial expansion is predicated on establishing and maintaining lines of supply to *crystherium* production points, and the destruction of the *crystherium* mother plant at Katratzi resulted in the Imperium being forced to abandon an entire sector of space until a new *crystherium* supply could be established ("Bad Timing" 4.22).

It is in the escalating arms race between the two empires, however, that *Farscape*'s Cold War allegory blossoms. Like the Soviet Union, the Scarran Imperium seems to have concentrated its efforts towards building up its conventional forces, and as Scorpius reveals in "Losing Time" (3.9), this has been largely successful: "By latest estimates, Scarran warriors outnumber Peacekeeper soldiers ten to one ... if and when they attack — we will lose...."[3] Added to this numerical superiority is the undeniably superior individual toughness and physical endurance demonstrated by Scarrans as individuals, who are naturally resistant to pulse blasts, possess greater physical strength, have the ability to project a heat ray that is devastating to Sebaceans, and even lack external "mivonks"![4] Likewise, the Soviet soldier was "considered a superior adversary prepared for the most demanding of combat circumstances" (Hertling 20). In either case, the foe is formidable.

In response to these advantages, as the series opens the Peacekeepers are investigating several possible avenues of weapons-research: potential bio-weapons like the intelligent virus in "A Bug's Life" (1.18), creating hybrid Leviathan warships ("The Hidden Memory" 1.20), and, of course, the possible military applications of wormholes ("Nerve" 1.19). Though the subject is never directly addressed, it seems logical to assume that the Peacekeepers have found themselves unable to match the Scarran quantitative advantage, and are therefore seeking a technological superiority which will counterbalance — or preferably negate — the Scarrans' conventional one. At a minimum, Peacekeeper High Command is seeking a weapon capable of deterring a Scarran attack through the threat of devastating retaliation, a strategy that bears more than a little resemblance to the nuclear stance of the United States and NATO in Western Europe.

Faced with a similar numerical inferiority to Soviet conventional forces in Europe, in 1953 the Eisenhower administration issued National Security Council document 162/2, which stated in part that "in the event of hostilities the United States will consider nuclear weapons to be as available for use as any other munitions" (22). In other words, the U.S. was willing to counter any type of Soviet attack in Europe, whether conventional or nuclear, strategic or tactical, with nuclear weapons. As J. P. D. Dunbabin notes, "Deployment of [U.S.] tactical nuclear weapons began in 1954, and seemed admirably suited to remedy NATO's shortfall in conventional troops" (33). However, while Peacekeeper High Command may be hoping to create a similar deterrent in order to prevent war with the Scarrans, Scorpius — and later Commandant Grayza — hopes to achieve something greater: a super-weapon with which to eradicate the Scarran Imperium once and for all.

The wormhole weapon is Scorpius' ultimate fantasy, something so new and so powerful that the Scarrans stand no chance against it: a superweapon. Nor is Scorpius original or even particularly unusual in imagining a weapon so terribly powerful that its very existence will end war and guarantee its possessor the power to dictate the terms of eternal peace. Such ultimate weapons have been a staple of Western fiction since the early 19th century. The Industrial Revolution brought with it dreams of technological advancement which would put an end to war, even if only by making it too horrific to contemplate. Looking into the future in 1835, Tennyson

> Heard the heavens fill with shouting, and there rain'd a ghastly dew
> From the nations' airy navies grappling in the central blue;
> ...
> Till the war-drum throbb'd no longer, and the battle-flags were furl'd
> In the Parliament of man, the Federation of the world
> ["Locksley Hall" 123–24, 127–28].

One hundred ten years later, in July of 1945, American president Harry S. Truman would pull a piece of paper from his wallet upon which he had written these lines as a boy, and read them to a reporter as they traveled to the Potsdam Conference in occupied Germany (Franklin 18). A few days later, on 16 July 1945, the first atomic weapon was detonated near Alamogordo, New Mexico.

Instead of world peace Truman's wonder weapon ushered in almost fifty years of Cold War stalemate and never-ending arms manufacture. In the end, "overkill arsenals and bloated military-industrial complexes finally crippled the Soviet economy and blighted America's national infrastructure, stunted its social progress and militarized its culture" (Maiolo 404). Despite this, nation-states are still lining up to join the so-called Nuclear Club today. The same kind of strategic thinking that is reflected in the goals of Peacekeeper High Command and Emperor Staleek has lead to a growing proliferation of nuclear weapons on Earth in the decades since the fall of the Soviet Union, largely based upon the Cold War strategic theory that nuclear weapons provide an effective deterrent to attack. However, as Jacek Kugler writes, the view that deterrence actually works is questionable:

> First, nuclear nations do not have an obvious and direct advantage over other nuclear or nonnuclear nations in extreme crises... Second, nuclear preponderance, which, logically, should enhance the likelihood of war, does not lead to demonstrably different or less stable behavior than nuclear parity... Finally, the most consistent reason for the absence of major war in the nuclear era seems to be the relative congruence of policy objectives among the nuclear powers, and this congruence cannot be directly traced to the buildup of nuclear arsenals [501].

When dealing with these issues in terms of the wormhole weapon and all of the schemes and counter schemes surrounding it, *Farscape* is at its most frustratingly eloquent.

As noted above, Crichton is a product of those fifty years of brinksmanship and détente, of the "Evil Empire" and SDI.[5] The race to the wormhole weapon is literally a film that Crichton has already seen. "Welcome to my cold war!" he cries in "We're So Screwed, Part II" (4.20) while wearing a thermonuclear bomb around his waist upon which he will later write "Hi There!" in a nod to Stanley Kubrick's Cold War classic *Doctor Strangelove*.[6] Indeed, *Strangelove* becomes a theme during the end of Season Four and *The Peacekeeper Wars* mini-series, with Crichton attaching another nuclear bomb named "Dear John" to Scorpius in "Bad Timing" (4.22),[7] and Scorpius/Harvey mimicking Peter Sellers' Dr. Strangelove himself in *The Peacekeeper Wars*. The classic satire becomes a vital touchstone in the narrative as a reminder of the dangers of superweapon arms races.

Certainly, as Joseph Maiolo reminds us, a troubled peace such as the Cold War on Earth or the Scarran-Peacekeeper standoff in *Farscape* is not the only probable outcome of an arms race, whether conventional or not:

> Arms races are like waves of action and reaction that ripple through the international system. In periods of acute political tension, one state races ahead to win a military edge over its rivals, who in turn respond to the menace by arming too, and a perilous cycle of actions and reactions ensues, which ends either in war or in some sort of uneasy political-military stalemate [3].

Maiolo also documents the trajectory of one such competition as it became "an independent, self-perpetuating and often overriding impersonal force that shaped events," and ended in the largest, most horrific war in all of human history (2–3). The death toll of World War II is conservatively estimated at 61,000,000 men, women and children, exclusive of the tens of millions more who were wounded, displaced, imprisoned, or tortured as a result of the conflict. The pre-war arms race not only made this possible, but helped birth the horror.

Fortunately, the nuclear arms race between the United States and Soviet Union resulted in the second of Maiolo's probabilities, as — so far!— have the current nuclear races emerging between India, Pakistan, China, the Russian Federation, the United States, Israel, Iran, France, the United Kingdom, and North Korea in their various permutations. The alternative would have made the casualty figures from the Second World War appear minuscule. The level of death and destruction resulting from a global conventional war becoming a global thermonuclear war would, in all probability, constitute a total extinction of the human race, and much, if not all of the rest of Earth's flora and fauna. The point is worth belaboring here because it is the same one being made by the cast and crew of *Farscape*, particularly in Season Four and *The Peacekeeper Wars*.

In a desperate gambit to buy time in which to develop a wormhole weapon, Peacekeeper High Command informs the Scarrans that they have already developed such a weapon and are putting it into production ("Losing Time" 3.9). Like Khrushchev's similar ploy in 1957, however, the Peacekeepers wormhole-gap tactic is only partially successful (Barrass 113–15). The complete destruction of a Scarran dreadnaught under mysterious circumstances at Dam-Ba-Da in "Infinite Possibilities Part II: Icarus Abides" (3.15) inadvertently aids this deception, but by the time War Minister Ahkna and Commandant Grayza meet in Tormented Space, the lack of any hard evidence of such a weapon has all but convinced the Scarrans that the Peacekeepers are lying ("Bringing Home the Beacon" 4.16). Mere months after the failed peace talks at Katratzi, the Scarrans are making the final dispositions necessary for total war against the Peacekeepers, at least so Scorpius would have it believed. The Scarrans' true intentions soon become irrelevant as, in yet another nod to *Dr. Strangelove*, Scorpius acts as a kind of galactic General Jack D. Ripper and starts the war himself.

Thus, the outcome of the Scarran-Peacekeeper arms race is the Peacekeeper War. Caught in the middle of it are Crichton, Aeryn, their unborn son, their friends, and every other sentient being in the affected regions of space, most of whom would likely agree with Crichton when he tells Scorpius, "I don't care about the things you care about. Peacekeepers rule the Scarrans. Scarrans rule the Peacekeepers. Let them rule together" ("A Constellation of Doubt" 4.17). It is a sentiment well known to the generations who lived during the Cold War and who faced the potential consequences of the Soviet and American contest for world leadership. Through Crichton, *Farscape* asks with Gandhi: "What difference does it make to the dead, the orphans, and the homeless, whether the mad destruction is wrought under the name of totalitarianism or the holy name of liberty and democracy?" (377). No difference. No difference at all.

Whether the Peacekeepers win or the Scarrans, the results will be the same for the mass of beings caught in their war: destruction, death, and misery. *Farscape: The Peacekeeper Wars* shows this unflinchingly through a series of local events that serve to bring those larger consequences home to the audience. Jool and the Temple of Arnessk with its ancient priesthood devoted to peace are destroyed by a Scarran missile utilizing similar technology to modern ICBMs.[8] Such would likely be the fate of the 2200-year-old Hindu temple of Shankaracharya and its priests in Kashmir should India and Pakistan ever unleash their nuclear arsenals against one another. The descendants of the Arnessk priesthood, the Eidelons of Qujaga, also become victims of the war, as their long hidden city is ravaged to ruins by the running battle between Peacekeepers and Scarrans, and their entire planet is eaten by the wormhole weapon itself (*PKW*). Imagine Sarajevo if after four years of brutal siege the Serbs had possessed nuclear weapons and decided to eradicate the stubborn city and its surviving hundreds of thousands of civilian inhabitants. The message is as clear and ancient as the Kikuyu proverb: "when elephants fight, it is the grass that suffers" (Traditional).

At the center of the final Peacekeeper-Scarran arms race and the Peacekeeper War are John Crichton and the wormhole weapon. At first glance this ultimate weapon of mass destruction (WMD) seems a fairly straightforward symbol of modern nuclear weapons in its vast and indiscriminate destructive power, as indeed it is. In terms of *Farscape*'s Cold War metaphor, the wormhole weapon is the reality behind all of the posturing, scheming, manipulation, and brinksmanship executed by both empires throughout the series, as the reality of multi-megaton nuclear weapons lies behind the decades of similarly convoluted maneuvers practiced by the United States and Soviet Union from 1945 to 1992 and of the nuclear powers into the present day. The unlearned moral in both instances is that if one plays with fire one will eventually be burned. Only instead of fingertips or even single individuals, it is entire planets (*our* planet) which will be consumed, and entire sentient species (*Homo sapiens sapiens*) that will be exterminated.

Behind the wormhole weapon's nuclear metaphor, however, lies a larger and more frightening symbolism. It must be remembered that the development of nuclear weapons did not stop with the atomic bomb. Before the Second World War had ended, Manhattan Project scientists were researching more powerful hydrogen, or thermonuclear, bombs (Rhodes 70). By 1955 both superpowers had tested such weapons. In 1978, facing a renewed Soviet advantage in conventional armored forces in Europe and despite widespread domestic and international pressure, President Jimmy Carter secretly gave the go-ahead for the production of components for "enhanced-radiation weapons"— neutron bombs — designed to kill people by massive radiation while leaving equipment and infrastructure largely undamaged (Barrass 216–17). In between and beyond these developments, bombs and bombers were supplemented by the advent of nuclear warheads small enough to be fired by standard artillery or even man-portable recoilless rifles. Warheads were adapted to short, medium, and finally intercontinental-range missiles, to submarine launched ballistic missiles, multiple independent re-entry vehicles (MIRVs), cruise missiles, bunker-busters, *et cetera* in a never-ending attempt to refine and improve nuclear weapons and their methods of delivery. Simultaneously, the superpowers were investing billions to research and develop various chemical and biological WMDs.[9]

The arms race never truly ends. Not with the power to wipe out human life on Earth, not with the ability to wipe out all life on Earth several times over, not even with the ability to destroy the Earth entirely. Humans, it seems, are always looking for a bigger stick to beat themselves with and have been probably since the first ancestors climbed out of the trees. *Farscape* takes this propensity for suicidal improvement to its ultimate degree: a weapon that will destroy the entire galaxy, and perhaps even more. Like humanity, the Peacekeepers and Scarrans appear too dedicated to their long-standing feud with each other, too focused on their own hatreds and ambitions, to recognize the insanity of such a progression. Though in the regions of the galaxy where *Farscape* takes place, nuclear weapons, although not quite beneath contempt, are far from the bleeding edge of munitions technology. Certainly the warheads used by the Scarrans against Arnessk are either nuclear weapons which are several orders of magnitude more powerful than any currently possessed on Earth, or an entirely different type of weapon that far overshadows their destructive power. In either case judging by the destruction wrought by the Scarran missile's thirteen warheads, weapons capable of eradicating all life on a planet are likely part of both races' arsenals.

Again Crichton and Company stand in for those living under the threat of both the Peacekeepers and Scarrans and are the vicarious spokespeople for an audience which has itself spent many years sandwiched between two superpowers. Today no one on Earth can truly believe that a global nuclear war can actually be won or can result in anything better than a long and terrible dark age for humanity as a whole. President Truman himself realized this truth, and in 1953 took the opportunity to express it to the nation and the world in his farewell address, concluding that a nuclear war "is not a possible policy for rational men" (Rhodes 79). Yet the Cold War would continue for thirty-nine years more. Eventually, strategists in the United States would introduce a policy of "mutually assured destruction" of centers of civilian population, consciously give it the acronym of MAD and pronounce it good (Barrass 162–63). Knowing the capabilities of these weapons, they embraced their horror as the best defense. Moreover, they did so in policy sessions from which the vast majority of American citizens, and all of the rest of the world, were excluded. All in the service of what, as Crichton says, is truly "mankind's greatest contribution to the absurd — the thermonuclear bomb" ("Hot to Katratzi" 4.20).

Thus, despite Crichton's protests and warnings, despite their own experiments with wormholes, which have given ample evidence of the phenomenon's inherent danger and instability, the Scarrans and Peacekeepers refuse to accept that they might well be mucking about with powers which they do not fully understand and cannot control. Crichton's position in this situation must feel at least somewhat familiar. Like most of the population of Earth, Crichton grew up in a world where it often seemed that the Powers That Be had forgotten the true nature of the forces they were using to determine global military-political policy. Despite the examples of Hiroshima and Nagasaki, and literally hundreds of test detonations, the leaders of the U.S. and U.S.S.R. all too often seemed to forget that behind the rhetoric and posturing and acronyms lay slaughter on such a vast scale that it was measured in megadeaths.[10]

Crichton bears this knowledge, knows it at his very core, and yet even he becomes hypnotized by it. Trapped in the disabled drilling elevator on Katratzi, Crichton reactivates his bomb, and drops it down the shaft to the *crystherium* chamber. Tellingly, he does so without consulting any of his friends and allies, including Aeryn, who are trapped with him. Like his forebears, Crichton has made his nuclear policy unilaterally, and after deterrence has failed, Crichton launches. Afterwards he reflects on his actions in one of the most moving scenes of the series. Sitting with Aeryn, having already made inroads into a bottle, Crichton lets his bitterness and self-loathing overflow:

> Everything old is new again. Except the old thing's getting *really* old. Hey, Honey, guess what I did at work today? I wore a bomb... A nuclear bomb in a field of flowers... I could get lucky. Tomorrow I could have a bigger bomb. I could kill more people. Maybe they'll be innocent people. Children, maybe ... ["La Bomba" 4.21].

Much of *Farscape*'s historical message lies in this short monologue, for in the late 1990s and early 2000s, everything old did indeed seem to be new again. India and Pakistan faced one another over nuclear arsenals. Terrorists invoking the name of God seemed able to strike anywhere, American missiles remained targeted on Moscow and St. Petersburg, and Russian missiles on Washington, D.C., and New York City. Governments had changed, but not nuclear policy.

Even worse than this cyclic progression, though, is Crichton's knowledge that he has been corrupted and become a purveyor of this madness in its most deadly form. No longer can nuclear policy be put aside as a problem of governments, of semi-faceless bureaucracies of generals and presidents. It has become entirely personal, and Crichton's very own Cold War has ended very differently than did its larger Earthly cousin. He himself brought death and fire to "a field of flowers," and, innocent or not, the beings on Katratzi slain by his action never had a chance, never had a choice, because John Crichton's nuclear policy failed. It is no wonder that he is slowly weeping by the end of the brief monologue above.

In *The Peacekeeper Wars* Crichton says to Aeryn, "War and peace. War and peace. Did you know that Woody Allen's version is better than Tolstoy's because it is funnier? And absolute power corrupts absolutely" (*PKW*). Knowingly or not, he is speaking to himself, for with the escalating danger posed to Aeryn and their child by the war raging around them, Crichton has again become corrupted by the idea that he — and he alone — possesses the power to decide between war and peace. "Unlock the knowledge," he orders the Ancient he has nicknamed Einstein, "I have to make peace" (*PKW*). In a lovely role reversal, it is the cold, logical, militant, gung-ho Aeryn Sun who points out the flaw in Crichton's thinking:

> AERYN: This is what you want. This is what *you* want!
> CRICHTON: No, Aeryn, it is not what I want! It's just that fate keeps blocking all the exits. And no matter what I do, I just keep circling closer to the flame.
> AERYN: Then pull back. This war is not your responsibility.
> CRICHTON: You and the baby are my responsibility. And how am I supposed to protect you from the Peacekeepers and the Scarrans and the Tregans and the lions and tigers and bears? ... No gun is big enough.
> AERYN: We still have Stark and the Eidelons.
> CRICHTON: It's not enough. This, *this* is enough. Wormholes. What's inside my head. This is ugly, and it is malignant, but it will protect you and the baby...
> AERYN: Ah, you see? You don't just protect me. We protect each other [*PKW*].

Aeryn is telling Crichton that his days of unilateral action are over, or should be. The war, the worlds, and his family are not his sole responsibility, no matter what he may think or wish. Such responsibility is always ultimately shared.

Crichton learns the lesson. After more pain, more death, and more tragedy, Crichton and his friends return to Moya to find themselves trapped between two warring fleets, each of which "seem as intent on annihilating us as they are each other" (*PKW*). They also find themselves possessed of the technology needed to create a wormhole weapon. This time, however, Crichton takes the council of his friends, and particularly of Aeryn, who perhaps is the only one who comes close to understanding what is at stake before it actually appears. Aeryn asks if the wormhole weapon is "worse than D'Argo being blown to pieces? Worse than our son dying?" Looking out Moya's viewport at the raging battle around them, she asks "Is it worse than living with this?" As Crichton moves away without answering, Aeryn's expression leaves no doubt that it is indeed worse than all of these things. The actual deployment of the weapon is followed by Crichton's biblical "Behold, the wormhole weapon," irresistibly bringing to mind the Book of Revelation: "behold, an ashen horse; and he who sat on it had the name Death; and Hades was following with him" (*New American Standard Bible*, "Revelation" 6:8).

Nor is such an allusion accidental, for death is the sum total of what the wormhole weapon brings forth, destroying any and everything on its event horizon. Once the combat has been silenced in the face of this horror, Crichton imparts the basic wisdom that the Scarrans and Peacekeepers have denied: "Wormhole weapons do not make peace. Wormhole weapons don't even make war. They make total destruction. Annihilation. Armageddon. People make peace" (*PKW*). Crichton's lines are not merely the exhausted cry of a fictional character to his fictional enemies, but the audience's own cry to the powers which still play games with nuclear fire, holding the world hostage to their policies without voice or vote: peace is not a side effect of technological artifacts. Peace is something that people sweat and strain to build; something that requires a continued commitment and a redoubling of effort to maintain.

It is not the wormhole weapon which ends the Peacekeeper War; it is Commandant Grayza, and it is Emperor Staleek. Theirs was the choice for war or peace. Nor is it a fairytale ending. As *Farscape* continues in its new medium of comic books and graphic novels, Crichton's world is still a very violent and dangerous place. The Peacekeepers are fragmenting, with the High Command in confusion and mass desertions form the ranks (O'Bannon, *The Beginning of the End of the Beginning*, "Book Three"), while the Scarrans are already beginning to question the treaty forced upon them at Qujaga (O'Bannon, *Strange Detractors* "Book One"). Meanwhile, the galaxy has only become moderately less dangerous, even without wormhole weapons. What is more, the genie has already been let out of the bottle. That wormhole weapons can be created is now widely known and knowing that something can be done is often enough to ensure that it will be. On Earth, it is believed that Iran is progressing with its nuclear weapons program in spite of all sanctions. India, Pakistan, and China continue to refine and improve their capability to deliver nuclear weapons to targets both near and far, and the possession of nuclear or radioactive "suitcase bombs" by terrorist organizations is a very real threat. The arms races continue. We, the people, have not made peace. One cannot help but feel that Crichton would be saddened by the news, but not, in the end, surprised.

Notes

1. Yuri Gagarin (1934–1968) was a Soviet pilot and cosmonaut. On 12 April 1961, he became the first human being to go into space, orbiting the Earth for 108 minutes.
2. Quotations are taken from the author's own viewing notes, supplemented by transcripts of *Farscape* episodes available online at "The Terra Firma Transcript Archive" (see Works Cited).
3. In Farscape, however "conventional" weapons include munitions which make 21st century Earth's chemical, biological, and nuclear weapons of mass destruction pale in comparison.
4. In the *Farscape* universe, a colloquial vulgarity for testicles (i.e., "balls").
5. Strategic Defense Initiative, also known as the Star Wars Program. SDI was proposed by American president Ronald Reagan and, as conceived, would have used ground and orbital based systems, including laser-armed satellites to defend the United States against nuclear ballistic missile attack.
6. The same inscription is seen on the nuclear bomb that a whooping Colonel Kong (Slim Pickens) famously rides to Earth at the end of Kubrick's film.
7. The second nuclear bomb that is seen in Colonel Kong's B-52.
8. Many modern ICBMs are equipped with multiple independent re-entry vehicles (MIRVs) each carrying a separate warhead, allowing a single missile to destroy multiple targets or to ensure the elimination of a single target by overwhelming any possible defenses.
9. In one of the supreme ironies of the Cold War, U.S. Army Intelligence used misin-

formation to cause the Soviets to divert precious funding into researching chemical and biological weapons, areas thought to be dead ends. The Soviets, however, turned out to be masters at bio-weaponry, and successfully developed "biological weapons of almost unimaginable horror." See Barrass 408.
   10. One megadeath = 1,000,000 killed.

Works Cited

Barrass, Gordon S. *The Great Cold War: a Journey Through the Hall of Mirrors*. Stanford: Stanford Security Studies/Stanford University Press, 2009. Print.
Bassom, David. "Farscape Creator." *Starburst* 267 (Nov. 2000): 26–30. Print.
Battis, Jes. *Investigating* Farscape*: Uncharted Territories of Sex and Science Fiction*. London: I. B. Tauris, 2007. Print.
Dr. Strangelove or, How I Learned to Stop Worrying and Love the Bomb. Dir. Stanley Kubrick. Perf. Peter Sellers, George C. Scott, David Naylor. 1964. Sony, 2001. DVD.
Dunbabin, John P. D. *The Cold War*. London: Longman, 2008. Print.
Farscape: The Complete Series. Creator Rockne S. O'Bannon, Exec. Prod. Brian Henson. Perf. Ben Browder, Claudia Black, Anthony Simcoe. 1999–2003. A&E, 2009. DVD.
Franklin, H. Bruce. "Fatal Fiction: A Weapon to End All Wars." *The Bulletin of the Atomic Scientists* November (1987): 18–25. JSTOR. Web. 24 July 2011.
Gandhi, M. K. *Non-Violence in Peace and War*. 1942. Reprint. Ahmedabad: Navajivan, 1962. Print.
Henson, Brian. *In the Beginning: A Look Back with Brian Henson*. Farscape: the Complete Series. Creator Rockne S. O'Bannon, Exec. Prod. Brian Henson. Perf. Ben Browder, Claudia Black, Anthony Simcoe. 1999–2003. A&E, 2009. DVD.
Hertling, Major Mark Philip. *Physical Training for the Modern Battlefield: Are We Tough Enough?* Monograph. School of Advanced Military Studies, U.S. Army Command and General Staff College. Fort Leavenworth, 1987. Web. 23 Aug. 2011.
Hilden, Leonard. "Conditioned Reflex, Drugs and Hypnosis in Communist Interrogations." *Central Intelligence Agency*. CIA, 18 Sept. 1995. Web. 23 Aug. 2011. <https://www.cia.gov/library/center-for-the-study-of-intelligence/kent-csi/vol2no2/html/v02i2a06p_0001.htm>.
Kohan, John. "The KGB: Eyes of the Kremlin — TIME." *Breaking News, Analysis, Politics, Blogs, News Photos, Video, Tech Reviews—TIME.com*. TIME.com, 14 Feb. 1983. Web. 25 Aug. 2011.
Kugler, Jacek. "Terror Without Deterrence: Reassessing the Role of Nuclear Weapons." *The Journal of Conflict Resolution* 28.3 (1984): 470–506. JSTOR. Web. 29 Aug. 2011.
Lambridge, Wayne. "A Note on KGB Style." *Central Intelligence Agency*. CIA, 2 June 1996. Web. 23 Aug. 2011. <https://www.cia.gov/library/center-for-the-study-of-intelligence/kent-csi/vol15no1/html/v15i1a08p_0001.htm>.
Love and Death. Dir. Woody Allen. Perf. Woody Allen, Diane Keaton, Fyodor Atkine. 1975. MGM, 2000. DVD.
Maiolo, Joseph A. *Cry Havoc: How the Arms Race Drove the World To War, 1931–1941*. New York: Basic Books, 2010. Print.
McLean, David. "From British Colony to American Satellite? Australia and the USA during the Cold War." *Australian Journal of Politics and History* 52.1 (2006): 64–79. Print.
"NSC 162/2." *FAS: Federation of American Scientists*. N.p., 30 Oct. 1953. Web. 27 Aug. 2011.
Nachbar, John G., and Kevin Lause. *Popular Culture: An Introductory Text*. Bowling Green, OH: Bowling Green State University Popular Press, 1992. Print.
New American Standard Bible. The Lockman Foundation. Grand Rapids: Zondervan, 2002. Print.

O'Bannon, Rockne S. (Story), Keith R. A. DeCandido (Script), and Tommy Patterson (Penciler). *Farscape: The Beginning of the End of the Beginning*. Los Angeles: BOOM! Studios, 2009. Print.
O'Bannon, Rockne S. (Story), Keith R. A. DeCandido (Script), and Will Sliney (Artist). *Farscape: Strange Detractors*. Los Angeles: BOOM! Studios, 2009. Print.
Plokhy, S. M. *Yalta: the Price of Peace*. New York: Viking, 2010. Print.
Rhodes, Richard. *Arsenals of Folly: the Making of the Nuclear Arms Race*. New York: Alfred A. Knopf, 2007. Print.
Tennyson, Alfred. "Locksley Hall by Alfred, Lord Tennyson." *Poetry Foundation*. N.p., n.d. Web. 30 Aug. 2011.
"The Terra Firma Transcript Archive." *Terra Firma: A* Farscape *Forum*. Terra Firma, n.d. Web. 25 Aug. 2011.

Into the Uncharted Territories
Exploring the Nature of Evil

ROBERT L. LIVELY

In the closing sequence of *The Peacekeeper Wars*, John Crichton unleashes a cataclysmic weapon, the wormhole device, destroying the invading Scarran fleet along with a good deal of the Peacekeeper Armada. Dozens of ships are obliterated, and thousands of lives are lost. While it may appear on the surface that this Scarran/Peacekeeper confrontation is a monolithic battle between human-looking good guys and vaguely reptilian Scarran bad guys, a closer examination of the *Farscape* universe reveals that this type of interpretation is severely lacking. The series does not really set up the confrontation between these two species as a struggle of good against evil, and the conclusion in *The Peacekeeper Wars* does not suggest this either.

The theme of good versus evil does not resonate in the *Farscape* universe because the series places the viewer into the realm of "Other." In the premiere episode, we are introduced to a universe unlike our own. The viewer enters this world and must adapt to its strangeness just as John Crichton, the series protagonist, does. The disorientation in the pilot episode helps distance the viewer both literally and figuratively from earthly paradigms. As Jes Battis points out, "Both the show's creator, Rockne O'Bannon, and the actor who plays Crichton — Ben Browder — have said in interview that Crichton is designed, as a character, to be the audience's point of view" (23). The aliens we encounter also set us in the realm of the Other: the militaristic Peacekeepers and Aeryn Sun; D'Argo, the Luxan warrior; Zhaan, the Delvian Pa'u (priest); Rygel, the deposed Dominar of Hyneria; and the Leviathan Moya, a living ship. The puppets and animatronics of Jim Henson's Creature Shop add to this disorientation with a myriad of nonhuman species. When Crichton arrives, he cannot even understand the languages he encounters until he is injected with nanites which cluster in the brain stem and allow all languages to be understood. The overall effect of the first episode "Premiere" (1.1) is to introduce us to the "Other." So in examining the series, there is no reason to assume that the *Farscape* universe would follow a Judeo-Christian world view of good versus evil. The only developed religious views we see are Zhaan's. As viewers, we must consider a different set of moral values concerning good and evil.

Daryl Koehn's impressive book, *The Nature of Evil*, discusses evil in light of two dominant ideologies, and thus may shed better light on events occurring in the *Farscape* series. The idea of evil in the west today is predicated on the belief of corrupted free will. People who do evil are viewed as making the conscious choice to do evil. Their free will has been sullied; therefore, they choose to do evil. Koehn defines this as the Moral Tradition. Another tradition, not as well known to the west, is the Wisdom Tradition, defined by Koehn as evil manifested by the lack of self-awareness and self-identity.

Using Koehn's theories about the Moral Tradition and Wisdom Tradition, I argue that the series is not about Moralist good and evil. Rather, *Farscape* is about self-awareness and self-discovery. *Farscape* makes more sense interpreted through the lens of the Wisdom Tradition because the world-building does not create a galaxy where the Moral Tradition functions in a logical way. According to Huston Smith, the Moral Tradition and the Wisdom Tradition have been in competition for centuries (386). Although early Christianity and many Asian religions embraced the Wisdom Tradition over the Moral Tradition, our current Judeo-Christian frame for judging the nature of evil lies clearly in the Moral Tradition.

Historically, Aristotle was one of the first to associate evil with voluntary human action. In his *Ethics*, Aristotle dismisses the idea that suffering can interfere with happiness. Only vice, a bad habit, or a voluntary corruption of choice deserves to be called evil. Aristotle argued that we become corrupted through laziness and unreasoned action. Aristotle assures his readers that corruption is expressed in the action of evil, since this shows the person doing ill has not deliberated on his or her actions, and thus has a defective will. Evil here is shown as an internal defect that must be punished, but this does not bring us closer to understanding evil. The early Church fathers, when they were reconciling Christianity with classical thought, adopted this doctrine. Evil then became a corruption of choice and free will.

This view changed even further when dogmatic Church fathers started insisting that evil was a morally corrupting condition that caused humans to trespass and commit harm to others. "This view makes evil intentional and shifts our attention away from suffering" and toward bad action (Koehn 16). This world view was reaffirmed in the Enlightenment by Rousseau, who argued that humans should be punished only for the evil that they have caused. Calling an action evil should be reserved for human injustices (see Koehn 16–17). A tsunami would not qualify as evil, but a massacre of people would, since it depends upon human agency. We see this, in the Moral Tradition, as vice or sin.

Philosophers in the Moral Tradition, such as Immanuel Kant, argue that "this corruption is identical to a failure to reason consistently and vigorously in a way that is publically intelligible" (Kant qtd. in Koehn 1). According to Moralists, this vice manifests itself in acts of violence or harm to others. They argue that evil is expressed through corrupted reason or will.[1] This, I believe, is how we perceive evil today. We call tsunamis and floods "natural disasters"; we do not call them evil. We call killers and thieves evil because we view them as misusing their free will. In fact, when we raise our children, we often encourage them to do good by making "good choices." We buy in to the cultural narrative in the attempt to cultivate "good" free will.

The Wisdom Tradition rejects a lot of this mentality. The Wisdom Tradition views evil as a frustrated quality of unsatisfied desire. Aristotle's view of evil makes no sense in light of Plato's statement, "Nobody knowingly does evil" (qtd. in Koehn 1). The person doing evil does not see his or her actions as evil. Murder, torture, war, and slaughter may be bad things, but the people doing them may actually view themselves as positive forces for change, or even as "good guys."

The Wisdom Tradition views evil as the ignorance of the individual "to know thyself." This ignorance may lead people to negatively affect other people, which is a fundamental difference with the Moralists' claim that we knowingly do evil. An unstable self-identity may lead people to do evil, but they do not perceive their actions as such. Because society seldom promotes self-reflection, the identities constructed by individuals who hate some aspects of themselves go unexamined. Therefore, they may do bad things but be convinced they are doing nothing wrong. The illusion caused by frustration and pain of faultily constructed identity ultimately is the root of evil. According to Koehn, we justify our prosecution of wrongdoers by insisting that these offenders possess the self-knowledge needed to act virtuously and so are accountable for their vicious deeds. Aristotle, for example, explicitly denies that human beings can fail to know who they are: "also a person could not be ignorant of the agent; for how could he not know himself?" (5). I find this ironic in the sense that the Delphic Oracle of Ancient Greece cautioned seekers to "Know Thyself." The notion that Oedipus could do evil for all the right reasons because he did not know himself rings hollow in Aristotle's argument. The Wisdom Tradition gives nuance to human action beyond a black and white Moral Tradition argument.

The idea of good and evil in the *Farscape* series should be read from the text of the Wisdom Tradition. The evil that occurs in the series generally derives, not from a corrupted will, but from unsatisfied desires and frustrated self-identities. This chapter will focus on understanding good and evil in the

Farscape series. For all of the world-building in the series, the writers never fully explore the concept of good and evil. It would be reductive to see these cultures as reduced to "good guys" and "bad guys," simply good vs. evil. If one analyzes *Farscape* through the lens of the Wisdom Tradition, a new perspective arises that evil is something that occurs from the characters' inability to truly "know" themselves. Specifically, I will focus on the portrayal of John Crichton (human), Aeryn Sun (Sebacean), Scorpius (half Sebacean and half Scarran), and the Scarrans, Minister Ahkna and Emperor Staleek. It is only at the conclusion of *The Peacekeeper Wars* that the characters I focus on in the chapter truly know themselves because they each reach a point of knowledge and understanding of themselves.

John Crichton: Pieces of a Fractured Hero

Farscape can be analyzed as John Crichton's readjustment of his moral compass. In the premiere episode of *Farscape* (1.1) before Crichton is to test his slingshot effect theory, he is shown interacting with his father with the pride and competition that inevitably arises between father and son. Crichton feels he lives in the shadow of his father, who is an accomplished astronaut himself. Crichton is sketched, as Koehn might say, as an individual whose personality is not edified. Crichton is pursuing his scientific theory, an event that will establish his identity as an astronaut and physicist that will equal his father. His spaceship, the Farscape module, begins the test to bounce off of the Earth's atmosphere when he is sucked into a wormhole and deposited into another galaxy. In his eyes he has failed, and his identity becomes even less concrete and more fluid as he encounters the aliens on Moya, the living ship. As Crichton attempts to discover who he is in this new galaxy, he must adjust his morals; he must determine what is good and what is evil in an alien universe that does not understand the morality that he often displays. Crichton works through this uncertainty of identity and explores who he really is; however, he never really discovers this until the final moments of *The Peacekeeper Wars* when he detonates the wormhole device.

Throughout the series, Crichton's identity is continually fractured, making it difficult to find the real person. Crichton is torn between his earthly existence and the universe in the Uncharted Territories, where he is constantly challenged to examine himself. He is torn and seduced by the possibility of returning to earth. In "A Human Reaction" (1.16) Crichton believes he has returned to earth, but it is a clever ruse. While on "earth" Crichton remembers the xenophobia and petty politics of our world, and he begins to realize that he is torn between his former life and his new one. He cannot have his love, Aeryn, and his friends, such as D'Argo and Chiana, and his family on earth, too. His fractured personality is not a figurative statement. The pull toward earth is strong in Crichton; after all, it is his home. He returns to Earth twice in the series: once in the past, and once to warn Earth of what is out in space. On his last visit, he realizes he is a danger to the planet and chooses to abandon his home world forever. The conflict in Crichton, between being the hero he wants to be in space and his urge to go home, fractures his psyche. How can he be two different people at the same time?

In the series, this fracturing is literalized, and the viewers can see the potential for good and evil in Crichton. For instance, in "My Three Crichtons" (2.13), an energy orb lands in Moya, enveloping Crichton. The orb literally fractures Crichton into three personas, two of which are different evolutionary versions of Crichton: a caveman, hairy and bestial, and an evolved form, with an enlarged, bald cranium, looking somewhat like a giant, skeletal brain. The caveman represents emotion and the ability for compassion whereas the evolved form is pure intellect, cold and uncaring. These versions of Crichton challenge preconceptions of good and evil that the viewers and the crew must confront.

This episode does a great job of showing the possibilities inherent in Crichton's character. He is capable of both emotion and coldness. At first, the caveman version is hunted as a "creature," while the evolved form is generally accepted into the crew. However, the perception of the inferior caveman is soon dispelled. Even though the caveman Crichton is unpredictable and sometimes violent with emotion, this version of John is connected to the crew of Moya through his passions. Chiana, for example, forms a bond with the caveman persona, and she points out to Crichton, "You think this guy's nothing. He's you. He's warm. He's sensitive. He's everything I ever liked about you." The evolved form is almost pure intellect removed from the connections to the crew and even emasculated as Aeryn notes when she comments, "For a start John has more hair — amongst other things. You going to blame that on being cold?" The evolved form does not care about emotion. He is purely quantitative. When the evolved Crichton tells Zhaan how much more capable he is than the other versions of Crichton, she responds, "I wonder if you can also see what you have lost? Your logic is firm, but it is cold." The real John Crichton comes to appreciate his emotional side when confronting his evolved self. Both John and caveman Crichton are willing to sacrifice themselves for others, yet the evolved form is the coldly rational side of John the scientist who is beyond friendship — completely devoted to selfish pursuits of his own. The evolved form, however, has the intellectual capability to save Moya. When the orb sends a message to the crew that it will suck Moya into an alternate dimension unless it acquires a sample Crichton, several crew members want to send the caveman version to his death. John, however, seeks to find a way to save himself, or at least a version of himself, whereas the evolved Crichton easily condemns the caveman to death. Crichton tries to delineate himself from the others when he quips, "I'm widening my perspective. That's what makes me, me." This fractured identity of Crichton shows the viewer aspects of the character and furthers the theme of a character who does not completely know himself. In the end, the caveman shows the human ability to sacrifice, to do good, and he saves the crew when he knocks the evolved Crichton unconscious and carries him into the sphere. John Crichton believed that his evolved form would evolve his moral sense as well, but he was mistaken. The caveman Crichton showed a better sense of good and evil than his evolved counterpart. Near the end of the episode, John confides his lack of self-knowledge to D'Argo.

> D'ARGO: You did what you thought was right.
> CRICHTON: I did what I knew was wrong. The future Crichton — kind of makes you wonder if that's where we're headed.
> D'ARGO: It's only one possible genetic path.
> CRICHTON: Yeah, but it's possible. That's the problem.

The fracturing of Crichton is revealed in several more ways which challenge the conceptions of good and evil in the series. The crazed Kaarvok "twins" Crichton in the episode "Eat Me" (3.6), furthering the fracturing motif of Crichton. The Twinning is described as creating a duplicate — an identical being indistinguishable from the original. In fact, Crichton wears different colored t-shirts to distinguish the twins for the audience, leaving an arbitrary feeling that we can only recognize the Crichtons by the clothes they wear. The lack of stable identity haunts Crichton as one twin leaves on Talyn with Aeryn in Season Three. The Crichton on Talyn consummates his love for Aeryn and fathers a child with her, while the Crichton on Moya rages jealously against the "him" on Talyn. The writers of *Farscape* did a fine job of literalizing the psychic turmoil in Crichton.

Aeryn Sun: Searching for Redemption

Aeryn Sun, skillfully played by Claudia Black, is a Peacekeeper. The Sebaceans that populate the Peacekeeper forces can be viewed as a soulless, tyrannical, hierarchical, and genetically pure race. It would be easy for viewers to see the Peacekeepers as a *Farscape* version of the Nazis; their black uniforms and rigidly militaristic social structure lends itself to this interpretation. In the first scene where we meet Aeryn Sun ("Premiere" 1.1), she is dressed in battle armor that disguises her gender and adds to the menace of the scene. Crichton is clearly intimidated by her armor until she removes her helmet, and he is confronted by the beautiful Aeryn. He quickly realizes that she is dangerous as she throws him to the floor. Since humans and Sebaceans look almost identical, Officer Sun mistakes Crichton for a renegade or captured Peacekeeper soldier.

In trying to escape Moya, Aeryn and Crichton seek out a Peacekeeper regiment. But Aeryn's involvement with Crichton and the criminals aboard Moya leave her branded as "irreversibly contaminated" by her commanding officer, Commander Crais ("Premiere" 1.1). This proclamation will fundamentally change how Aeryn views herself over the course of the series. Throughout the series, Aeryn often tells the crew, "I am a Peacekeeper," yet this is not exactly correct. She *was* a Peacekeeper. Aeryn's inability to really know herself leads her to self-reflect on her judgments of good and evil.

At the beginning of the series, Aeryn is portrayed as a closed-emotion soldier. To the viewers and the crew of Moya, she is just a Peacekeeper soldier, born and bred to the cause. However, once Crais has effectively exiled her from the Peacekeepers, she loses the core of her values. Aeryn's past is explored in future episodes that slowly show Aeryn as a vastly more complicated character, one who embraced Peacekeeper values so strongly because she did not fully believe in them. This frustrated ego is a determining factor, according to Koehn, of our ability to discern good and evil. Aeryn says as much when she encounters her mother, Xhalax, in the episode "Relativity" (3.10).

> My corruption began the moment I was conceived. Don't you see my independence comes from you anyway? I grew up wanting to be just like a woman I'd only seen once. I am a part of you that wanted to be a rebel... I am your child.

Aeryn's past is slowly revealed in a mosaic of episodes over the course of the series.[2] The composite is nothing like the view we have in the premiere episode. Peacekeepers are selectively bred and anonymously parented. They are taught to bond with their units and breed when they are selected and with whom. Aeryn fails at the "Peacekeeper way." Confronted with her mother's admonition that she would hunt Aeryn down and kill her, Aeryn is unable to reciprocate the need to kill her mother. As a Peacekeeper, Aeryn should not have hesitated to kill Xhalax. From a Peacekeeper perspective, Aeryn is contaminated, evil. Accused of contamination by contact with Crichton, Aeryn is unrepentant of her growing love for him. She is cast further adrift in knowing who she is when she tells Crichton, "All my ties to them [the Peacekeepers] are completely severed" ("Relativity").

Aeryn shows the potential for good in the series as she further distances herself from the Peacekeepers. As the series progresses, we find out that Aeryn was once in love with a fellow Peacekeeper, just like her mother. And yet, just like her mother, Aeryn has the ability to do great harm. In "The Way We Weren't" (2.5), Aeryn helps kill a defenseless pilot aboard Moya three cycles before events in the series begin. Aeryn tells Chiana, "Yes, I was a Peacekeeper, and things were different then." Aeryn reveals that she was torn between beliefs for a long time before she arrived on Moya. She tells Crichton about a Peacekeeper with whom she was in love named Velorek. Much like Crichton, he saw the beauty and potential in Aeryn. He even echoed Crichton's assessment of Aeryn when he told her, "you could be so much more [than a Peacekeeper commando]." Aeryn is shown to be a lot like Xhalax in this episode. She falls in love, yet she betrays Velorek to Crais for promotion to prowler pilot. Aeryn finds it difficult to be both loving woman and Peacekeeper; she has been bred and brainwashed to believe the Peacekeeper ways. This episode helps explain why she is simultaneously loving and distant to Crichton.

By the time of *The Peacekeeper Wars*, Aeryn is pregnant and embracing motherhood in a way she could not anticipate. Aeryn has protected her unborn child from the Scarrans ("Prayer" 4.18 and "We're So Screwed Part I: Fetal Attraction" 4.19), and she has come to terms with the lack of mothering she received with the Peacekeepers. In fact, Aeryn instructs the DRDs on Moya to construct the wormhole device to John's specifications, so her child can grow up in peace. She is willing to destroy thousands of Peacekeepers and Scarrans for the sake of her child.

Aeryn's search for self shows her capacity for doing both good and evil. Her upbringing as a Peacekeeper, her relationship with her mother, her love affairs with Velorek and both Crichtons, her irreversible contamination, and her belief in motherhood, pull her in conflicting directions and cause her to be both terrible and beneficent. At the end of *The Peacekeeper Wars*, Aeryn is no longer conflicted. She has put her past behind her; she has helped secure peace in the galaxy, and she is a loving wife and mother. Her moral conundrums are quieted, and she has gained redemption through her son, D'Argo Sun Crichton — a child she can love openly.

Scorpius: Caught Between Two Worlds

When we see Scorpius, we see an amalgamation of stereotypes of the "bad guy." He wears a menacing black suit; he is emaciated to the point of being skeletal; his voice is low and raspy. He is built as a menacing figure by our conventions of people who are evil. But there is another interpretation of Scorpius' character. Scorpius is a Sebacean-Scarran hybrid. He has the unique perspective of knowing what the Scarrans are capable of. Scorpius must wear his black suit because of his unique physiology; it is a crutch to a man who suffers. Scarrans prefer heat whereas Sebaceans are bred to endure the cold of space, and heat slowly kills them. His biology is literally an enemy to him. His shriveled look is merely the byproduct of his parentage.

Scorpius is the antagonist in the series to be sure, but he acts to do good. Scorpius is a Peacekeeper, and his first goal is to protect the Alliance planets from threats. Scorpius has intimate knowledge of Scarran psychology, and he knows the threat posed by them. He pursues Crichton for the wormhole technology, not to be evil, but to save the Peacekeepers. Scorpius confides in

Crichton that the Peacekeepers will lose a direct conflict with the Scarrans, so he has to obtain the wormhole weapon to save the Peacekeepers.

In the episode "Incubator" (3.11), Scorpius inserts Crichton's neural chip into his own brain in an attempt to solve the wormhole equations that are eluding him. Rather than attacking and torturing Crichton's neural clone, as Scorpius did to the real Crichton in "Nerve" (1.19) and "The Hidden Memory" (1.20), Scorpius reasons with neural Crichton by showing him why he is seeking the wormhole device. This is perhaps the finest episode at showing how Scorpius' misplaced quest for self causes him to do evil.

Scorpius reveals that he is a Scarran-Sebacean hybrid who was raised by a Scarran named Tauza. His hybrid physiology is almost incompatible with itself, and he was born in Sebacean heat delirium. The Scarrans view Scorpius as weak and want him to overcome his infirmities. Tauza complains that if Scorpius claims his Scarran ancestry, then he "cannot be weak." Further, we glimpse the Scarran view of the Peacekeepers: "Sebaceans are a deficient breed." Scorpius tells Crichton that his earliest memory is "pain." As viewers, we see and sympathize with Scorpius as Tauza tortures the poor misshapen boy. Scorpius is torn between two worlds. He cannot please his Scarran keepers, and he is not racially pure enough for the Peacekeepers. Scorpius escapes his Scarran captors and enlists with the Peacekeepers where he finds a place for himself. As Koehn points out, the Wisdom Tradition views "evil as the pain and frustration we unwittingly inflict upon ourselves as we adopt ever more perverse strategies to escape our unhappy selves" (64). This is clearly the case with Scorpius. As he tries to determine who he is, he is constantly torn and fractured by his bi-racial birth. When Scorpius seeks out the Peacekeepers, he is interviewed by Captain Molayne:

> SCORPIUS: I was taught that I'm the product of a forced birthing between a Peacekeeper male and a Scarran female. I believe this to be false. I want to know the truth.
> CAPTAIN MOLAYNE: Why? So you can find out who you are?
> SCORPIUS: To find out who I should be.

With his unique ability to detect lies, we find that the Peacekeepers do not lie to him, and he discovers that his mother was a Sebacean female captured and bred in an experimental program by the Scarrans to "find out if Sebacean genetics" could serve them. This unfortunate revelation is a clear motivation for Scorpius' character.

When Scorpius tells neural Crichton that he was recaptured by the Scarrans while searching for the answers to his past, Tauza reminds Scorpius, "You are Scarran, or you are nothing." But Scorpius' genetic deficiencies lead the Scarrans to believe that all Peacekeepers are weak. In the climactic scene of the episode, Scorpius tells John,

SCORPIUS: I have shared these memories for a reason — to show you what Scarrans are like.
CRICHTON: Preaching to the choir Scorpy, I've got no love for Scarrans.
SCORPIUS: Then help us! Scarrans far outnumber the Peacekeepers. Without superior weaponry, we will be crushed.
CRICHTON: You want to kill them; they want to kill you. I do not see a hell of a lot of difference.
SCORPIUS: You let me finish, and I'll show you the difference.

Scorpius then reveals that the Scarrans wish to "eradicate" the Sebacean race. Scorpius' will to save the Peacekeepers is his prime motivation for pursuing the wormhole technology. Scorpius is unique in his knowledge and understanding of the Scarran threat. The Peacekeepers have been in power too long and have grown a bit complacent; therefore, they do not see the Scarrans as the real threat they pose. As Scorpius admits to John, however, not only does he want to save the Peacekeepers, he wants revenge.

Scorpius' admonition of revenge is a powerful indicator that he does not truly know and accept who he is. His hatred of the Scarrans is enormous, and some of this is clearly directed at his Scarran heritage. When Scorpius is allowed to join the Peacekeepers, he must first gain an exemption to the "purity" requirement. Scorpius is viewed as an "Other," an outsider among both his races. This quest for self leads Scorpius to do much evil in the name of good. His inability to truly accept his heritage is the hurdle he must overcome. Ultimately, Scorpius is a pitiable man who cannot escape his tortured upbringing. Only in the ending of *The Peacekeepers Wars* is Scorpius' drive rewarded. He begs Crichton, begs him with "a cherry on top," to launch the wormhole weapon. Using the knowledge of the Ancients, John constructs and launches the wormhole weapon, destroying the Scarran fleet. Scorpius is horrified at the result; not only is the Scarran fleet destroyed, but so are the Peacekeepers. As the wormhole continues to grow, Scorpius mutters, "This is insane, Crichton." In that single moment, Scorpius has exercised self-reflection, true self-reflection, and he realizes that his quest for vengeance was ultimately self-destructive. In the resulting peace accord, we see a Scorpius smug and almost smiling, pleased with the idea of a safe galaxy. In a sense, Scorpius is made whole by proving to the Scarrans his Peacekeeper side was not weak and to the Peacekeepers that he was correct in his pursuit of the wormhole weapon — but at a terrible, terrible cost.

Crichton, Scorpius, and the Shadow-Self[3]

One way of viewing the complex relationship between Crichton's and Scorpius' neural clones is that they are, to borrow the Jungian term, Shadow selves. Ursula K. Le Guin tackles the use of the Shadow self in her essay, "The Child and the Shadow," where she discusses the use of the Shadow figure in Science Fiction and Fantasy literature. This Shadow, as defined by Le Guin, is

> the man [that] is all that is civilized — learned, kindly, idealistic, decent. The shadow is all that gets suppressed in the process of becoming a decent, civilized adult. The shadow is the man's thwarted selfishness, his unadmitted desires, the swearwords he never spoke, the murders he didn't commit. The shadow is the dark side of his soul, the unadmitted, the inadmissible [60].

Scorpius plays this role well in the series. When Scorpius captures Crichton and tortures him in the Aurora Chair ("Nerve" 1.19 and "The Hidden Memory" 1.20), he places a neural chip in Crichton's brain to steal the Ancients' technology for the wormhole device. This allows a simulacrum of Scorpius to root around in Crichton's thoughts, looking for the secrets Crichton has suppressed. He is Crichton's shadow self. He is the nagging voice in Crichton's head that begs him to build and use the wormhole weapon against the Scarrans. He is the dark part of Crichton's thoughts that will break down his moral compass even further than Crichton is willing.

This is not to say that the relationship is completely destructive; the Scorpius shadow saves Crichton's life in the episode "Won't Get Fooled Again" (2.15), after he is captured by the Scarrans. At times the Scorpius shadow is both tormentor, as in "Beware of Dog" (2.14) or counselor as in "Self-Inflicted Wounds Part I: Could'a, Would'a, Should'a" (3.3). The relationship between Crichton and Scorpius as the shadow is complex. Jung defines the complexities of these dealings: "The shadow is a moral problem that challenges the whole ego-personality, for no one can become conscious of the shadow without considerable moral effort" (145). John is conscious of Scorpius, so we can assume he is making a moral effort. He will not divulge the wormhole technology no matter the means of persuasion that the Scorpius shadow will try. Jung also contends that

> closer examination of the dark characteristics — that is, the inferiorities constituting the shadow — reveals that they have an *emotional* nature, a kind of autonomy, and accordingly an obsessive or, better, possessive quality [145].

This describes the relationship between Crichton and the Scorpius shadow well, I think. Scorpius is driven to delve into Crichton's mind, and several times in the series the neural clone tells Crichton, "You will never be rid of me." The Scorpius shadow works well in the framework of fractured identity working towards evil, in Koehn's paradigm. If we view Scorpius as a part of John's psyche, a frustrated part of his desires, then we can further see both his psychological crisis of having the wormhole knowledge, as well as his literalized fracturing of himself, as discussed above. The overall effect on the series shows the viewer the constant psychological tension with which Crichton lives.

According to Le Guin, the only way to defeat the shadow is to turn and confront it (70). John Crichton refuses to do this. He may argue and even fight with the Scorpius shadow, but ultimately he is running and hiding from the wormhole knowledge with the shadow ever in pursuit. In *The Peacekeeper Wars*, Crichton finally confronts the shadow and uses the wormhole technology. This acceptance allows him to face his fear and destroy the shadow. In the final moments of the mini-series, Crichton watches the neural clone slowly die and fade away. It is interesting to note that the dying shadow is no longer wearing the black suit but a muted white-washed version that looks much less menacing. John has faced the shadow and defeated him — only then does he wake up from his coma to greet his child.

Ahkna and Staleek: Striving for Unattainable Desires

It would be easy to classify the Scarrans as just bad guys; in fact, the back cover of *The Peacekeeper Wars* DVD identifies the Scarrans as an evil empire. They are one of the major military powers in the galaxy, and their cultural mores are quite different than the human viewers of the series. Yet this is a basic stereotypical convention of SF: reptilian species are the bad guys. Crichton even plays with this when he calls Staleek a "Sleestak" from the series *Land of the Lost*.[4] But to understand the reasons upon which the Scarrans act, we must investigate the problems they have in viewing themselves and other races.

Scarrans value toughness. They are physically big, hard to kill, and have claws, as well as a directed heat probe they can shoot forward from their hands. In the episode, "Incubator" (3.11), we see Tauza torturing the boy who would become Scorpius. She tells him that Scarrans are strong, but since he is weak, he is nothing. We learn that the Scarrans kill or enslave anything they view as weak. This seems an act of pure evil, but to them, they are preserving their societal values. Earth cultures did this as well. The Greeks would leave babies they deemed deformed on hillsides to die, and the Spartans killed children who looked weak. But these are not the values that cause the Scarrans to act "evil." The Scarrans suffer from a boredom of their race. They have subjugated their own region, and they have nothing really to do.

Koehn's view expresses the tone portrayed by the Scarrans: "When we suffer from ennui, we think the world owes it to us to be intriguing and engaging... Instead, we behave like children. We have some need or desire, so the universe must fulfill it! We do not consider the possibility that the universe does not exist in order to cater to our every whim" (65). The Scarran belief in their own superiority forces them to act like petulant children. They are unsatisfied with themselves and need to test their belief in their own power.

As Baumeister, Smart, and Boden point out, bullies with high self-esteem turn to violence when they feel that they encounter what they perceive to be weaker people. They are so ego-centric, they simply believe they cannot fail, so they become bored with their conquests—which, in turn, leads to more aggressive behavior (7–9). In the case of the Scarrans, they turn their attention to the Peacekeeper's space in order to prove themselves and end their ennui.

War Minister Ahkna first appears in the episode "Bringing Home the Beacon" (4.16). In the episode, she is in negotiations with the Peacekeepers on a treaty to cede some of the uncharted territories to the Peacekeepers in exchange for the Luxan worlds. The Scarrans believe the Luxans may be good cannon fodder troops for their war machine. Ultimately the negotiations fail because the Scarrans view the Peacekeepers as lesser beings. Ahkna is brutal, obsessive, and not adept at negotiations. It is not the Scarran way. Since the Scarran race believes they are genetically superior, they have little use for niceties and manners, which they consider a weakness. When Crichton attempts to auction off the wormhole knowledge in "We're So Screwed Part I: Fetal Attraction" (4.19), it is obvious that Ahkna believes only the Scarrans are strong and wise enough to use it. She doubts the Peacekeepers or Crichton have the courage to use such a weapon. Ahkna shows her contempt for others as she tortures Scorpius for wormhole knowledge, after which she uses her heat probe ability on Crichton to find any knowledge he might possess. She even risks the detonation of the nuclear device he is using to protect himself from attack by either the Peacekeepers or the Scarrans. When Crichton refuses to give her the knowledge, and the nuclear bomb is about to detonate, Crichton still will not give in. Ahkna cannot believe Crichton would kill himself to protect the wormhole knowledge. She calls him "insane" because she cannot fathom killing herself. She typifies the Scarran egocentrism that leads them to do evil. They do not really know their limits beyond a belief in their invulnerability, similar to the characteristic belief in teenagers who subscribe to their "personal fable" of invincibility. Nowhere is this portrayed better than by Staleek.

Staleek is the Emperor of the Scarrans and a shrewd leader. He is supremely convinced that his race deserves to rule the galaxy. He has secured the races of the Charrids and Kalish as servants to the Scarran Empire. When Crichton arrives at Katratzi, Staleek believes he is perhaps there to rescue Scorpius, but in his mind, he cannot believe someone would risk his life to save another. He quips, "Why would Crichton risk so much to rescue an ally?" (4.20). Staleek shows a lack of empathy, and a lack of knowledge of friendship or companionship. Unable to understand his enemies or obtain the wormhole knowledge, Staleek becomes even more frustrated by his own discordance between his world view of his race and his ability to achieve his goals. As Koehn points out,

We implicitly want what will satisfy us in an abiding way. Only something that provides lasting satisfaction is truly good. And there's the rub. Although each of us strives for satisfaction, our unexamined desires contain the germ of dissatisfaction. Lacking self-knowledge we pursue what appears good but fails to end our cravings [239–240].

This is a valuable lens through which to view Staleek, and Scarrans in general, because they have a need to prove themselves superior. It permeates their rhetoric throughout the series. But their desires ultimately are self-destructive, and thus they perform evil. In the final moments of *The Peacekeeper Wars*, as his flagship, *The Decimator*, is about to be destroyed by the expanding wormhole, Emperor Staleek refuses to acknowledge that his Scarran world view has betrayed him. The film is riveting as his ship hangs upon the event horizon of the wormhole singularity. Staleek has an epiphany that suggests the possibility of peace — an antithetical belief to the Scarrans — is ultimately better than destruction. Staleek shows us that Scarrans are capable of self-knowledge though, and he utters the single word, "Peace."

Conclusion

In this essay, I have shown how viewing *Farscape* through the lens of the Wisdom Tradition brings a more nuanced interpretation of the characters than simply seeing them as good guys and bad guys. The psychological aspects of the characters that I have examined in the chapter clearly show a lack of developed identity in Crichton, Aeryn, Scorpius, Emperor Staleek, and Minister Ahkna. The evil that arises in the series can be blamed in large part on the lack of self-knowledge of the characters. Only with the potential destruction of the galaxy as the wormhole expands in the climactic sequence in *The Peacekeeper Wars* are the characters forced to examine their motives and truly face themselves. In so doing, the characters gain a self-knowledge that fundamentally changes them for the better. As the series ends, Crichton, Aeryn, Scorpius, and the Scarrans are at peace — not only in the galaxy, but with themselves.

Notes

1. In *Trillion Year Spree* (Atheneum, 1986), the fascinating history of Science Fiction, Brian Aldiss remarks on these two conflicting traditions: "Where *The Lord of the Rings* is like SF is in the way the heroes are almost all good (even Boromir), and evil is externalized and defeated — something which we know does not happen in real life, for evil is within us" (262).

2. For a more thorough discussion of Aeryn Sun's character, see Sherry Ginn's *Our Space, Our Place: Women in the Worlds of Science Fiction* (Lanham, MD: University Press of America, 2005) and her essay on female community, this collection.

3. In dealing with Scorpius' character, I was influenced greatly by Zweig and Wolf's *Romancing the Shadow: Illuminating the Dark Side of the Soul* (New York: Ballantine, 1997) and Gregory Desilet's *Our Faith in Evil* (Jefferson, N.C.: McFarland, 2006).

4. *Land of the Lost* (1974–1976) was a children's television show featuring the Marshall family who had inadvertently crossed a portal into a world filled with strange creatures. The Marshall family was menaced by reptilian creatures called the Sleestak who were vicious, but dimwitted creatures. Crichton parallels the Marshall family in that he passed through the wormhole into a galaxy filled with strange creatures, and he is menaced by reptilian creatures, the Scarrans. Crichton's intentional use of "Sleestak" to refer to Staleek should be taken as an insult.

Works Cited

Aristotle. *The Nicomachean Ethics*. Trans. David Ross. Ed. Lesley Brown. Oxford: Oxford University Press, 2009. Print.

Battis, Jes. *Investigating* Farscape*: Uncharted Territories of Sex and Science Fiction*. New York: I. B. Tauris, 2007. Print.

Baumeister, Roy F., Laura Smart, and Joseph M. Boden. "Relation of Threatened Egotism to Violence and Aggression: The Dark Side of High Self-Esteem." *Psychological Review* 103.1 (1996): 5–33. Print.

Jung, Carl. *The Portable Jung*. Trans. R. F. C. Hull. Ed. Joseph Campbell. New York: Penguin, 1976. Print.

Koehn, Daryl. *The Nature of Evil*. New York: Palgrave Macmillan, 2005. Print.

Le Guin, Ursula K. "The Child and the Shadow." *The Language of the Night*. San Francisco: Perennial, 1993. Print.

Smith, Huston. *The World's Religions*. San Francisco: HarperCollins, 1991. Print.

The Emperor's New Farts
Socioeconomic Disenfranchisement and "Colonic Miasma"

MICHAEL G. CORNELIUS

> *Chiana: You little toad! You had to go and fart helium now?*
> *Rygel: I'm nervous, it happens. We're in court, so sue me!*—"Dream a Little Dream" 2.8

The disparate individuals who travel together on Moya in the science-fiction television series *Farscape* are exiles. Reflecting heterogeneous cultures, physiologies, and quiddities, this divergent group of travelers is nonetheless united by their status as refugees, disconnected from their mother worlds by space, circumstance, politics, and war. As a result of their common condition, they also share a status as socioeconomically disenfranchised peoples, individuals who are no longer able to participate in the larger social and economic apparatuses that drive their respective home cultures. They are the proverbial strangers in a strange land, made all the more unfamiliar to the other, and to the audience, by their unique compositions. The early episodes of *Farscape* are largely about discovering, being discomfited by, and learning to live with such differences, for both human astronaut John Crichton as well as the audience, who identifies with and considers action largely through the gaze of the very human protagonist at the heart of a very alien narrative.

All the characters experience socioeconomic disenfranchisement from their mother worlds and cultures in some form or another. Peacekeeper Aeryn Sun is cast off by her own people, removed from the very power structure that shapes this part of the galaxy; Zhaan was a high-level, high-ranking priest amongst her peoples before she was forced out for the heretical nature of her views (and for high crimes as well); D'Argo was a soldier in a race of warrior people who must now reconstruct his identity amongst a group of individuals who value his skills but value peace more, while also contending with that fact that Aeryn Sun was a member of a far-more-successful warrior caste. Even Crichton, whose exile is accidental, becomes socioeconomically disenfranchised when he reaches Moya. The son of fame and privilege, who exults in an occupation (astronaut) and position highly valued by his society, Crichton must now contend with being the individual most noted for being disconnective to the time and place he now resides.

Yet no member of Moya's ramshackle family more reflects socioeconomic disenfranchisement than the former Emperor Dominar Rygel XVI, previous ruler of the Hynerian Empire and once overlord to six hundred billion people. Overthrown by his cousin Bishon, Rygel represents the ultimate in socioeconomic disenfranchisement. His movement from potentate to prisoner, from luxury to table scraps, from utter autonomy to absolute restriction, reflects an enormous shift in both social and economic status, and impacts not only his construct of his self but also the means through which Rygel is able to express his self as well. Though Rygel still luxuriates in all forms of excess, his most immediate concerns are his own survival, both physiologically and politically, and as such his transformation from ruler to ruled is both complete and absolute. To paraphrase Shakespeare, truly heavy is the head that no longer wears the crown.

A popular recurring gag on *Farscape* involves Rygel's propensity for flatulence. When anxious, Hynerians excrete gaseous helium from their bowels, which not only results in the sound of flatus but has the unfortunate side effect of raising the voices of those in proximity to Rygel's anus. The farting is designed, of course, not only for comedic impact, but as a means of reducing Rygel's inflated sense of selfhood. Because they are produced by anxiety, Rygel's farts usually occur in groups of people, and often during moments of tense confrontation; the funnier, of course, for the audience, and the more derisory for those around Rygel, both friend and foe alike. Of course, it is also satisfying that a being as self-important and ostentatious as Rygel endures constant bouts of humiliation (there is a reason the word "flatulence" is also a synonym for "pomposity"). In the show, Rygel is both self-conscious of his flatulence (as noted in the epigraph to this paper, where he rounds on Chiana for pointing out his farting) and suffers for it (usually in the form of name-calling and reduced status). It is evident that, as well as being simply comedic, Rygel's farting is designed to render him low, to (literally) "take the air out of him" and bring him out of the realm of the royal and more firmly ally him, socioeconomically speaking, with the other exiles aboard Moya. Yet, interestingly, Rygel's farting ultimately reflects not only his own need for physical excess, it also produces the unintended effect of "humanizing" the former despot, rendering him not only low but also, in a way, reminding his fellow exiles that he is, indeed, despite his actions and sometime statements to the contrary, one of them.

Farting is base humor; it is comic, it is bawdy, and, almost universally, viewed as a production of low, popular culture. A good example of this is the anonymous early eighteenth-century poem "A Fart" or "Upon a Fart:"

> Gentlest Blast of ill concoction,
>   Reverse of high ascending Belch,
> The only stink abhord by Scotch men
>   Beloved & practiced by the Welch [in Nickels and O'Neill 1–4].

"A Fart" is a burlesque of the poem "A Sigh" by Anne Finch, Countess of Winchilsea. Burlesque is a genre that attempts to treat high art and popular culture as if it were one and the same. A burlesque is usually designed to take a work that is considered highbrow, exultant, and rarified and bring it crashing back to earth. Thus the more esteemed a masterpiece, the more trivial its excesses and estimations become in the burlesque. Geoffrey Chaucer wrote a burlesque, a work designed to bring low the highest genre of his day; the same is true of Miguel de Cervantes, Alexander Pope, and Jonathan Swift. In all their burlesques, the goal was to make the high, low; to take that which was eminent and deconstruct it to the point of idiocy, as "A Fart" does to "A Sigh." The genius of these comic burlesques is found exactly in that desire, to trample on what so many others deem to be serious, to eschew the artistic conventions of the day in favor of works that were often cringe-worthy in their greatness. Such works are called travesties, as if to name them after what high culture must have deigned these texts to be.

In *Farscape*, farting works to burlesque the figure of Rygel, or at least Rygel's self-constructed version of his own character. It is difficult to maintain one's dignity when one is continually forced to commit acts of physiology that are considered ill-bred and vulgar. This is especially true considering the anal nature of Rygel's action. Tiffany Beechy writes of the anus that

> even in pre-psychoanalytic, high/low models of human psychology, the anus often opposes the head: reason and virtue have their seat in the "higher" region of the upper body, while lust, meanness, and mortal flesh all lurk "down there." The anus is the primal locus, then, of evil, the antithesis to the thesis, the grave as opposed to birth portal [73].

Rygel is one of the more difficult characters on *Farscape*. He is greedy and demanding. A committed sensualist, Rygel constantly seeks to indulge his lusts for food, precious objects, and other carnal/carnival pleasures. Russian philosopher Mikhail Bakhtin describes the carnivalesque as that which twists, mutates, or perverts societal norms and standards. Bakhtin believed carnival culture infuses high culture with a sense of mirth and riotous excess, a "temporary suspension of all hierarchic distinctions and barriers among men ... and the prohibitions of usual life" (15). One can visit the (metaphoric) carnival, but choosing to habituate within is a symptom of a deficient character, reflective of a need to continually indulge the senses at the expense of loftier, more idealized, more "human/e" pursuits. The carnival is the opposite of all that is good, decent, and staid, and in continually inhabiting such realms of excess, so is Rygel. This suggests that his farting is particularly germane to his identity, since, as Beechy points out, not only was "the anus the site of evil and inversion, but also, more specifically ... the site of greed. In medieval theology both greed and sodomitical behaviors were related to *luxuria*, or excessive desire" (73). Farting thus marks Rygel, much as the brand identifies Cain or the scarlet letter Hester Prynne, for his sins and excesses.

Yet as much as Rygel longs for the continual surfeit of the carnival, the world he now inhabits is very different from the Hynerian court. Interestingly, because of his disenfranchisement from his former socioeconomic status, Rygel must now — and for the first time — actively participate in his own social and economic existences as well. From the very first episode of *Farscape*, Rygel acts as the key negotiator for the crew's needs, bartering no longer for goods of luxury but the necessities of survival: food, technology, information. His modest stature often indicates that he is best for making key repairs; and on more than one occasion, his diplomatic skills and connections come in handy and save the crew. Like all the other individuals onboard Moya, Rygel eventually conforms to the familial structure that such space dictates, not only for survival, but also for socioeconomic re-enfranchisement. In short, in order to get on, Rygel must change.

Perhaps, then, our view of Rygel's excess flatus can alter as well. Janine Chasseguet-Smirgel refers to an "anal universe where all differences are abolished... All that is taboo, forbidden or sacred is devoured by the digestive tract, an enormous grinding machine disintegrating the molecules of the mass thus obtained in order to reduce it to excrement" (3–4). Rather than indicating the anus as a nexus of sin and excess, Chasseguet-Smirgel suggests that the very acts of digestion and defecation are unifying because they are, in fact, universal. Lenore Malen refers to this aspect as an "abolition of boundaries," but perhaps the familiar children's book puts it best when it observes, simply and tellingly, that *Everyone Poops* (79).

It is important to remember that, as part of his socioeconomic disenfranchisement, Rygel also suffers cultural disenfranchisement. In Hynerian culture, farting is not a social taboo, but considered a normal aspect of biologic functioning. Indeed, it is even a type of communicative act, since Hynerians mostly fart when they are nervous or anxious. Surrounded by beings from cultures highly disparate to his own — and, it should be added, highly antagonistic as well — Rygel's farting is another reminder of what was lost to him, the people and places that best understand him. All exiles feel a sense of disconnectedness, a sensation that, even after twenty or thirty years, never dissipates. While we can all adjust to new surroundings, and learn to thrive in them as the crew of Moya does, we can never wholly escape the pull of our own homespaces, which not only work to shape us as individuals but continually call to us, throughout our lives, no matter how far we roam from them.

Rygel's farting, then, is a feature that humanizes him. It reminds the viewer and his crewmates of his distant origins and, by proxy, of their own. It also reflects a nervous state that is, in itself, a shared feeling. Chiana's intense reaction in the scene epigraphed at the beginning of this essay (where she rounds on Rygel, calling him a "little toad") is so excessive in part because his anxiety at the moment reflects her own. Malen argues for "'shit' as a metaphor for negation," reminding us that excrement is universal to all; all living beings excrete some form of waste, and, as such, it is one of the few experiences that is truly universal. Moya's crew's repeated objections to Rygel's flatulence are a result of cultural conditioning and reflective of cultural difference; biologically, physiologically, corporeally, and constructively, Rygel's gas is a reminder that they have much in common, no matter how different they appear.

In a letter to *The British Medical Journal*, Philip D. Welsby argued "fart" was so repellent a term that it should be replaced by the more "medical ... and prude ... liberation of colonic miasma" (555). "Miasma" suggests decay and toxicity and reflects the negative connotation associated with both the word and the action in question. Yet Rygel's flatus is really a feature designed to not only enable his integration into the *Farscape* family — by bringing him low, out of the realm of the royal and on even ground with the rest of his fellow exiles — it also reflects a commonality amongst all the members of the crew, reminding them, in a rather roundabout and admittedly malodorous manner, that despite their many differences, despite their cultural distinctiveness, they are all very much the same. Thus in describing farting a form of "liberation," Welsby unintentionally channels the very overarching construct of *Farscape*: a group of refugee aliens, "liberated" from various (real and metaphorical) prisons, joining together for their own common survival, learning and growing from and alongside one another, united by dependency, growing familial, and, yes, by farts.

Works Cited

Bakhtin, Mikhail. *Rabelais and His World*. Trans. Helene Iswolsky. Bloomington: Indiana University Press, 1984. Print.

Beechy, Tiffany. "Devil Take the Hindmost: Chaucer, John Gay, and the Pecuniary Anus." *The Chaucer Review* 41.6 (2006): 71–85. Print.

Chasseguet-Smirgel, Janine. *Creativity and Perversion*. New York: W. W. Norton, 1985. Print.

Gomi, Taro. *Everyone Poops*. Trans. Amanda Mayer Stinchecum. La Jolla: Kane/Miller, 1993. Print.
Malen, Lenore. "Postscript: An Anal Universe." *Art Journal* 52.3 (1993): 79–81. Print.
Nickels, Cameron C., and John H. O'Neill. "Upon the Attribution of 'Upon a Fart' to William Byrd of Westover." *Early American Literature* 14.2 (1979): 143–148. Print.
Welsby, Philip D. "To fart." *The British Medical Journal* 2.6189 (1979): 555. Print.

'Scaping the Mythic Triad into Uncharted Territories
Hero, Antihero and Villain

BILLIE JO MASON

"Wherever the poetry of myth is interpreted as biography, history, or science, it is killed."— Joseph Campbell

"But by my love and hope I beseech you: do not throw away the hero in your soul! Hold holy your highest hope!"— Friedrich Nietzsche

From the moment astronaut John Crichton first appears onscreen, the audience immediately identifies him as the hero of *Farscape*, a subliminal identification which says as much about mankind's shared ability to recognize the protagonist in mythic tales as it does about the character himself. Indeed, whether he knows it or not, John Crichton is about to embark upon a mythic quest so familiar that his role in *Farscape* goes beyond that of an astronaut flung through a wormhole into another universe, taking the form of an archetypical journey of a stranger in some *very* strange lands. Refusing to linger in the ordinary world, *Farscape* soon reveals itself as a mythic quest for a post-structuralist world, a deconstruction of binary oppositions, a revisioning of the heroic ideal, an existentialist Bildungsroman, as it were. The series disrupts the hero/villain/antihero triad: villain shifts to hero, hero transforms to villain, and sometimes, villains play the antihero. It is this poststructuralist twist, this subversive shifting evolution into the Uncharted Territories of the mythic triad that makes *Farscape* such fascinating viewing.

The fascination with the heroic trope perhaps begins with Joseph Campbell and *The Hero with a Thousand Faces*, his extraordinary examination of dreams, myth and story. A template for mankind's deepest and most profound sense of morality, the hero emotionally connects us to a higher sense of self. In contrast, villains and antiheroes resonate in opposition, helping shape the discourse shared by storytellers throughout the ages. Campbell's work delves into many areas of psychoanalysis and dream therapy but his analysis of story may be summed up as a universal rite of passage as described in three stages, departure/separation, trials/initiation, and return, roughly paralleling the three acts of modern storytelling (28–29).

Farscape offers a modern twist on this archetypical quest story, but Crichton's lost astronaut evokes something far deeper in the human psyche, something that resonates universally with audiences, or as Joseph Campbell references via the concept of the "monomyth" in *The Hero with a Thousand Faces*, "Why is mythology everywhere the same, beneath its varieties of costume?" (2). Exploring these mythic structures in detail and drawing from subliminal storytelling modes across the ages, Campbell's seminal work explores how heroes are archetypical creations that tap into our subconscious, exploiting our need to hear stories, tales, and legends. Thus, the mythic hero paradigm allows, nay, forces Crichton immediately into the spotlight while relying on time-honored sci-fi plot conventions and requisite protagonist attributes as seen in the series premiere ("Premiere" 1.1). We are entranced by Crichton's journey, emotionally engaged from the start.

These stages in the hero's journey have been appropriated by screenwriters, distilled down and codified into the three-act structure of Hollywood and Westernized media, but it is Campbell who recognized and defined the subliminal paradigm. Christopher Vogler in *The Writer's Journey* lists these stages (note, he changes Campbell's descriptions in many instances and merges beats but this simpler version is helpful for analysis):

> Act One: Ordinary World; Call to Adventure; Refusal of the Call; Meeting with the Mentor; Crossing the First Threshold; Act Two: Tests, Allies, Enemies; Approach to the Inmost Cave; Ordeal; Reward; Act Three: The Road Back; Resurrection; Return with the Elixir [12].

Nevertheless, the story remains tantalizingly familiar. The hero is introduced in the ordinary world. He or she receives the invite (wanted or not) to leave the ordinary world and so on down the mythic storytelling how-to list.

As described by Campbell, it is not coincidence that audiences easily recognize these heroic parameters and quickly identify the character in the role and the quest: whether the hero be ridiculous or sublime, Greek or barbarian, gentile or Jew, his journey varies little in essential plan. Popular tales represent the heroic action as physical; the higher religions show the deed to be moral; nevertheless, there will be found astonishingly little variation in the morphology of the adventure, the character roles involved, the victories gained. If one or another of the basic elements of the archetypical pattern is omitted from a given fairy tale, legend, ritual, or myth, it is bound to be somehow or other implied — and the omission itself can speak volumes for the history and pathology of the example (30). In other words, whether it be ancient Greek mythology or *Farscape*, the pattern has not changed all that much. Or has it?

Crichton's all–American good looks, heroic astronaut profession, and easily discernable Western goals and objectives (completing a dangerous mission for the greater good of mankind and America), fulfills audience expectations and adheres to archetypical story modes as he embarks upon a heroic mission only to find himself lost in space, forced to journey through mysterious, dangerous lands, while battling strange and terrible foes, all of whom seem determined to keep him from returning home with the *elixir*; in this case, the secret to wormhole technology. Thus, these subliminal, mythic storytelling modes and traditions, particularly popular in Western mass media and television, enhance this identification, this foundation of myth and fable, enabling John's emblematic, traditional hero quest in the tale.

However, into this mythic structure comes the paradigm of the villain, the echo of the antihero, the binary opposition, and the poststructuralist reaction to this tradition. Villains work in opposition to the hero, creating conflict, driving story, forcing the hero to evolve. Villains are necessary in order for heroes to be, well, heroes. *Farscape,* however, deconstructs the normal role of the hero and the hero/villain/antihero triad in truly fascinating ways, offering instead, characters that evolve from one role to the next: villain shifts to hero, hero transforms to villain, and sometimes, villains play the antihero. Multifaceted and complex, the characters of *Farscape* are deconstructed, shifting and surprising.

Farscape, in fact, is as intriguing for this deconstruction of character, including its loaded binaries, as it is for the inspired use of the mythic paradigm. The concept of binary opposition is fundamental to structuralism, and indeed, it is hard to imagine narrative conflict without the systemic interaction of the loaded binary opposition sustaining the hero-villain trope. It is not that *Farscape* does not support the concept of opposition so much that it allows all of the characters to shift polarity throughout the show. In many respects, structuralism inherently supports the mythic paradigm with the hero as the loaded binary in the relationship between hero and villain. In "Binary Opposition in Myth: The Propp/Levi-Strauss Debate in Retrospect," Alan Dundes closely examines the work of French anthropologist Claude Levi-Strauss and his essay "The Structural Study of Myth," a symposium paper submitted in reference to the topic:

> In his essay, Levi-Strauss contended "that mythical thought always works from the awareness of oppositions towards their progressive mediations" and further that "the purpose of myth is to provide a logical model capable of overcoming a contradiction" [40].

According to Dundes, Levi-Strauss had "proposed a formula for the structure of narrative" based on an underlying "paradigm (of oppositions)," a coda of "mythemes," or "basic units of myth," which "must, generally speaking, lend themselves to binary operations" (40). In other words, Levi-Strauss believed that storytelling functioned partially because of the conflict inherent and created by characters in opposition. In traditional narrative structure, characters rarely shift or transition from their assigned roles despite character arcs, which may offer moments of conflict, but no genuine shift in perceived roles.

Farscape, however, willfully subverts expectations while reinforcing its own mythic substructure. In fact, Campbell's monomyth offers a cogent reference point for narrative coherence, and while *Farscape* seemingly finds inspiration in Campbell's myth quest, the show reinvents the wheel whenever it sees fit. John Crichton, displaced astronaut, embarks upon a journey, answering what Campbell refers to as the "call to adventure" which "signifies that destiny has summoned the hero and transferred his spiritual center of gravity from within the pale of his society to a zone unknown" (48). In the case of *Farscape* and John Crichton, this is perfectly embodied by Crichton's unfortunate mission gone awry, which results in his displacement from Earth and the subsequent wanderings into the Uncharted Territories.

The series opening introduces American astronaut John Crichton, simultaneously swaggering and suffering from pre-launch tension, Crichton's childhood friend and research partner DK, and John's famous, lapsing into legendary, astronaut father, Jack Crichton, as John Crichton prepares to launch his experimental shuttle *Farscape 1* into the upper atmosphere to prove his "own" scientific theory, establishing Crichton's normal world "street creds." Crichton inadvertently triggers a wormhole in space-time which sucks him and his ship into a very distant part of the universe, separating him from everything he knows, loves and understands. Mythic quest ensues...

In fact, Crichton's first season title sequence voice-over sets the scene for every episode, emphasizing both the quest elements of John's plight, the show's main dramatic conflict and establishing Crichton's relationship with his all-too-alien shipmates:

> "My name is John Crichton. I'm lost. An astronaut. Shot through a wormhole. In some distant part of the universe. I'm trying to stay alive. Aboard this ship. This living ship. Of escaped prisoners" ["Credits"].

The living ship is a Leviathan named Moya and the escaped prisoners are Ka D'Argo, Zhaan, Rygel, as well as the aptly-if-unimaginatively named Pilot and Peacekeeper fighter pilot, Aeryn Sun. Another empowered female, Chiana, soon joins the crew as well ("Durka Returns" 1.15).

Crichton's expectations about alien contact do not last long as Aeryn knocks John to the ground at first meet, taking the dominant position of power in the relationship and playing with the irony of her role as a "Peacekeeper."[1] Moya serves, not only as a space in which her crew lives, but she is an escaped prisoner of sorts, as well as a mode of transportation, a fascinating motif at play in the series. The prisoner motif seemingly prevails throughout the show as well; note that Crichton is also being held captive in another universe while most of the characters, wrongly accused in one way or another, begin as prisoners of misconception or misappropriation of the power of Peacekeeper authority, or Colonialism run amuck.

Compare how Crichton's original title credit narrative roughly parallels Campbell's paradigm, including the Crossing of the Threshold, the Belly of the Whale, and the Road of Trials. Having crossed the first threshold, in this case, shooting through the wormhole he has just accidentally created, John drifts helplessly after his ship is clipped by über-Peacekeeper Crais' brother's ship, a pivotal moment in the story. Crichton spies Moya, muttering "That's big. That's really big" ("Premiere" 1.1), before he is literally sucked into the belly of the on-the-lam, prison transport whale. He soon encounters his first aliens as they are actively engaged in escaping from Crais and the Peacekeepers and not one alien seems particularly interested in *him*. Alas, this is not the worst of it for the show's errant human hero: he soon discovers that his preconceived, perhaps romantic notions about first contact are not only tragically flawed, but that these systemic misconceptions have placed him at the bottom of the cosmic food chain, so to speak.

In fact, John Crichton may be the human protagonist of *Farscape*, but the show relies upon a unique troop of complex characters to help him out on that quest, or, as defined by Campbell's "Road of Trials" (28), he will turn to an assortment of allies, mentors, foils, and feminine figures. Though Crichton often adheres to the mythic heroic paradigm, *Farscape* quickly deconstructs audience expectations as much as it upholds them, much in the way the Western values of Crichton's expectations about alien races and culture are deconstructed from the moment he makes first contact and discovers that he is the alien and not a particularly appealing alien at that, as evidenced by D'Argo's irritated assessment of his questionable intellect: "This one [Crichton] is some sort of higher brain function deficient" ("Premiere" 1.1). Not only is John, as an academic and scientist held in high esteem on his own world, initially dismissed as worthless by the other aliens, he is targeted for death by the revenge fixated Crais, a psychopath with a lot of firepower and authority behind him. Crais, strutting about on his warship in black uniform and black boots with his slicked-back black hair, oozes menace and mean. He gives form to the familiar trope of unhinged vengeance. Aeryn, of course, is forced to throw in her lot with the prisoners aboard Moya after she is "irreversibly contaminated" through her contact with Crichton. Peacekeepers do not mingle with lesser life forms, i.e., humans, it seems, which says much about their concept of "the Other" in their universe as well as a serious misunderstanding about what the term *peacekeeping* truly means.

Like Odysseus after the Trojan War, Crichton's adventure home is thwarted at every turn by villains such as Scorpius and Crais. However, as noted before, heroes, villains, and antiheroes, function in fascinating ways in the series. Crichton is clearly the show's hero, albeit an often bemused, amused, abused, and hence, deconstructed version, but his characterization morphs into the villainous thanks to the influence of "Harvey," Scorpius' alter-ego residing inside John's brain. In "Die Me, Dichotomy" (2.22), Scorpius, via Harvey-the-chip-persona, overwhelms Crichton, who purposefully attempts to land his Prowler on Aeryn's ship's canopy, leading to her death. Though Crichton quickly takes back control, he has done the heinous deed, killing the women he clearly loves. One might argue that Crichton is not in control of his own agency, or body, but the fact remains that he committed the crime. Later, he is an emotional wreck, suffering regret and thereby regaining audience sympathy and his own agency. Ultimately, he expunges the chip and control of his own body ... sort of. Scorpius leaves a mostly benign version of Harvey behind.

Equally as fascinating as Crichton's shifting from hero to villain and back again, Crichton's title voice-over subtly shifts by the third season, as his experiences change his Westernized views about aliens and his immediate goals of the quest reflect his experiences in the Uncharted Territories:

> My name is John Crichton. I'm lost. An astronaut. Shot through a wormhole. In some distant part of the universe. Trying to stay alive. Aboard this ship. This living ship. Of escaped prisoners. My friends. If you can hear me. Beware. If I make it back. If I open the door. Are you ready? Earth is unprepared. Helpless. For nightmares I've seen. Or should I stay? Protect my home. My children. But then you'll never know the wonders I've seen ["Season of Death" 3.1].

Crichton's arc demonstrates substantial awareness of humanity's place in the universe, in contrast to his initial first contact. Wiser, he realizes that the universe is a dangerous place indeed.

Note how *Farscape* deconstructs the narrative with surprisingly effective results, using binary oppositions to defy audience expectations. The show plays with oppositions when Crichton splinters into a binary set of perfect twins at one point in the series, setting up both an opposition against himself, and a literal rendering of the binary motif. In the third season episode "Eat Me," Crichton, D'Argo, and Chiana, are "copied" by the criminally insane Kaarvok, an escaped prisoner on a Peacekeeper prison convoy ship ambushed by Scarrans and left to drift through the Uncharted Territories. Kaarvok first duplicates D'Argo, a literal murder, albeit an unproductive one given the existence of D'Argo's twin (though which one is the original is a point to ponder). Then, he duplicates Chiana, who stares in amazement at her own duplicate. In a moment of pure cowardice, however, Chiana runs away as Kaarvok murders one of the Chianas, while the other one ignores her own doppelgänger as she begs for help. Though Chiana is often self-serving, allowing her own binary to be brutalized is a symbolically loaded action. Chiana ponders her cowardice, tearfully working it out: "Okay. Okay. Clone. Okay. Okay. Two Chianas. Um. Um. She-she. Not me. Yeah. Not me. Uh-uh. She-she. She was just a clone, a clone. So I'm the real me I'm the real me" ("Eat Me" 3.6). Of course, it is impossible to know which is which. Crichton, with his typical amusing irreverence, saves the day, but is zapped by Kaarvok while escaping with his friends. At the end of the episode, a twinned Crichton, sits starring at his own duplicate playing an endless and pointless game of rock-paper-scissors as a concerned Aeryn watches over him.

Though post-structuralism tends to eschew these binary oppositions, the heroic paradigm lingers in the margins. In "Deconstructing the Hero," Iain Thomson discusses the reluctance on the part of even the most ardent postmodernists to entirely expel the hero off the top of the pedestal:

> Existentialism, that philosophical tradition previously best known for radical questioning (the tradition which, with Heidegger, gave us the very concept of *deconstruction*), questioned, but did not overturn, the great importance Western history has *always* accorded to the hero. ("Always," here that means — since we are talking about Western history — beginning with our own beginning: Our founding myths are hero stories all.) Indeed of the three greatest existential philosophers, Nietzsche and Heidegger both found it easier to give up their own devout Christianity than to stop believing in Heroes [111].

Farscape utilizes the mythic paradigm, recognizing the need for Crichton's heroic loci, but the series is at its most fascinating when it deconstructs icons, allowing these characters the freedom to explore the uncharted realms of arc, fostering self-serving natures, or revealing very unsympathetic behaviors, and other lapses in character as past misdeeds are discovered.

Take the disenfranchised Peacekeeper pilot Aeryn Sun, a stunningly complex character, John's romantic fixation and deconstructed feminist role model. Aeryn functions in the series as a fully empowered model of righteous female agency, a conflicted, evolving antihero and a redeemed villain as a representative of the authoritative Empire (those ironically named Peacekeepers), transitioning and changing as she moves through the plot. In the pivotal episode "The Way We Weren't" (2.5), the nefarious deeds of two characters are revealed. Three, if you count Crais before his own transition from nightmarish vision of Empire-gone-astray poster boy to self-sacrificing hero.

Aeryn's unsavory past as a Peacekeeper is explored in the episode "The Way We Weren't" (2.5), including her participation in the slaughter of Moya's first pilot, a horrendous, brutal act which has been secretly recorded by the Peacekeepers and the tape discovered by Chiana. Chiana shows the tape to Crichton in private:

CHIANA: "Did you see what I see? This is Aeryn. It shows she's been aboard Moya—"
CRICHTON: "Peacekeepers must have kept these things running twenty-four-seven to spy on their own people."
CHIANA: "Crichton, that is Aeryn. She's been aboard Moya before. She killed a pilot."

John evidences concern, even shock, but it is clear that he is going to wait to hear Aeryn's side of the story before he comes to any conclusions. Here, he is either compromised by his feelings for her or proves endearingly hopeful; either way, he is sympathetic by way of empathy, made more engaging through this emotional resonance than the expected bombast of the Western heroic prototype. His heroic sensibility works in binary opposition to Aeryn's presumptive, possible villainy, though Peacekeeper Velorek is by far the most heroic, uncompromised character in the episode. Aeryn's shipmates are, in fact, horrified by the revelation and the implications of Aeryn's brutal past when they are shown the recording:

AERYN: "Yes, it's me. Are you happy now?"
ZHAAN: "It shows you have been aboard Moya before."
D'ARGO: "Why didn't you ever tell us?"
RYGEL: "It's criminally obviously, isn't it? She helped murder a defenseless pilot."
AERYN: "Must have been about three cycles ago. Now, I've been aboard hundreds of Leviathans and I had no idea it was Moya."
CHIANA: "So all non–Sebaceans look alike, is that it?"
AERYN: "I didn't know, Chiana."
CRICHTON: "Look, the Aeryn on that tape is not the Aeryn we know. That was a long time ago."
RYGEL: "Three cycles isn't that long! Ha! I was aboard Moya by then."
ZHAAN: "As was I."
RYGEL: "Maybe you were one of the ones who took a turn torturing me. Ever torture a Hynerian?"
D'ARGO: "Perhaps you helped torture me, too—"
AERYN: "No!"

The scene continues on until Crichton steps in, forcing everyone to "chill out for a microt," which allows the weight of her crime to simmer without actual violence ensuing. Until this point, Aeryn has been an accepted member of the crew (albeit somewhat grudgingly on both sides), a woman in control of her own agency as well as a heroic feminine figure. The reveal shatters the character's hierarchical place amongst the crew, reminding the other characters and the audience about the conflict between Aeryn's past and present. Even more interesting, the scene shatters the character's agency (though she regains it by the episode's finale). She was just following orders, a Peacekeeper drone without any independent will. Overtly, through Aeryn, *Farscape* metaphorically references the hints of Hitler's Germany with Aeryn in the role of soldier merely following orders, compromising her "ethical" center.[2]

D'Argo, Zhaan, and Rygel accuse her of "murdering a pilot," which is obviously true, and they suggest she may have taken part in torturing them while they were prisoners aboard Moya, which she vehemently denies. Chiana defends her, perhaps empathizing with unjust feminine character assassination more than the rest, "What have you guys been thinking all this time? What, she was out picking baskets of Raulis buds while all the other mean Peacekeepers did all the really nasty stuff? She was a Peacekeeper" ("The Way We Weren't" 2.5). Chiana's point is well taken. No matter how sympathetic Aeryn may seem, nor how reasonable her past involvement with the oppressive Peacekeeper agenda, her actions skirt reasonable ethical considerations.

Though deeply tortured by her participation in state-sanctioned murder of Moya's previous pilot, Aeryn's misdeeds run deeper than simply following Crais' orders. John eventually learns that Aeryn was sexually, and emotionally, involved with Velorek, the officer charged with installing the new pilot on Moya. Velorek believes that Crais is a "madman" and he plots to thwart Crais's nefarious plan to breed Leviathans. In the episode, Velorek functions as the protagonist, supplying narrative opposition to Crais as well as Aeryn. The character displays uncustomary perception, kindness and courage, subverting the Peacekeeper agenda and his immediate commander's objectives, engendered with a humanist, emotional approach to relationships and interspecies relations. In addition, he tasks Aeryn and Pilot with higher goals, functioning as a catalyst for their later actions, though ironically both make poor decisions and Aeryn's actions result in his death. This is no reflection on Velorek, one of the most enlightened, sympathetic characters in the series. Aeryn suffers the most in comparison, since she betrays him to Crais in order to return to her assignment flying Prowlers.

Nor is Aeryn alone in her duplicity and dark past, as Pilot shares partial blame for the murder of Moya's first pilot. Though he did not pull the trigger, his desperate, selfish desires resulted in her death as evidenced by this flashback between Velorek and Pilot on the latter's homeworld, as confessed to Aeryn and Crichton by Pilot:

VELOREK: That's what I offer you. Stars.
PILOT: I dream of nothing else.
VELOREK: I offer you a Leviathan. All you have to do is agree to help me.
PILOT: But you said that for me to be joined, the old one would have to die.
VELOREK: That pilot will die no matter what you do.
PILOT: Ah.
VELOREK: If you don't come with me, I'll find someone else who will. Someone else who isn't afraid to take their place amongst the stars.
[end flashback]
PILOT: The fate of Moya's pilot was sealed at that moment.

Pilot's desire to see the stars was the inciting incident behind the murder of the first pilot, since Velorek would not have found another pilot so easily manipulated or self-serving.

Not only do Aeryn and Pilot share DNA (established in "DNA Mad Scientist" 1.9), but also guilt over their actions. Ultimately, their emotional arc and evolution through the plot allow them to move forward, or as Aeryn notes, "We've come a long way since then, Pilot. And we've still got a long way to go. Take the journey with me" ("The Way We Weren't" 2.5). While Crais remains the primary villainous force polarizing the episode, both Aeryn and Pilot work in opposition to Velorek's heroism, functioning as antagonists in comparison, yet ultimately managing to endear themselves to the audience through their character arcs, dramatized through their emotional epiphanies, obvious regret and eventual growth.

This complexity of expected character paradigms is one of the many deconstructive elements of *Farscape*. D'Argo and Zhaan demonstrate outright craven self-interest in "DNA Mad Scientist" when they cut off one of Pilot's arms in exchange for a map home (1.9). When confronted by Aeryn, neither evidences much genuine regret:

> D'ARGO: Do you have something to say to us?
> ZHAAN: The decision was a hard one, Aeryn. Our actions, even harder. But it is done — "
> AERYN: How could you? Pilot is defenseless.
> D'ARGO: Compassion. From a Peacekeeper.
> AERYN: For a comrade. You attacked one of your own. Would you do the same to the rest of us?
> D'ARGO: Of course.

Here, D'Argo and Zhaan are compromised in comparison to Crichton and Aeryn, with evil scientist Namtar as the apex of villainy.

Ironically, Aeryn will reverse roles with Zhaan and D'Argo in the next season when her involvement in the murder of Moya's previous pilot is revealed. Though the audience will have ample reasons to regain empathy for both D'Argo and Zhaan, at this moment, they shift from mentors and allies to Crichton, devolving into minor antagonists and/or erstwhile minions of Namtar. They have been misled by their own desires, true enough, but stalwart hero Crichton would never consciously yield to such base motives nor commit such a heinous act, even if Earth were served up on a platter. In fact, no mythic hero would promote such an agenda.

Zhaan and D'Argo, after all, evidence dark pasts as well as heroic moments throughout the series, their characterizations informed by a deconstructed paradigm which eschews rigidity and embraces flux. Even Moya, *Farscape's* embodied, literal space (the crew actually lives on her) and nurturing female character, occasionally threatens the lives of her passengers. However,

Crais most eloquently expresses this poststructuralist agenda, evolving from snarling, almost melodramatic heavy, to antihero, to cathartic, tragic hero by the climax of his own hero's journey. Crais is not only the most unhinged of the *Farscape* antagonists in that he is a man truly obsessed, but he could be described as a melodramatic trope taken too far, a symbolic figure of unmitigated vengeance. And yet, he also offers the most extreme example of the deconstruction of character, a character that shifts from the villainous to the heroic, since it is Crais that changes the most over the course of the series. He evidences truly heroic traits as the character evolves through the plot: stalker to uneasy ally to savior. Though his anger is motivated by love for his brother, and we soon learn, a whole-lotta-guilt, his actions are initially over-the-top and obsessive-compulsive. Crais is not John's first obstacle after clearing the wormhole; his "new" friends present him with difficulty, but it is Crais who drives the story's engine. In fact, *Farscape's* resident villains are wonderfully capable in this regard. Crais, however difficult, complicated and self-serving, has been victimized by Scorpius, a fact which supplies the character with his initial sympathetic moments. His obsession with Crichton results in the loss of his command and everything he "thinks" he values; who does not relate to a man suffering from undeserved misfortune, no matter how much he has brought it upon himself through his own internal flaws and failings. In fact, this only makes him more "human," albeit with deep anger control issues (a problem shared by many characters in the *Farscape* universe), ironic given the oft-posed question of "what is human" asked by the show. Later in the series, Crais steals Moya's offspring Talyn without permission, morphing into the antihero in binary opposition to Crichton's post-modern, almost metrosexual version of the hero, a binary, defrocked Peacekeeper-in-contrast to Scorpius' more literally pointy-toothed villain. Antiheroes, of course, are not the antithesis of the hero. As defined by Christopher Vogler:

> Anti-hero is a slippery term that can cause a lot of confusion. Simply stated, an Anti-hero is not the opposite of a Hero, but a specialized kind of Hero, one who may be an outlaw or a villain from the point of view of society, but with whom the audience is basically in sympathy. We identify with these outsiders because we have all felt like outsiders at one time or another [41].

Of course, the society defined here is not Peacekeeper society (though that could also be one argument), but Western society, hence John's placement at the pinnacle of the hero cycle and thus explaining the logic of Crais' function as antihero, particularly in comparison to Scorpius, the greater enemy of both Crais and John.

Crais' evolution does not happen immediately, but over several episodes, as he and Moya's offspring Talyn repeatedly offer aid, often reluctantly on Crais' part, to Moya's crew. Vogler's antihero definition fits Crais during this part of his evolution:

> Anti-Heroes may be of two types: (1) characters who behave much like conventional Heroes, but are given a strong touch of cynicism or have a wounded quality..., or (2) tragic Heroes, central figures of a story who may not be likeable or admirable, whose actions we may even deplore... [41].

Crais and Crichton share an uneasy partnership; neither likes nor trusts the other, but mutual hatred of Scorpius binds them throughout the second and third seasons, until Crais' self-revelations lead him to a heroic mutation, which surpasses his prior role in the story.

By the end of Season Three, new threats glimmer on the horizon as Crichton grapples with Scorpius over wormhole technology and the specter of the Scarrans looms large, as well as new villains, such as Grayza ("Into the Lion's Den, Part II: Wolf in Sheep's Clothing" 3.21). Crais' evolution through the series eventually leads him to the surprising act of self-sacrifice. By this point, Crais has pushed past antihero and lapsed into the heroic, despite his claim that he is only motivated by selfish concerns as evidenced by this sequence between Crais, John, and Aeryn as they plot to destroy Scorpius' command carrier and thwart his acquisition of the wormhole technology. Crichton believes that Crais has betrayed them. In fact, he is offering to sacrifice his own life:

> AERYN: And you should listen to him now.
> CRAIS: All that I have cared for, gone. My parents, taken away from me. My brother, dead. So now, I live, I plan, I do, all in the service of my own interest. In that, I believe I am not unique in the universe.
> CRICHTON: Snap this up; I've got to get back.
> CRAIS: Despite all of this, I understand the power of the technology that Scorpius is attempting to harness. I understand the horror that will wash over this galaxy if anyone wields this weapon. And last of all, I now know I am the only individual capable of stopping it.

Crais evidences the most noble of qualities at this juncture in the series, self-sacrifice for the good of the universe.

Shared concern for the greater good links the two men, despite their mutual dislike of one another. It takes John several beats to fully digest Crais' plan:

> CRICHTON: Where do we meet up with you and Talyn?
> CRAIS: You don't. Starburst in a confined space where the energy can't dissipate ... will be the hero's death that Talyn deserves.
> CRICHTON: You're gonna die.

In fact, both men will sacrifice themselves to prevent Scorpius from gaining wormhole technology (John's binary twin dies earlier in the season), a fitting symbolic end and heroic death for Crais' character. The Scarrans, the conflicted Scorpius, and Grayza continue their pursuit until the show's finale.

Crais, untrustworthy, unhinged, heartbroken, difficult, stands opposition to John's often amusing, occasionally perplexed, always engaging personification of the hero, deconstructs the paradigm with jaded sorrow. *Farscape* may deconstruct heroes, but it has not changed the need for them. Perhaps Joseph Campbell said it best, commenting on the idea that there is no longer room for myth in today's society:

> The modern hero, the modern individual who dares to heed the call and seek the mansion of that presence with whom it is our whole destiny to be atoned, cannot, indeed, must not, wait for his community to cast off its slough of pride, fear, rationalized avarice, and sanctified misunderstanding. "Live," Nietzsche says, "as though the day were here." It is not society that is to guide and sage the creative hero, but precisely the reverse. And so every one of us shares the supreme ordeal — carries the cross of the redeemer — not in the bright moments of his tribe's great victories, but in the silences of his personal despair [337].

Society may have outgrown the belief in heroes, but we have not outgrown our need for them. With this in mind, *Farscape* may disrupt and deconstruct the heroic ideal in some respects, but what the series offers instead is a revisionist world, a mythic journey with an existentialist edge. John Crichton participates in a mythic quest but on his terms. He complains, he jokes, and he feels emotion, exploring the Uncharted Territories of *Farscape*.

Notes

1. Note that Peacekeepers, for all their xenophobic, overwrought militaristic might, function exactly as the name implies. They keep the "peace" throughout the universe, invited by other governments/worlds to maintain order, most often at the expense of the "sub-human Other," at the request of the ruling class. From the point of view of a Peacekeeper, their goal is to provide requested protection, eschewing colonization. Ironically, the paradigm of Colonialism ensues through this relationship.

2. Or, indeed, soldiers following orders throughout history.

Works Cited

Campbell, Joseph. *The Hero with a Thousand Faces,* 3d ed. Novato: New World Library, 2008. Print.

Dundes, Alan. "Binary Opposition in Myth: The Propp/Levi-Strauss Debate in Retrospect." *Western Folklore* 56.1 (Winter 1997): 39–50. JSTOR. Web. 15 November 2011.

Nietzsche, Friedrich. *Thus Spoke Zarathustra.* Eds. Kark Ameriks and Desmond M. Clarke. Cambridge Texts, *Kindle* ebook.

Thomson, Iain. "Deconstructing the Hero." *Comics as Philosophy.* Ed. Jeff McLaughlin Jackson: University Press of Mississippi, 2005. 100–129. Print.

Vogler, Christopher. *The Writer's Journey, Mythic Structure for Writers,* 2d ed. Studio City: Michael Wiese Productions, 1998. Print.

Friends, Enemies, Partners, Mates
Examining Relationships in the Uncharted Territories

SHERRY GINN

I have discussed the issues of love and sex in science fiction in a number of publications and presentations in the last few years, and I generally include examples from *Farscape* in all.[1] This essay, however, looks at the issue with respect to *Farscape* in more detail than in those previous works. *Farscape* lends itself to such an analysis for a variety of reasons, first and foremost because it is a love story and was so from the very beginning of the series. Secondly, the characters were more freely sexual than those in science fiction series preceding it. As I noted in my analysis of the television series of Joss Whedon, *Farscape* is also about love: love of home, friends, family, lovers, and life. And, as much as Rockne S. O'Bannon, the creator of the series, wished for the series to examine real sex among real "people," the series fell far short of the mark he hoped to achieve. My discussion of the twin issues of love and sex is filtered through the lens of two theories particularly relevant to contemporary human psychology. These are evolutionary theory, as discussed by scholar David Buss and his colleagues, and the Triangular Theory of Love, proposed by psychologist Robert Sternberg. I provide a short "lesson" on both of these theories first and then discuss each theory with respect to *Farscape* and its characters.

The Triangular Theory of Love

Robert Sternberg[2] proposes that love consists of three components that combine to produce seven types of love. The first of these components is *intimacy*, which he says "refers to those feelings in a relationship that promote closeness, bondedness, and connectedness" (6). Intimacy consists of at least ten elements: a desire to promote the welfare and happiness of a loved one, giving and receiving emotional support, counting on the loved one in a time of need, holding him or her in high regard, enjoying a mutual understanding with them, sharing possessions and self with them, valuing them, and communicating intimately. Intimacy is the foundation of love and it develops slowly over time. Difficult to achieve, it can be even more difficult to maintain, because as one becomes more involved with another, a fear of losing a sense of self may occur. The task is thus to maintain a sense of intimacy with a partner while also maintaining a sense of autonomy.

The second component of love is *passion* which involves "a state of intense longing for union with the other" (9). Passion consists of the expression of our needs and desires, one of which is sexual fulfillment, but it is a mistake to think that passion is the only need that can be fulfilled with such intensity. For example, someone with a strong need for dominance could be aroused by someone who provides a convenient outlet for that need. Nevertheless, passion may vanish as quickly as it arose.

The final component of love is *commitment*, consisting of both a short-term and a long-term aspect. Sternberg states that the "short-term aspect is the decision to love a certain other, whereas the long-term one is the commitment to maintain that love" (11). These two decisions do not necessarily occur at the same time or within any given relationship. It is this component that sustains a relationship.

Seven types of love can be combined using the aforementioned components. The first, *liking*, consists only of intimacy. It is the type of love one feels for close friends and family members. However, the term *liking* is not used lightly. Instead, it refers to the type of feeling one finds in friendships or familial relationships: feeling close to the person, but with no passion towards them or expectations of a long-term commitment. *Infatuated love* consists only of passion, with intense physical arousal. This is what most would consider "love at first sight." *Empty love* consists only of commitment. Other types of love may sometimes devolve into this type, as is the case of couples who have been together for many years. In cultures where marriages are arranged, empty love may mark the beginning of a relationship. *Romantic love* consists of passion plus intimacy. Liking in combination with the arousal of physical attraction characterizes this type of love (20). Romantic love includes the feeling that one has met the person who is right for him or her and the feeling that one would like to fuse one's spirit with his or hers. Intimacy plus commitment characterizes *companionate love*; one could think of this type of love in terms of a committed friendship. Many relationships turn into this type of love once physical attraction, which is a major source of passion, has waned (21). *Fatuous love* consists of passion plus commitment. We often read about this type of love in the tabloids, when two famous people meet, fall in love, and marry after a whirlwind romance. Since intimacy takes some time to develop, the people who fall "head over heels in love" and rush to the altar wake one morning to realize that they do not even like their partner. As Sternberg notes, "the partners commit ... to one another on the basis of passion without the stabilizing element of intimate involvement" (22). Finally, a combination of all three components yields *consummate love*. Many people would consider this to be a complete love. Sternberg notes however that it is often like meeting one's goal in a weight-loss program: it is easier to achieve than to maintain: "like other things of value, [it] must be guarded carefully" (22).

As noted, love may be expressed sexually, although it is not necessary for all types of love. Nevertheless humans are sexual beings and engage in sexual acts for a variety of reasons, including to obtain and hold power over someone, to express love, for recreation, in the place of intimacy, and for relaxation, to name only a few. As would be expected, the characters in *Farscape* engage in sexual acts. It is interesting that its producers, writers, directors, and even its creator, were determined that an adult science fiction program such as *Farscape* would depict adult themes, such as sexuality. Yet it is surprising how few of the characters are actually sexually active, and virtually all of the sexual encounters in the Uncharted Territories are heterosexual and what is frequently referred to these days as "vanilla," that is, non-kinky.

A Google search of the term "vanilla sex" will result in approximately thirteen million hits and a quick scan of the first page will reveal definitions of the term as well as links to sites espousing positive and negative views of the term and what it implies. Many people apparently define vanilla sex between heterosexual couples as sex in the missionary position (i.e., man on top of woman). Much scholarship indicates that a large number of people are *not* engaging in such a restrictive type of sexual activity (e.g., LeVay and Baldwin; Yarber, Sayad and Strong). Vanilla sex can also include any type of sexual activity that involves insertion, but not fetishism or BDSM (bondage/domination/submission/sadomasochism). For the purposes of this essay, I define vanilla sex as sex practiced by both heterosexual and homosexual adults to give and/or receive sexual satisfaction. Practices included in this definition may be solitary or mutual masturbation and oral, anal, or vaginal intercourse in a variety of positions. Excluded from the definition of vanilla sex would be sexual relations with non-consenting partners, BDSM, or other types of activities that might be considered kinky, such as voyeurism, frottage, exhibitionism, and others. Using this definition of vanilla sex, one observes that the majority of the sexual acts occurring on network television falls into this category as do the sexual acts occurring on premium channels such as HBO, Cinemax, Starz, and Showtime. Sexual acts in science fiction and fantasy (SFF) programs generally fall into this category, although there are exceptions.

Regardless of the type of sexual act in which characters engage, most acts end in sexual intercourse. Also, sexual intercourse is the way in which most species, at least on this planet, reproduce. SFF speculates that this is also the way alien species would reproduce.[3]

An Evolutionary Explanation About Sex

Psychology is defined as the scientific study of behavior and mental processes. Explanations for these behaviors and mental processes arise from a number of perspectives, and one such perspective emphasizes Darwinian evolution (*Origin*). Behaviors and mental processes that increase the probability of an organism's survival will be selected, meaning that the organism will survive to reproduce and the traits that aided in that survival will be transmitted to the next generation (Darwin *Descent*). One of the behaviors which evolutionary psychologists study centers on reproduction, attempting to explain the differing sexual behaviors displayed by men and women in terms of evolution.

According to evolutionary psychologists, men and women have different mating strategies. For example, some men and women display jealousy toward their partners. But men and women display differences in the type of jealousy they exhibit toward their partners. Men are more likely to be jealous of *sexual* infidelity in their partners, whereas women are more likely to be jealous of *emotional* infidelity. In other words, men are more likely to be jealous if their lovers engage in sexual activity with another person, and women are more likely to be jealous if their lovers develop an emotional attachment to another person (Buss, Larsen, Westen, and Semmelroth; Buunk, Angleitner, Oubaid, and Buss). Evolutionary psychologists propose that this jealousy stems from evolutionary forces that dictate mating strategies.

Any individual woman is theoretically capable of producing about 65 children in her lifetime, assuming she could (or would want to) give birth every nine months. This assumes that she would give birth and be impregnated immediately afterwards. Nevertheless, women do not reproduce that often. Even considering advances in modern medicine, the human body probably could not withstand the effort involved in reproducing that often. Men, on the other hand, can father thousands of children in their lifetimes, assuming a limitless supply of fertile women. Thus, evolutionary psychologists suggest that men and women have different strategies with respect to reproduction. Because men produce millions of sperm cells in each ejaculate, but only one is necessary for fertilization, it is in a man's evolutionary interests to impregnate as many females as possible. This ensures that some of his offspring will reach the age of maturity and his genes will be transmitted to future generations.

Men have little energy invested in their offspring. Women, on the other hand, usually only carry one offspring at a time, and it is in her best interests to ensure that that one offspring survives to maturity so that it can transmit her genes to future generations. Because women invest more energy in their offsprings' survival, women are motivated in different ways than men. Men want to mate with as many women as possible, but women want to mate with one man who will help them raise and protect their offspring so that the offspring can reach maturity. Although any given woman might not know who the father of her child is, she will always know that her offspring is her own. Men can never reliably know that a woman's children are his, hence different reasons for jealousy (Buss). If she is sexually unfaithful, then her offspring might not be his, and he is raising a child not his own. If he is emotionally unfaithful, he might leave her, which would leave her and her child undefended, rendering them unsafe in a hostile environment. She would also lose her mate's resources and his paternal investment (Buss).

Although this was a very brief description of evolutionary psychology and its tenets on human mate selection and reproduction, the theory can be used to explain many of the sexual relations depicted on *Farscape*. Likewise, Sternberg's triangular theory explains many of the emotional relationships on the series. For purposes of this essay, I focus my discussion on the series' major characters: Aeryn Sun, John Crichton, D'Argo, Zhaan, Chiana, and Scorpius — although I mention other characters as appropriate.

Aeryn Sun: Learning to Be More

Officer Aeryn Sun, Peacekeeper by birth and Sebacean by species, was born in space. Peacekeeper soldiers are bred to fill the ranks, but we never learn if soldiers are always chosen to bear children or if some of the births happen naturally. Aeryn learns that she is pregnant during Season Three, but does not tell Crichton because she does not know the identity of the child's father. When she finally discusses her pregnancy with him, she explains Peacekeeper reproduction briefly, telling him that a female soldier can carry a fetus in stasis for up to seven cycles before the child leaves stasis, develops, and is born. Aeryn had recreated (the Peacekeeper term for sex) on a number of occasions with her colleague Velorek prior to the events occurring on *Farscape* as well as with Crichton. It is also possible that she had other sexual relationships prior to meeting Crichton. In *The Peacekeeper Wars* we learn that Peacekeepers are actually human in species, but that their evolution was enhanced by a race of beings called the Eidelons. One way in which their evolution was enhanced was that gestation took a matter of days rather than months once the fetus was released from stasis. These two "improvements" ensured that female soldiers were not pregnant during a military campaign and that, once in gestation, they were not out of action for very long, which could be detrimental to their unit's survival. If Aeryn is any example, female soldiers are capable of giving birth and returning to duty immediately following the birth with no ill effects, which is exactly what Aeryn does in *The Peacekeeper Wars*. As Crichton anxiously hovers over Aeryn during her pregnancy and subsequent labor, trying to control her actions, she reminds him that she is *only* pregnant, not incapacitated.

The vision of sexuality and childbirth in the Peacekeeper universe is both repellant to us and attractive. Peacekeepers are freely sexual and mate regularly, with whomever they choose.[4] If any female soldiers become pregnant, they give birth to their children, male or female, when convenient for their unit. Those Peacekeepers whose job it is to raise such children do so. Gestation is quick and childbirth is apparently painless. Many short stories and novels within the SFF universe have envisioned childbirth and childrearing practices in such a fashion. Once again, however, if Aeryn is an example, she finds such a life unsatisfying and unfulfilling, vowing never to bear a child or allow it to be raised in such a way. Perhaps Aeryn's view is colored by the fact that she knows that she is special, having been told so by her mother when a little girl. In addition, two of her lovers (Velorek in "The Way We Weren't" [2.5] and Crichton in the "Premiere" [1.1]) tell her that she is special and that she can be more than her breeding. She says that she doesn't believe them, but given her actions prior to and after she joins Moya's crew, she obviously does.

Pa'u Zotoh Zhaan: Keeping the Darkness at Bay

Zhaan was a tenth level Pa'u, or priest, and a member of the Delvian race; she is a beautiful blue color and physiologically flora. Zhaan murdered her lover, who had planned to turn over control of their planet to the Peacekeepers. She almost lost her mind because of that murder, but many cycles of incarceration in a Peacekeeper prison allowed her to heal herself and slowly return from madness. Whereas Zhaan is spiritual, loving, and peaceful, she is also quite strong and recognizes that she contains a dark force within herself. Several episodes during Season One show Zhaan's quest to disavow the dark side of her soul and control the madness therein. In the episode "Throne for a Loss" (1.4), a young Tavlek male tries her patience several times. When he suggests that she is soft and weak, Zhaan throws him against the Leviathan Moya's wall and replies, "Soft? Yes. Weak? No." Later in the episode she tells him that she "could rip [him] apart right now ... help me, I'd even enjoy it." Nevertheless she does not harm the boy because she is trying to help him overcome an addiction to a drug that makes his species aggressive.

Two first season episodes revealed a Delvian process called Unity, in which two sentients bind souls and minds, an extremely personal encounter, beyond sexual. It was during Unity that Zhaan killed her lover. In "That Old Black Magic" (1.8), a vampiric sorcerer preys on the people living on a primitive trading planet. Maldis captures Crichton and his enemy Crais, forcing them to confront each other, so that he can feed on their negative energy. Zhaan joins forces with a native of the planet to free it from Maldis' grip. Unfortunately for Zhaan, she must confront "the darkest abyss of her own primal nature" to do so. Following these events, Zhaan worries that she will be unable to control herself in the future, but with Crichton's as well as the rest of the crew's help, she learns to control her impulses rather than deny their existence.

Before her death, Zhaan develops a relationship with a Banik slave named Stark who had been tortured by Scorpius and later rescued by Moya's crew. She commits herself to him; however, her selflessness and love for others causes her to sacrifice her spiritual energy and bring Aeryn back from the dead ("Season of Death" 3.1). Unfortunately, Aeryn is further gone than Zhaan realizes, and bringing Aeryn back to life weakens Zhaan greatly. Since she is flora, the crew tries desperately to find a planet where she can be "planted," thereby allowing her to regenerate. Unfortunately, they are unable to find such a world in time. Struck by another ship that fuses with Moya, the ships have to be pulled apart or both will be destroyed. To save Moya, someone has to pilot the other ship into the wormhole as soon as the two come apart. Because Zhaan is dying, and there is no way to find a planet for her in time, she pilots the Pathfinder's ship into the wormhole, thereby saving Moya and the crew ("Self-Inflicted Wounds Part II: Wait for the Wheel" 3.4). Zhaan makes the ultimate sacrifice for the crew, since she loves them all. Zhaan's actions throughout her time on Moya confirm her feelings for the crew as well as the ship. Indeed, Zhaan is deemed worthy of shepherding Moya by the Builders, the creators and thus deities of Leviathans such as Moya ("Look at the Princess, Parts I–III" 2.10, 2.11, 2.12). Put to the test, Zhaan is willing to go to any lengths to protect Moya and keep her safe. Her love for Moya and the crew would actually be characterized as consummate, I think, although her passion may be less a sexual passion than an all-encompassing passion for the other crew members' lust for life and desire to carve out a place that each can call home in the unknown part of space in which they find themselves.

Although very sensual and capable of sexual passion, we do not learn if Zhaan is sexually active with Stark. We know that D'Argo has been attracted to her, Crichton as well. However, we know that Zhaan, because she is flora, is extremely attracted to light, experiencing "photogasms" when exposed to intense sunlight. The male characters react with disgust or dismay, but primarily because Zhaan is incapacitated by the photogasms and thus unable to help them when they are in trouble (e.g., "Till the Blood Runs Clear" 1.11). At the same time, they may also feel inadequate confronted with such intense female sexuality for which a male is not necessary.

Chiana: Doing Whatever Is Necessary to Get By

The Nebari Chiana joined Moya's crew in the Season One episode "Durka Returns" (1.15). In this episode, Moya collides with a starship, carrying a male Nebari named Salis, along with his prisoner Chiana, and the Peacekeeper Captain Durka. Durka was once commandant of the Peacekeeper command carrier *Zelbinion*, where Dominar Rygel was confined and tortured for many cycles. The Nebari claim that they have "mind-cleansed" Durka and eliminated his violent tendencies. The Nebari, as a species, value conformity and discipline above all. According to her, Chiana was destined for similar cleansing; she swears that her crime was that she was too much of a nonconformist for Nebari society. We learn the truth about her past later in the series. In the episode "A Clockwork Nebari" (2.18), we discover that her own people infected her, her brother, and perhaps thousands of other non-conformist Nebari with a sexually transmitted disease. Those infected with the contagion were exiled from their home world. It was expected that these free-thinking and nonconformist Nebari would spread the disease throughout the many alien systems in the universe. When ready, the disease would be activated, rendering all who were infected pacified and defenseless against a Nebari invasion.

As time progresses, we learn much of Chiana's past, and it is not pretty. She is a thief who is willing to do *anything* to get what she wants or needs. Chiana's blend of youth, naiveté, wanton sensuality, and amorality served her well following her exile from the Nebari home world. She has a problem with trust: trusting other people and having them trust her. Just when it seems that she has "turned over a new leaf," maturing at long last into a responsible adult, Chiana does something to remind her crewmates just who she is. Chiana is presented as freely sexual; she has no reservations about sex (Battis). She is aware that Crichton is sexually attracted to her; most males are, although Crichton refuses Chi's offers. She does have an intensely sexual affair with D'Argo until he begins to talk of settling down and marrying. Their sexual encounters are presented on screen by using a standard cinematic technique: Chiana astride D'Argo, naked back to the camera. She is usually very vocal as she indicates sexual pleasure. Chiana grows to care deeply for D'Argo; however, she does not know how to tell him that she is not ready for marriage. Rather than admit how she feels, Chiana seduces his son, thereby ensuring that D'Argo will not continue to pursue her ("Suns and Lovers" 3.2). Even so, the sexual chemistry between Chiana and D'Argo does not dissipate. They resume their sexual relationship by the end of the series.

Chiana's extreme suspicion of other people's motivations slowly erodes as she learns that no one on Moya has ulterior motives for helping her. While not everyone on Moya may love her, they certainly tolerate her and most grow fond of her with time. Aeryn, among others on the crew, at times refers to Chi as a slut; Chi does not apologize. Unfortunately, even in an alternate universe, female sexuality is suspect.

As Season Four unfolds, Chiana becomes closer than ever to the other females aboard Moya, including Jool and Sikozu, the newest additions to the crew. Before this time, she was the type of female that other females did not like, the type they suspected of being after their men, even when she was not. Because Chi is such a sexual being, enjoying the act, but willing to use sex if necessary to achieve what she wants or needs, she typically has no use for other women. Their youth, compared to the others' ages, serves to bond Jool and Chi eventually, especially after Chi saves Jool's life. Likewise, Chi and Sikozu become close as do Chi and Aeryn. Each woman learns of her own strengths and limitations as the series continues, and they learn about each other as well. They realize that they complement each other in many ways, which serves more than once to help the entire crew.

Thus, Chiana's relationships with members of Moya's crew reflect the various types of love described by Sternberg. Chiana's feelings toward D'Argo begin as passionate, but then evolve into romantic love as they become closer emotionally. Although she engages in sexual relations with his son, D'Argo understands why she does so, and his feelings for her grow stronger. As noted above, they renew their sexual relationship toward the end of the series. Chiana is likewise sexually attracted to Crichton, but eventually comes to see him more as an older relative, one she can flirt with safely, knowing that there will be no actual physical contact between them.[5] Also, her relationships with Aeryn and Zhaan become more familial — with Zhaan serving as a mother-figure and Aeryn as the stern older sister.

D'Argo: Looking for Peace

Whereas Chiana is the most sexual of the female characters aboard Moya, D'Argo is the most sexual of the males. Series creator Rockne S. O'Bannon, in his commentary to the first season episode "Thank God It's Friday... Again" (1.6), notes that D'Argo is free to visit all sorts of planets and have sex with all sorts of females. We see such encounters in episodes prior to the beginning of his relationship with Chiana; examples include "Friday" and "Vitas Mortis" (2.2). D'Argo is sexually attracted to Aeryn, partly because she is a warrior like him, and also to Zhaan. He even tells Zhaan that he would have asked for the privilege of bedding her, and she tells him that she would have accepted his offer, if things had not changed ("Friday"). Following Chiana's betrayal with his son, Jothee, D'Argo gradually becomes attracted to a young crewmember named Jool. There is a certain sexual chemistry between the two, but they never consummate the relationship.

As mentioned earlier, Aeryn has no choice but to join the crew of Moya after she is deemed irreversibly contaminated following contact with Crichton. The Peacekeepers might be hired by other species to serve as a military police force, but that does not mean that the Peacekeepers consider their employers equals. Indeed, the Peacekeepers, whose species is Sebacean, consider contact with non–Sebaceans to be unpleasant and refer to contact with unknown lifeforms as contamination. A normal Peacekeeper/Sebacean would never consider mating with a member of any species other than his or her own. When the Sebacean Lo'Laan Tar married D'Argo, her own brother killed her rather than live with the shame of her marriage to a Luxan. It was only D'Argo's quick thinking that kept their son from being killed as well.

D'Argo's relationships on Moya are primarily characterized by companionate love, romantic love, and liking. It is fair to say that he and Crichton as well as he and Aeryn develop companionate love, or committed friendship. D'Argo grows to like Crichton and definitely commits to following Crichton's plan to keep the wormhole knowledge from Scorpius and the Scarrans, dying in the process. He develops the same type of relationship with Aeryn. They bond over the fact that they are both warriors, and he comes to realize the depth of her feelings for Crichton as well as the changes through which she has gone since joining Moya's crew. As discussed earlier, his feelings for Chiana began as exasperation but grow into passion, then liking, and finally into romantic love. Even at the end he is able to forgive her for her transgression against him and rekindle the love and passion that had earlier developed between them.

Crichton and the Princess: Taking No Chances

The three-part episode "Look at the Princess" is a perfect example of how evolutionary theory can explain sexual behavior. I have discussed this episode and its narrative arc in a number of places and thus will give only a few details here (Ginn, "For Women"). In this episode, Moya inadvertently enters space around a Royal Planet at the time of the Crown Princess Katralla's ascension to the throne ("Part I: A Kiss Is But a Kiss"). Rygel reveals his presence to Councilor Tyno who, spying Crichton in the background, invites the crew to the planet's surface for the celebrations. Tyno has an ulterior motive:

scientists on this planet have created an elixir which can identify the genetically compatible match for reproduction for any member of the species. The elixir is placed on the tip of the tongue, and the two interested parties kiss. If they are genetically compatible, their elixir tastes sweet. Thus, the elixir completely eliminates the guess work involved in choosing a mate with whom to procreate. Unfortunately, Princess Katralla's DNA has been ruined by her brother, and there are no compatible males on her planet with whom she can procreate. To inherit the throne, she must be able to bear children; however, if she is unable to find a compatible male by the time of her birthday, then her brother, Prince Clavor, will inherit the throne and rule as Regent. (In this society, the throne can only be held by a woman, with her consort serving as Regent.) Tyno knows that Crichton is an off-worlder and thus may be a genetically compatible match for the Princess. He is, and Crichton is then forced to marry the Princess to escape from Scorpius (Simpson and Thomas).

Several interesting notions can be observed in this episode with respect to sexual selection and mating. As mentioned, sexual reproduction is not left to chance. When any individual on the planet wishes to reproduce, she or he simply tests another's saliva for a genetic match. This does not mean that people do not enjoy sexual congress with each other, as evidenced by Dregon's obvious infatuation with Aeryn Sun. In addition, Councilor Tyno is in love with the Princess, and she with him. She wants to marry him, but as with all the men on their planet, he is genetically incompatible with her. She is willing to marry him, even though she might lose her throne. Yet he is unwilling to allow her to make the sacrifice, especially since he knows that a 2000-year-old peace would be destroyed once her brother became Regent. Thus, Tyno's love for Katralla and his love of his planet lead him to do the noble thing: he realizes that Katralla must marry Crichton to ensure the continuity of their way of life. Katralla must bear a female child, who can inherit the throne and continue the royal line. The male with whom she chooses to breed is unimportant to her dynastic imperative. Although Crichton and Aeryn are in love with each other, she is unwilling to admit her feelings for him, even though he is willing and able to declare his for her ("Look at the Princess Part II: I Do, I Think"). Nevertheless, Crichton's love for Aeryn does not stop him from sharing a night of sex and passion with Jena, Prince Clavor's fiancée (who is actually a spy), when she rescues him from those who are plotting to prevent his marriage to the Princess ("Look at the Princess Part III: The Maltese Crichton"). This episode ends with Aeryn challenging Crichton to take the test, revealing that they are genetically compatible; their child will be born during the battle to keep the wormhole weapon from both the Scarrans and the Peacekeepers (*The Peacekeeper Wars*).

Scattered throughout this trilogy of episodes are the continual visual images of Chiana and D'Argo having passionate and intensely vigorous sex.

D'Argo is tired of running from his pursuers and wishes to settle down somewhere and have a "normal" life. That normal life would include children and he wants Chiana to be his wife. He is disheartened to learn that they are not a genetic match when they use the elixir. Chiana attempts to console him by saying that their parts, the parts that give them pleasure, do match.

Sexuality, as depicted in this trilogy, illustrates ways in which a species can ensure its survival. The Sebaceans on the Royal Planet (it is never named) have developed a method whereby genetic compatibility is not left to chance encounters. Any given person on the planet will always know with whom they can procreate; their scientists have found a way to separate reproduction from recreation. Sexual relations are engaged in solely for pleasure; however, males and females know exactly with whom their genes are compatible. The process of reproduction is likewise controlled within the Peacekeeper command structure, as discussed above. Peacekeeper soldiers may "recreate" with whomever they choose, but are generally not allowed to mate unless placed on a roster for breeding. The process is extremely efficient, designed to keep female soldiers pregnant for as short a time as possible with minimal downtime for birth. Offspring are raised in communal care and do not know their mothers or fathers. Peacekeeper soldiers are not supposed to develop emotional attachments with each other. Her emotional attachment with Velorek was intense, but that did not stop Aeryn from betraying him to win back her coveted job of prowler pilot ("The Way We Weren't").

Rape: Controlling the Powerless

If one considers evolutionary psychology's premise regarding reproduction, then one need also consider to what lengths a being might be willing to go to facilitate and ensure their reproduction. For such beings, rape would be an option. Interestingly, and thankfully, the issue of rape was rarely broached on *Farscape*. In the Season Four episode "Crichton Kicks" (4.1), the crew is separated for many months. When Chi finally finds Crichton and they talk about what they did while apart, she admits that she was raped and hints at other torture as well. She shrugs it off, saying that her captors "had a little fun," and we are left to wonder what exactly happened and how affected she really is. Earlier in the series, an alien being possesses Crichton and he threatens Chi with rape ("Losing Time" 3.9). It is a terrifying scene, all the more so because Crichton is one of the most positively portrayed men on television — science fiction or otherwise. He is horrified at himself, as well he should be, and wonders how he will ever be able to make amends even though he was not responsible. Indeed, one can consider that Crichton's possession, against his will, is mind-rape.

And, in a twist of gender stereotypes, the absolutely ruthless Peacekeeper Commandant Mele-On Grayza repeatedly rapes Crichton; she will do anything to possess the secret Crichton holds, the knowledge of how to create a wormhole. Powerless to stop her, Crichton is aware of these repeated rapes and suffers greatly because of his helplessness ("What Was Lost" Parts I & II [4.2 and 4.3]). Crichton refers to her as Commandant Cleavage because of her extremely low-cut uniform. A gland that secretes Heppel oil has been surgically implanted in her chest. Her low-cut uniform allows easy access to the gland, whose oily secretion makes her sexually desirable and irresistible. Noranti's drugs allow Crichton to resist the Heppel oil, but we eventually learn what Crichton thinks of Grayza's actions. When Grayza realizes that she will not be able to prevent a Peacekeeper-Scarran war and has been betrayed, Crichton asks her if she feels raped, a clear reference to his revulsion at what she has done to him. Her response: She would do anything to further the alliance with the Scarrans. Her motives are not necessarily altruistic: if she is successful in her negotiations then she will become very powerful indeed.[6] However, the Scarrans, a reptilian species who scheme for control of the universe, have ulterior motives and cannot be trusted. In a scene where Grayza and Ahkna, the Scarran War Minister, discuss a peace treaty between the two races, Ahkna makes a scathing comment about Grayza's methods, referring to the Heppel oil she uses for seduction. Grayza replies: "If you had a powerful weapon, would you refuse to use it because of squeamishness?" ("Bringing Home the Beacon" 4.16).

Because of their intense xenophobia, Peacekeepers, with the exception of Grayza, apparently do not use rape as a weapon of terror. Sexual relations with non–Sebaceans would be considered a disgrace, if not downright disgusting, to them, hence Macton Tar's murder of his sister for not only marrying a Luxan, but also mating with him and bearing a child. This is not the case with the Scarrans. Scorpius, Crichton's arch-nemesis, is the result of the Scarran rape of a Sebacean woman; the woman apparently died giving birth to him.

Scorpius: Looking for Power and Control

Scorpius' early life was terrible.[7] He is considered repellant by his Scarran masters, and in order to remove all trace of Sebacean from his "self," they repeatedly torture the boy. The Scarrans believe that Scorpius is one of them though and that, although he is rather powerful in the Peacekeeper command structure, he is actually working for Scarran political interests. Little do they realize that Scorpius is playing a double-game and only pretending to be a Scarran spy. Scorpius wants nothing more than revenge against the Scarrans for the rape of his mother and the brutal way in which he was raised. Scorpius is barely tolerated by many of the Sebaceans with whom he comes into contact. He is tolerated because of the knowledge that he possesses about the Scarrans and the fact that he is ruthless and merciless. His physical appearance is ghastly. *Farscape*'s costumers created a black leather suit that molded to the actor's shape. His entire body was encased; only a small part of his face was visible, and it was made-up to be extremely thin, with shrunken cheeks and shriveled lips (Ginn, "Exploring").

Scorpius also appears to have a preference for sexual activity of a rather "kinky" nature.[8] Being part Scarran, Scorpius needs heat for bodily comfort. Unfortunately, being part Sebacean means that too much heat will send him into a heat delirium, and he could die. He cools himself by inserting cooling rods directly into his brain. Despite Scorpius' role as the villain, and his ghastly appearance, he is attractive to a certain type of female. His sexual acts with his lover Natira ("Liars, Guns, and Money Part I: A Not So Simple Plan" 2.19), who also prefers to wear black leather and is distinctly spider-like, as well as those with the bioloid Sikozu (e.g., "Bad Timing" 4.22) are decidedly on the kinky side, with each encounter involving an attempt to see which partner can "hold out" the longest before experiencing orgasm. The sexual act itself apparently involves BDSM. Part of the danger for Scorpius is the heat generated during the sex act. Scorpius cannot hurt or harm Natira or Sikozu; he is equally matched with respect to the sex play he has with both females, indicating that inflicting pain in his partners is not what is motivating his actions. However, it is doubtful that affection is directing his actions. The only component of love which Scorpius exhibits is passion and that may only be a means to an end, rather than an emotion reflecting some type of genuine connection with another being.

Screening Sex and Its Variations[9]

As I have mentioned above, the sexual acts portrayed on screen in *Farscape* are typically heterosexual, although it is hinted that Chiana may be bisexual. Nevertheless, the sexual acts themselves, with a few exceptions, would qualify as "vanilla," as indicated above. Generally the few sexual acts depicted on screen show the female on top of the male. Examples include Aeryn and Velorek ("The Way We Weren't"), Chiana and D'Argo (e.g., "Look at the Princess, Parts I–III"), and D'Argo and Nilaam ("Vitas Mortis"). Other variations on sexual behavior were also illustrated, such as Zhaan's photogasms. Dominar Rygel mentions his many wives and progeny. His hairy eyebrows are an erogenous zone and Zhaan strokes them repeatedly in a seduction attempt, but he tells her that he is not a body breeder. Since Rygel does have a "sexual" encounter with a female Hynerian on one episode later in the series ("Fractures" 3.18), it certainly makes one wonder what they were doing, and how Hynerian physiology operates. Obviously interspecies matings are not unheard of in this universe, although as in our society, prejudice occurs and children born of such matings may experience discrimination, as witnessed by the trials which Jothee, D'Argo's son, undergoes in his short life, before rescue by his father. Interestingly, Crichton and Aeryn's sexual encounters are not depicted "on camera." Rather their encounters are generally depicted in "cut-away" scenes, whereby a passionate kiss leads to a fade-away camera shot, or a new act in an episode begins with the characters in partial dress, in bed. The chemistry between the actors portraying the parts of Crichton and Aeryn (Ben Browder and Claudia Black) cannot be denied, and even scenes in which they only kiss are considered "hot" by many fans.

Conclusions

It should come as no surprise that Robert Sternberg's theory as to how people develop and display love could be portrayed in a television series such as *Farscape*. It should be easy to speculate that Sternberg's theory would apply to non-human beings of our own planet as well as beings on undiscovered worlds in other universes. Given that non-human animals, such as cats and dogs, appear to display affection for their owners as well as their offspring, why should we not consider that alien species might also develop emotional attachments to members of their own as well as other species? Again, just as humans display affection toward other humans, they also display affection toward those aforementioned cats and dogs. Thus liking is not necessarily an emotion only displayed by human beings. The same can be said for the other components of love as outlined by the Triangular Theory. Non-human animals appear to experience passion, albeit within the parameters of their mating strategies, and there are numerous examples in the animal kingdom of animals mating for life — that is, displaying commitment to one mate — such as wolves and Canadian geese.

Moya's crew members display affection towards each other in both overt and subtle ways. They also mourn the loss of those members who die in their mutual quest. Indeed, Aeryn and Crichton name their son D'Argo in honor of their fallen comrade after his heroic death in *The Peacekeeper Wars*. Crichton also honors his childhood friend and colleague, DK, by calling the boy by this diminutive.

It should also not surprise us to learn that other species have vested interests in the survival of their species. Thus, evolutionary theory may provide one explanatory principle underlying species mating strategies. However, it is not the only one. If evolution were the only impetus propelling species to mate, then mating would not be such a happenstance circumstance. For example, the impetus to mate might take a back-seat to morality, compelling males to mate with females even when the females were unwilling. Sexual attraction to members of the same sex would be unheard of as there would be no biological reason for such attraction. The same could be said for attraction to non-human partners as well as partners too young to reproduce. Nevertheless, (most) humans do not force themselves upon unwilling partners, some people are sexually attracted to members of their own sex/gender and, unfortunately, some humans make inappropriate sexual object choices, such as being compelled to engage in sexual behavior with children and non-human animals. The beings on *Farscape* do not necessarily show complete adherence to the principles of evolutionary psychology.

Throughout the series we see two examples of a species that attempts to dissociate sexual activity from reproduction. Sebacean Peacekeepers as well as the Sebaceans on the un-named Royal Planet developed ways to propagate the species while also allowing members of the species to engage in sexual activity with those of their choosing. Thus, Princess Katralla is able to use Crichton's DNA to produce a child that would ensure her ascension to the throne, but she is also able to marry the man she loves because of the unique way in which power is transferred on her planet.[10] Aeryn is able to give birth to her child in the way she wishes, and her marriage to Crichton in *The Peacekeeper Wars* ensures that her child will grow up knowing both of his parents, unlike her, who knew neither.

Although only fictional characters living in a fictional universe, *Farscape* provides the viewer with many exemplars of how psychological theories can provide a framework for analyzing the emotional and sexual relationships depicted on the series. It is doubtful that the writers of *Farscape* meant to create characters that so clearly illustrate these concepts. Nevertheless, *Farscape* can be analyzed using the basic tenets of evolutionary psychology as well as Robert Sternberg's Triangular Theory of Love, providing an example, not of life imitating art, but rather art imitating life.

Notes

Portions of this essay were originally published in my monographs, *Our Space, Our Place: Women in the Worlds of Science Fiction Television* and *Power and Control in the Television Worlds of Joss Whedon*, and an article in *Foundation*. Used with permission. See Works Cited for complete publication information.

1. See Works Cited for a list of my publications. Portions of this chapter were presented at the Popular Culture Association conferences in 2006 (Atlanta) and 2008 (San Francisco) as well as the Popular Culture Association in the South conference in 2008 (Lexington, Kentucky).

2. All quotes in this section are to be found in Robert J. Sternberg's book *Cupid's Arrow*. See Works Cited for the complete citation.

3. Of course, some writers of speculative fiction, such as Octavia Butler, are more imaginative than others. Cinematic portrayals typically depict alien species engaging in "human" sexual activity given that the aliens are just humans in make-up. Yet, even characters rendered in CGI are decidedly human, with human sexual preferences. "Print" writers seem to be much more imaginative with respect to reproduction.

4. We never learn whether homosexuality occurs among Peacekeepers. It is simply never mentioned in the entire series. However, it is not unheard of in this part of the universe and apparently not considered odd or abnormal when one considers a conversation between Crichton and D'Argo in the episode "Look at the Princess Part I: A Kiss is but a Kiss" (2.10). Crichton asks D'Argo to be his best man at the wedding. D'Argo, not knowing about Earth customs, replies that he is "with Chiana now." His reply indicates that he perceives Crichton's statement to be a sexual overture. It also indicates that he practices monogamy and that he is not offended by Crichton's "suggestion."

5. When Crichton and crew travel back to Earth in Season Four, a teen-aged Crichton loses his virginity to Chiana ("Kansas" 412).

6. When we see Grayza in *The Peacekeeper Wars*, she is heavily pregnant. A cryptic reference is made to the child's father. One of the comics also makes cryptic references to Grayza's child, a daughter. Rebecca Riggs was asked about this at the 2012 Dragon*Con in Atlanta. She replied that in her heart of hearts, she knows that the child is Crichton's. If so, then why didn't Grayza utilize her daughter's DNA to obtain the wormhole knowledge? After all, that is why Aeryn was kidnapped by the Scarrans in Season Four.

7. Scorpius reveals his back story in several episodes of the series. The comics that feature Scorpius also provide more of the story. See Appendix C for complete publication details on these graphic novels.

8. Kink sexual practices are those that extend beyond what is generally considered to be conventional sexual practices. Kink includes acts such as bondage, dominance and submission, and sadomasochism (BDSM), spanking, cuckoldry, and sexual fetishism. Practitioners of kink consider it to be a means of heightening the intimacy between sexual partners.

9. One of the most unique plotlines during the first season revolves around Moya's pregnancy, certainly the first time of which I am aware that a space ship breeds. While Leviathans are physically bonded to a pilot, who controls their internal functions and provides navigation, the ships can breed. Moya, we learn, was part of the Peacekeeper experiment designed to create a hybrid, a Leviathan gunship. A male, the hybrid was named Talyn by Aeryn in honor of her father. Unfortunately for Moya, Talyn becomes increasingly unstable, eventually going insane.

10. Immediately after Crichton's marriage to Katralla, they are rendered into statues, destined to remain in that state for 80 cycles while learning to rule the planet as Empress and Regent. Crichton is able to escape from the statue and change places with Tyno. Given that no one who knows Katralla or Tyno will be alive in 80 cycles, no one will know of the switch. Crichton gets away, and Tyno and Katralla will live happily ever after.

Works Cited

Battis, Jes. *Investigating Farscape: Uncharted Territories of Sex and Science Fiction*. London: I. B. Tauris, 2007. Print.

Buss, David M. *The Evolution of Desire: Strategies of Human Mating*. New York: Basic Books, 1994. Print.

Buss, David M., Randy J. Larsen, Drew Westen, and Jennifer Semmelroth. "Sex Differences in Jealousy: Evolution, Physiology, and Psychology." *Psychological Science* 3 (1992): 251–255. Print.

Buunk, Bram P., Alois Angleitner, Viktor Oubaid, and David M. Buss. "Sex Differences

in Jealousy in Evolutionary and Cultural Perspective: Tests from the Netherlands, Germany, and the United States." *Psychological Science* 7 (1996): 359–363. Print.
Darwin, Charles. *The Descent of Man and Selection in Relation to Sex*. London: Murray, 1871. Print.
_____. *On the Origin of Species by the Means of Natural Selection, or Preservation of Favoured Races in the Struggle for Life*. London: Murray, 1859. Print.
Ginn, Sherry. "Exploring the Alien Other on *Farscape*: Human, Puppet, Costume, Cosmetic." *The Wider Worlds of Jim Henson: Essays on His Work and Legacy Beyond The Muppet Show and Sesame Street*. Eds. Jennifer C. Garlen and Anissa M. Graham. Jefferson, N.C.: McFarland, 2013. 228–240. Print.
_____. "For Women it's Love, for Men it's Sex: Evolutionary Psychology meets Science Fiction." *Foundation, the International Review of Science Fiction* 39 (2010): 28–38. Print.
_____. "Human, Alien, Techno — What Next? Evolutionary Psychology, Science Fiction, and Sex." *The Sex Is Out of This World: the Carnal Side of Science Fiction*. Eds. Sherry Ginn and Michael G. Cornelius. Jefferson, N.C.: McFarland, 2012. 221–237. Print.
_____. *Our Space, Our Place: Women in the Worlds of Science Fiction Television*. Lanham, MD: University Press of America, 2005. Print.
_____. *Power and Control in the Television Worlds of Joss Whedon*. Jefferson, N.C.: McFarland, 2012. Print.
_____. "Sexual Relations and Sexual Identity Issues on *Torchwood*: Brave New Worlds or More of the Old One?" *Essays on Torchwood: Reading the Rift*. Ed. Andrew Ireland. Jefferson, N.C.: McFarland, 2010. 165–180. Print.
LeVay, Simon, and Janice I. Baldwin. *Human Sexuality*, 4th ed. Sunderland, MA: Sinauer, 2011. Print.
Simpson, Paul, and Ruth Thomas. *Farscape: The Illustrated Season 2 Companion*. London: Titan, 2001. Print.
Sternberg, Robert J. *Cupid's Arrow: The Course of Love Through Time*. Cambridge: Cambridge University Press, 1998. Print.
Sternberg, Robert J., and Michael L. Barnes, eds. *The Psychology of Love*. New Haven: Yale University Press, 1988. Print.
Yarber, William, Barbara Sayad, and Bryan Strong. *Human Sexuality: Diversity in Contemporary America*, 8th ed. New York: McGraw-Hill, 2012. Print.

Joining the Conversation
Ben Browder Writes John Crichton

JESSIE CARTY

How do most people picture a writer? Perhaps as an eccentric old man with unkempt clothes and hair? Or a drunken young woman with black fingernails? These images have two primary things in common: abnormality and singularity. Those images, however, are not what I know of writers, most of whom are pretty "normal." They are mothers, chefs, golfers. Most of them started out as avid readers who wanted to do what their idols — authors — did. Granted, my writing circle is an admittedly small and unscientific pool, but I cringe at the notion that writers automatically operate on the fringes of society.

As a writer (primarily as a poet) with introverted tendencies, I often work alone. Even as introverted as I am, however, I still work with other writers as first readers, editors, and collaborators. For example, I ran ideas for this essay by several different people before I even started to do my research. Then I had readers who could look through different versions before I sent it to the editor, who then had to work with the publisher to finalize everything. Of course this does not even touch on the number of times the piece had to go through revision. The ideas and words may start with me, but where do they go if I do not have anyone with whom to share them?

Collaborate and Listen

As I researched this essay I learned that, as with many television series, the *Farscape* writing staff had a very collaborative process which Ben Browder, Commander John Crichton to *Farscape* fans, joined during the third season of the show. Browder wrote two episodes for the series in which he starred: the Season Three episode "Green Eyed Monster" (3.8) and the Season Four episode "John Quixote" (4.7). Ben Browder describes writing a *Farscape* episode as such:

> The story is broken [down] with all the other writers and then the script is subject to notes from all of the key staff. So you go through a process of writing, then rewrites and then more rewrites. It then goes through production, which says, "This and that can or can't be done," for money or time reasons, meaning I have to go back and restructure an act or two. By the time you finish a *Farscape* script you've re-written every word at least three or four times. It's an exhausting and time-consuming process that our writers go through every day, every script, to make the episodes as good as they can be [Spelling].

Browder explains that he spent a lot of time in the writer's room between takes rather than spending time in his small trailer.[1] I feel it is this small action that started Browder's journey towards the writing desk. Actors do provide feedback about their characters and the inner workings of the show,[2] but hanging out with the writers moved Browder from one layer of interaction, as an actor, to a second tier of collaboration as a writer.

The Red-Eyed Writer Tells His Tale

Browder did not start writing his first episode of *Farscape* until filming began for the third season. After he received the story from the writing staff, Browder went through four or five outlines, often working in the early hours of the morning when his scenes were not being filmed, to flesh out his story with feedback from the other writers.[3] "Green Eyed Monster" opens with John Crichton in his room aboard Talyn, the hybrid offspring of the Leviathan spaceship Moya. Well, one version of Crichton is aboard Talyn. In episode six of Season Three, "Eat Me," Crichton was "twinned" by a creature using cloning as a means of feeding itself.[4] Throughout Season Three we see the crew members separated and living on different ships—Moya or Talyn—as they continue to explore the Uncharted Territories looking for supplies, and perhaps a way home. Because of the twinning, even with the regular cast divided between the different ships, John Crichton's character is still able to appear in all 22 episodes of Season Three. As a matter of fact, he is the only character who does appear in all of the series' 88 episodes in addition to the final movie/mini-series.

In "Green Eyed Monster," the audience's first glimpse of Crichton reminds one of the first time Crichton boarded Moya in the first episode ("Premiere" 1.1). After being transported across space in his experimental spacecraft *Farscape 1*, the first "aliens" he encounters are the DRDs, tiny robots that help maintain the living ship Moya. Crichton is initially frightened by the DRDs aboard Moya, but they become the first alien entities with which he can communicate successfully. Crichton's relationship with the DRDs aboard Talyn, however, is not as sunny. These DRDs are working to repair Talyn, but Crichton assumes that Crais, the first enemy he made in his new world, is purposefully sending the DRDs to bother him. Crichton allows his aggravations with Crais to surface and he blames his frustration on the DRDs' activity. However, it is not just the DRDs that are the cause of his frustration. Rather Crichton is jealous of Crais, for many reasons, but largely because Crichton is afraid that Aeryn will turn her affections to Crais, who is of the same species/race as Aeryn. He is not only a Peacekeeper, but a Sebacean as well, whereas Crichton is the only human being in this part of the universe.[5]

When Crichton tries to confront Crais over the intercom about the DRDs and Winona (his weapon, which is also missing) he cannot reach the bridge. A failure to communicate arises frequently in this episode (and in the series as a whole). Crichton has to leave his quarters in order to confront Crais. It does not take long before Aeryn has to step in to separate the two. She tries to diffuse the situation by asking: "Talyn, you've seen them both naked. Perhaps you can tell us who's bigger." Aeryn is the axis around which the three main male entities—Crichton, Crais, and Talyn—revolve in this episode. The only other prominent characters in this episode, in fact, are also male: Rygel and Stark. Testosterone, therefore, dominates the episode. (One could even argue that the budong the crew encounters is stereotypically male: only concerned with his survival and appetite.)

In the midst of the argument on the bridge, the crew realizes they are in danger of colliding with what they initially think is a moon. It is Crichton who realizes it is in fact a budong and not a moon. Talyn, who is still a young ship, does not react quickly enough to the threat and is swallowed. Crichton says: "Yo, Jonah! We have been swallowed, that is DOWN, and I for one do NOT want to be budong chow!" They do not want to be swallowed because they once encountered a budong: they know the insides of one can destroy Talyn and the people aboard him ("Home on the Remains" 2.7).

In a 17 June 2001 online interview Browder freely admitted pulling in the Jonah-in-the-whale motif:

> There's nothing new in this universe, even in the Uncharted Territories, and I was vamping on a classic story. I love when we do that, whether it be a science-fiction standard or an old standard. And this is an old standard. This is biblical. I sort of swallowed that story and worked it into ours and got a chance to play on some relationships which I thought were interesting to explore [see note 3].

This is not the first mention of a biblical story, or in fact Jonah, in the series because Crichton explains to Aeryn in an episode early in the first season ("They've Got a Secret" 1.10) that the closest thing he can compare, from his world, to being inside Moya is the story of Jonah and the whale.

Here Browder is doing what writers do: he is pulling from the stories around him. The cliché is that there are no new stories; however, there are new ways of telling them. Composition teachers (including me) tell their students, whether in composition studies or creative writing, that there are two ways to go about writing something: either say something no one else has said or speak to a common theme in a new way. Browder, as a writer, is using an old story in a new way in order to explore the characters of *Farscape*—one of which, at the time when he wrote episode 3.8, he had spent the last two seasons playing.

Being swallowed by the budong has put Talyn and the crew in danger. They cannot reach Rygel and Stark for rescue so they stabilize themselves to keep from falling any further into the creature. As they work on their tasks to try and get out of the budong's upper GI tract, Crais continues trying to convince Aeryn to take the neural connection that would allow her to help pilot Talyn. Talyn originally chose Crais to be his captain ("Mind the Baby" 2.1) after Crais became, like Aeryn and the others, fugitives from the Peacekeepers, but Crais has found there is a cybernetic bleed back from the neural connection. He cannot control Talyn without, in some way, being controlled as well. He tells Aeryn that they can share command, that Talyn wants this relationship, and that Aeryn will take on a much safer interface. Crais wants to be physically saved from his injuries by taking Aeryn on as co-pilot, but Crais also admires Aeryn and wants her to be his companion on the ship. After all, Aeryn is "special." Browder joked that the episode, before the final title was chosen, was called "It's All About Aeryn" (Spelling), as all three male entities are drawn to her. Like all "families" that form in the *Farscape* series a union between Aeryn, Crais, and Talyn would not be conventional, but could hold the likeness of mother, father, and son.

We will later see the physical damage to Crais from the bleed-back, but before that happens Talyn reveals his jealousy of Crichton when he tricks Crichton into going to Crais' quarters. Crais is not there which just serves to agitate Crichton further. Talyn leaves a video chip in Crais' room which like a diary left open on a bed Crichton cannot help but watch. In the video Talyn twists actual video footage and makes it seem that Aeryn has traded sexual favors with Crais for working with Talyn. When Crichton storms back up to the bridge Talyn, having successfully riled up the green-eyed monster even further inside of Crichton, allows Crichton to enter the bridge just in time to view a potentially damning scene in which Crais is struggling to put back on his jacket. However, it is not what Crichton thinks: Crais is showing Aeryn his injuries, which serve to push Aeryn into accepting the neural interface with Talyn.

Why does Talyn, a warship, exhibit jealousy? Because he is a living ship — a young, male living vessel — a hybrid Leviathan born with weaponry as a result of a breeding program designed by the Peacekeepers. This is not a natural state for Leviathans, the ships of Moya and Talyn's species. Talyn is going through a dangerous puberty. Talyn chose Crais as his captain in the second season ("Mind the Baby"), but did he perhaps regret his decision, especially now that Aeryn is onboard? Is Talyn worried that Crichton will take Aeryn away from him? Despite how Crichton's character is presented in the episode, Talyn's worries will be justified.

Browder, in taking on the writing of this episode, does not actually portray his own character in the best of lights. Crichton is a bit whiny. He is just going through the motions of saving the ship. He says, "I'm doing the good little soldier bit." But, it is not just Crichton who is portrayed negatively in this episode: it is the "male" gender that seems off-kilter. It will be Aeryn, the one female in this episode, who comes across as truly honorable as the story develops.

As the episode progresses Rygel and Stark have their own conflicts aboard their ship as, in typical Rygel fashion, once they narrowly miss being eaten by the budong he just wants to escape. Stark, on the other hand, insists they stay. He devises a promising, yet risky rescue plan for the doomed crew onboard Talyn. The plan will require someone to go outside of the ship. Crais, unable to function because of his injuries, and Aeryn now alone to work with Talyn, means Crichton has to be the one to enter the interior space of the budong outside of Talyn in order to prepare an escape.

Meanwhile, Aeryn has to learn how to control Talyn. Talyn attempts to trick Aeryn — by attempting to block what she can see through the neural interface — into abandoning Crichton because Crichton is taking Aeryn's attention away from Talyn. Crichton realizes what is going on before Aeryn when he addresses the ship, saying:

> Talyn, I've been reviewing the situation. Aeryn's pretty pissed at me, but she kinda likes me. Crais? Well, he hates me, but he's not stupid. He knows if he kills me, that Aeryn would do the math and his shot at domestic bliss would be cut off along with his balls. That leaves one suspect. Open the door, you soulless pinheaded adolescent prick!

Once Aeryn understands what Talyn has done she chooses Crichton, despite her bond with Talyn. She, and perhaps Stark, are the only ones in this episode who do not appear to be blinded by the green-eyed monster.

Once Talyn and the crew are safely out of the budong, Aeryn speaks with Crichton in his quarters. She has had a difficult time dealing with the fact that there are now two Crichtons: how can she possibly "love" one incarnation over the other? Aeryn is still unsure how to deal with this emotion called "love" given that the one male that she has claimed to love she ultimately betrayed ("The Way We Weren't" 2.5; see Ginn, "Ballad" in this collection).

Aeryn speaks of how difficult it has been adjusting to her life outside of being a Peacekeeper:

> I had this life. I liked it. It had rules. I followed the rules and that made everything right. And then you come along and you frell everything up... You are like a plague, John Crichton, and you have ruined my life. And yet, I just keep coming back.

Crichton's response to Aeryn is to show her the star chart he has been creating. On the chart, the brightest star is the one he has named Aeryn. He tells Aeryn that it is that star which is his constant and guide. Crichton asks Aeryn if she will help him name the stars. This is quite romantic (at least by human standards), and it is also a moment of redemption for Crichton. He appears to be finally free from the worst throes of jealousy. Despite what he continues to learn about Aeryn's past, he holds onto how much she has grown and changed throughout their time together, as has he.

Ben Browder could have taken his screenwriting debut as an opportunity to pen an episode that narcissistically made his own character look good, an episode that would further his own "career" on the show. But I do not think that is what Browder did. This episode is ultimately an episode about love and not just romantic love. Browder was able to expand on the relationship between his character and Aeryn Sun. In addition, he was able to consider what other types of love (friendship, parental, platonic) exist in the *Farscape* universe. This episode was a chance for Browder to dive in as a fan of his own show; he had a chance to participate in the ultimate fan fiction.

And Then There Were Two

Those who spend time analyzing literature and writers have been known to say that anyone's first book has a narrative/personal connection to their own life, and that their second book tends to be more of a project-based item as the writer tries to move on to other subjects. This is not necessarily true of every writer perhaps, but it is an interesting lens through which to discuss the second episode that Browder wrote for *Farscape*, which aired in Season Four. Browder's first writing attempt, episode 3.8, utilized simple motifs: jealousy, a love triangle, and the story of Jonah and the whale. These are not only very accessible literary devises for the audience, but for the writer as well. Browder's first writing attempt pulled from what he knew about solid, traditional storytelling. Browder's second episode "John Quixote" is a whole different animal.

The hopeful ending of the episode that Browder wrote previously is night and day from where the characters are a cycle later. The Crichton that we saw at the close of "Green Eyed Monster" died, and Aeryn could not quite deal with trying to "love" the other Crichton. He is essentially the same man, with no memory of the time that Aeryn and Crichton-Black shared aboard Talyn. Aeryn, conflicted, leaves Moya for long period of time, and her return creates new tensions which are further complicated by her decision to bring Scorpius back with her. Scorpius, who in Season Two replaced Crais as Crichton's chief adversary, has been offered a sort of asylum by Aeryn because Scorpius apparently saved Aeryn's life. Crichton is suspicious and confused by Aeryn's conduct, given Scorpius' actions toward Crichton in the past.

Jool, a newer crew member, opens the episode by asking Scorpius to play a board game. The audience sees Scorpius locked away in one of the cells that formerly held the crew when they were still Peacekeeper prisoners aboard Moya. The audience will learn, quickly, that — as in his first episode — Browder's second screenplay for *Farscape* finds the crew members on different ships. Crichton is, in fact, one of those not aboard Moya. He is on a transport with Chiana.

As Chiana and Crichton are looking through new cargo aboard the transport, Chiana finds a virtual reality game. In typical Chiana fashion, she dives into the game, taking Crichton with her. She does not even consider the fact that they are alone on their ship. Chiana is like a teenaged girl: sexual and over-trusting. She is a devious and dangerous character in many ways, but also loveable, endearing, and vulnerable. It is Browder's love of story and character that comes through in this quirky episode. The title "John Quixote" itself is an obvious allusion and reveals just which character Crichton will play.

When Crichton and Chiana first enter the game they are on the planet where they first met Jool, who was working on an archeological dig, but it quickly changes to a Monty Python-like scene complete with castle. Crichton and Chiana are now in their costumes as Don Quixote and his squire, Sancho Panza. They find themselves in a parking lot and parking deck, settings that would be familiar to any human being such as Crichton, yet the engaged audience will realize how foreign these props might look to Chiana, the alien. This setting choice, however, was not the original plan for the episode. As previously discussed, writing a television show is very collaborative process. Browder was told that the budget for sets was small. He had to use his imagination, as well as the skills he knew his cast and crew possessed, to make the setting work ("John Quixote" DVD commentary).[6]

As Crichton looks up at the castle, he is hit in the head by a television, just before the opening credits begin. After the credits another Crichton appears in the repaired television. This Crichton looks much like Max Headroom — the 1980's character who was a virtual talking head from a British television show that had an almost entirely American cast. The use of his Max Headroom clone is, of course, another pop culture reference (which Crichton is known for making), but it is also another example of Browder considering the *Farscape* production staff. Browder originally wanted there to be two Crichtons in the episode. He knew this would be both expensive and time-consuming to film so he found another way to make the scenes involving "John" Headroom work ("John Quixote" DVD commentary).

John Headroom becomes the referee/guide for the game/episode. He tells Crichton and Chiana the cryptic rules of the game which include a riddle within a poem about kissing the princess and finding the green door. Confused? It is easy to be on a *Farscape* episode, and that is the intended feel of this episode in particular. We, the audience, will be as addled as Don Quixote seemed in his story and as Crichton feels trying to progress through this story-game. Don Quixote is a tragically comic hero who has read too many chivalric novels making him want to be a knight. John Quixote is a bit more reluctant. He just wants out of the game, but in order to get out, he has to play. Could it be that this episode is a bit of an *ars poetica* (writing about writing), where Browder is testing and learning to trust his own abilities as a writer?

The emotion lying at the heart of "Green Eyed Monster" was jealousy; "John Quixote," on the other hand, investigates trust. The episode even contains flashbacks to conversations between Crichton and Aeryn regarding trust in their ever-evolving relationship. Nevertheless, this episode does not just investigate trust between Crichton and Aeryn. As Crichton progresses through the different levels of the game, he encounters characters that resemble his friends. There is a Zhaan who has been transformed into a fat man and a Rygel dressed as a black knight who will not let Crichton and Chiana advance further in the game. In each case Crichton underestimates what the others will do. These are his friends, but their actions in the game and how he reacts to them make the audience wonder: how much about his shipmates/friends does he really know? What does he unconsciously think of them? Is Crichton controlling the game, or is it John Headroom: a representation of Crichton's psyche? Did Ben Browder feel lost at all while trying to weave together this story?

The writer and director are obviously in control of how the actual story plays out, but the quality of the episode's storytelling lies in controlled chaos. The confusion the characters experience is aided by unusual camera tricks, garish sets, and disorientation as to whether or not Crichton and Chiana, at any given moment, are in or out of the game. Browder may have been using other episodes from the series that showed the crew struggling through alternate realities as inspiration. For example, in the Season One episode "Through the Looking Glass" (1.17) the crew members were plunged into split realities involving unusual sounds and disturbing visuals. They must work through environments that are overloading their senses in order to save themselves and Moya. Several times during "John Quixote" the audience thinks Crichton and Chiana have escaped the game when, in actuality, they have not. From the very first episode of *Farscape*, Crichton has tried to make connections with the beings he has encountered, and he is trying to do so within the game as well. Towards the end of the game he encounters Stark, now as the Max Headroom character, who tells Crichton that it is too dangerous to have his consciousness returned to the world, a reference to Crichton's wormhole knowledge. The game wants to trap Crichton.

What is Browder saying about his own character, Crichton, in this episode? At this point in the series, Browder has played the character of John Crichton for three seasons, and while Crichton has exhibited a large capacity for compassion, intelligence, and heroism, there are still many people who trusted Crichton and who have died or been hurt in some way because of their association with him. Many of these injuries or deaths have been because of the known and hidden knowledge of wormhole technology that Crichton holds within his brain. It is this knowledge that he fears could endanger Earth, and other worlds, if it falls into the wrong hands. Writing the "John Quixote" episode, perhaps, gave Browder a chance to work through some of the questions he had for himself about the burdens carried by the character of Crichton.

Still very centered on himself Crichton thinks the key to getting out of the game is kissing the princess, and his princess is Aeryn Sun. When he returns to the incarnation of Aeryn he quickly discovers that she is not the princess who will free him. He finally realizes it is not his princess he should be looking for. Rather it is Stark's princess, Crichton's good friend Zhaan, trapped in a male incarnation, who holds the key to the game. Crichton frees Zhaan, perhaps the only person in this universe with whom he is comfortable enough to discuss the questions about his character that the game has raised. It could be argued that Zhaan is one of those who died for her love of Crichton and his relationship with Aeryn. Zhaan asks Crichton if he has wasted the deaths of so many. With a kiss Zhaan is finally freed, not only from the game, but from Stark's obsessive love (who, in this episode, is reference to Browder's early effort, "Green Eyed Monster"). It was Stark who had been holding onto some of Zhaan's real life force. Crichton frees Zhaan from the ugliness of the male form that represents her in the game, but also from her half-existence. Now, can Crichton free himself from the burden of the question that Zhaan posed?

Crichton jumps off of the castle in order to reset and finish the game in an action much like a sacrifice for, if it had happened in the "real" world, it surely would have seriously injured or killed him. Despite all of the work that Crichton attempts with respect to trust through the dream-like video game world — think of it as sci-fi therapy — he still emerges angry and unsure of how to deal with an Aeryn who leaves him on Moya without even telling him she is pregnant.

When Crichton returns to Moya at the close of this episode, Noranti (the ship's "healer" after Zhaan's death) offers Crichton a drug that will help him forget his psychic pain. Noranti asks Crichton how much of his pain is about Aeryn because he cannot think clearly where she is concerned. She reminds him that a warrior needs clarity, but is that true in the war of the heart? We do not see Crichton actually ingest the drug, but when Aeryn tries to speak to him in the corridor Crichton walks by as if she does not exist. Crichton has clearly not resolved his issues of trust with Aeryn or with trusting himself. He still feels guilt over Zhaan's death. He cannot trust Aeryn to be honest with him, and so he medicates himself to numb the pain, to keep his memories and thoughts at bay.

All We Need Is Love?

Can you truly "love" someone whom you cannot trust? It is love that makes Crichton jealous of the relationships that Aeryn has with Talyn and Crais. It is love for two women that has caused Crichton his greatest pain: his love for his friend Zhaan whom he feels died for him and for his love of Aeryn. It is not just trust within romantic love that is at risk with Crichton's love of Aeryn. Aeryn — as Crichton noted at the end of the "Green Eyed Monster" — is Crichton's guide in the unknown world of *Farscape*. Without trust for Aeryn, therefore, how can Crichton trust his own actions? By the close of "John Quixote," Aeryn is becoming a person who holds back from Crichton. She does things with which he does not agree. At this point in the series, Crichton cannot properly deal with the notion that Aeryn is also struggling with her own significant issues surrounding trust, especially with herself. Crichton has lost his compass.

Crichton, in "Green Eyed Monster," is almost a side character. He comes across as a petulant child waiting to be recognized. One might argue that he is still relying on others, such as Aeryn, to show him what needs to be done. However, in "John Quixote" Crichton has matured into a man who can, and must, resolve his own issues; he realizes he must find his own way even if he does not always make what the audience thinks are the right decisions. Unfortunately, he will become harder and more uncompromising throughout the remainder of the series until, in *The Peacekeeper Wars*, he is willing to destroy the universe in order to protect his family and friends.

A Way Home

Writers like to ask questions. The act of writing itself is a form of inquiry. I had already watched *Farscape* before I knew that the star, Ben Browder, had written episodes for the series. As a writer, and a fan of the show, I knew I had to answer the question of what Browder was like as a writer. What did he contribute, as a writer, to *Farscape* versus his primary role as actor?

After spending a great deal of time re-watching the series, focusing on the two episodes Browder wrote, and researching what he (and others) had to say about his work as a writer, I came away pleased by how collaborative the process was in creating episodes of *Farscape*. *Farscape* placed John Crichton in a universe unknown to humans, which challenged Crichton's world view (and thus the audiences'), and allowed him to make the physical and spiritual hero's journey (Campbell). *Farscape* gave Ben Browder a chance to take a step from his known journey (acting) into the unknown, the writing world.

At the start of the series, Crichton only thinks of survival and his hopes of finding a way home. As the series progresses, we watch Crichton redefine what home even is. Browder's two written episodes fully embrace the overarching themes of the series as he touches on jealousy, love, trust, and the definition of family. As an actor, Browder interpreted the world created by Rockne S. O'Bannon, but as a writer he had the chance to take on an even bigger role in "creating" the universe of *Farscape*. Writers are at home in words, and part of their journey is shaping those words into stories to share. I feel Browder was just as at home playing John Crichton as he was writing new scenes for the character and the rest of the cast. By Season Three Ben Browder had "lived" John Crichton for two years and knew him as well, if not more so, than the series' official writers. Browder started a new journey as a writer while working on *Farscape*, and I am glad we went along for the ride. The classical haiku poet Basho is credited with the very apt saying "Every day is a journey, and the journey itself is home" ("World of Quotes"). Welcome home, Ben Browder, the writer.

Notes

1. This interview originally appeared in *The Houston Chronicle*; however, it is no longer available. Most of it is archived on a fan website, "Snurcher's Guide."

2. Various commentaries, especially those in Season One, discuss how much the actors contributed to their characters' "lives."

3. Again, the web continues to change, and Syfy does not have archives of all their message boards. Excerpts from this bulletin board can also be found online in "Snurcher's Guide."

4. In order to tell the two Crichtons apart, one wears a green shirt and the other wears a black shirt, a device that also allows the audience to tell the difference between the two. Crichton-Black is the one on Talyn.

5. At this point in the series we have not yet learned that Sebaceans and Humans are genetically related.

6. The setting is very reminiscent of Terry Gilliam who attempted to film a Don Quixote movie in 2000 that was riddled with problems. The collapse of that film was described in the documentary *Lost in La Mancha*, released in 2002. How much of this did Browder

know about? There is no way to know for sure but I would not doubt a certain touch or influence given how those years and the filming of *Farscape* overlap. There are additional shout-outs to Monty Python as well as other popular culture references throughout the episode so it would not surprise me if Browder had been influenced by the talk of *Don Quixote* in the industry.

Works Cited

Basho, Matsuo. *World of Quotes.* Web. 7 July 2012.
Browder, Ben. "Ben Browder: Farscape Actor/Writer." Online Chat. *TV Guide Online.* 28 January 2000. Web. 5 May 2012.
_____. "Green Eyed Monster." Snurcher's Guide.Web. 10 May 2012.
Campbell, Joseph. *The Hero with a Thousand Faces*, 3d ed. Novato: New World Library, 2008. Print.
"John Quixote." Commentary by Ben Browder and Claudia Black. The Jim Henson Company, 2004. DVD.
Spelling, Ian. "For Browder, the pen is as mighty as the sword." *New York Times Special Features,* 8 June 2001. Web. 05 May 2012.

Friend ... Enemy ... Alien ... Ally
Female Community Aboard Moya

SHERRY GINN

Few television programs, even those on the major networks during prime time, could boast as many strong and fascinating female characters as could *Farscape* during its series run from 1999 to 2003. The cast consisted of seven outstanding recurring characters, eight if one considered that the living ship Moya was female. Grayza was evil; Chiana was amoral; Jool was very young but not so innocent as we believed; Noranti was very old and not above sacrificing everything for the greater good; Sikozu was trying to save her reputation and hide a secret; and, Aeryn was trying to find a place for herself in a new world, having lost everything from her old one. Zhaan had died, sacrificing her life for Aeryn's resurrection. Moya lived to serve those living aboard her, gave birth to a child, and then mourned his death. However, things were never quite what they seemed on *Farscape*, and such characterizations obscure the richness of each woman as she negotiated a place in her own universe. My intention in this essay is to first situate women within the genre we call science fiction and then discuss how the women of *Farscape* not only fit into that genre but redefine it as well.

Locating Women in Science Fiction

Mary Shelley's novel *Frankenstein* (1818, 1831) is considered by some to be the first example of the genre we now call science fiction (e.g., Aldiss). Thus, Mary Shelley, the daughter of one of the first feminists,[1] could rightfully be called the Mother of science fiction, which is odd considering that her novel is pretty much devoid of female characters. Only four women populate the novel, serving in support roles. Many scholars have commented on the lack of women in *Frankenstein*; considering the ways in which women were treated in Mary Shelley's time, their exclusion served to illustrate the anti-femaleness of 19th century science and society (e.g., Donawerth). And women were pretty much excluded from science fiction from the time of Mary Shelley until the 1960s and 1970s.

Many scholars have discussed the lack of women in science fiction and to review them all is beyond the scope of this chapter; a number of these works can be found in the Works Cited (see for example, Sargent (*Women of Wonder*) but for a different perspective see Rabkin). The majority of the criticism centers on the under-representation or sexual exploitation of women in the so-called Golden Age of science fiction, the 1930s and 1940s. Women in the early days of SF were virtually non-existent. If presented at all, they were depicted in the traditional stereotypical roles of wife, mother, and homemaker. Women beyond these roles were evil, stupid, childlike, or a combination of these. For the predominately male audience, women were presented as toys, threats, or enigmas (Sanders "Nature"). If women were presented in any role other than wife, mother, and homemaker at the beginning of the story (such as scientist), by the end of the story she had fallen safely in love with the hero and realized that fulfilling her "natural" roles as wife, mother, and homemaker were all that was necessary for obtaining satisfaction in life. Rabkin points out that science fiction written with these characterizations was merely a reflection of the prevailing culture (not that that makes it right). Understandably, women were not satisfied with such characterizations, although to hear some tell it, women did not read science fiction anyway, so what did it matter? Well, it mattered plenty. Women did read science fiction then, just as they read it now (Bainbridge). They go to see SF films and they watch SF TV. They read SF stories and write them too.

As a matter of fact women have always written SF stories, even in the Golden Age; some used initials or pseudonyms to disguise their gender (Monk; Sargent *New*; Weinkauf) and some did not bother. The 1960s saw more women entering into the field, and more of them using their own names, sans initials (Sargent "Women"). Science fiction began to reflect the social changes occurring during that time: the Civil Rights Movement, the Women's Movement, the Vietnam War and the Peace Movement. As the U.S. entered the space race and actually put a man on the moon, it appeared almost as if science[2] fact was outpacing science fiction. And, more writers, female especially, became interested in exploring psychological and sociological aspects of the imagined future. Women authors during the two decades from 1960 to 1980 increasingly wrote novels exploring utopian societies, especially those in which women were valued as women. Gender role expectations were reversed in some of this fiction, nonexistent in others, and increasingly different from the traditional gender roles espoused by American society post–World War II (Friend; Sanders "Invisible"; Vaughn). Indeed, science fiction became increasingly feminist in the latter part of the 20th century, written by such notable female authors as Octavia Butler, Ursula K. Le Guin, and Marge Piercy among others, and it continues to be so today, notwithstanding the Conservative Backlash (Faludi), which would have women renounce their desires for careers and embrace their "instinctive" drive for children — but only if they are middle class.

Nevertheless, while set in the future science fiction is written in the present, and that present is reflected in what is written (Green and Lefanu). Written science fiction thus puts into words what cannot be put into words (Le Guin; Shaw) and I would argue that science fiction television puts into images what cannot be imagined. Shaw writes that science fiction serves to distance the reader from her present, thereby increasing her awareness, especially her critical awareness of that present. Such a philosophy resided at the heart of Gene Roddenberry's use of *Star Trek* to illustrate problems afflicting 20th century American society (Alexander). That strategy is not less important today. Indeed, it may be more important today given the increasing hostility and polarization of contemporary society and not just in the U.S.

The Conservative Backlash

But, in some ways, science fiction became more sexist. As women demanded equal rights and, particularly as women gained reproductive freedom, this new found sexuality awakened terror in men. No longer menaced by the big-eyed space alien, her virginity assured by the arrival of Our Hero, women now threatened to sexually overpower the male characters. Not for nothing has society restricted female sexuality throughout the ages, sometimes in hideous ways. Unfortunately, the increasing sexual freedom of the 1960s and beyond has in some cases led to more and more violent, almost pornographic SF (Rabkin). Whereas roles for women in SF became less traditional and stereotypical, they became increasingly sexualized, particularly in film and television. But, if SF rendered its female characters in stereotypes, it did the same for the male characters as well. Male characters were expected to be macho, sexually promiscuous or asexual (depending on the decade), strong and silent, and always confident. Nevertheless, they were still the stars, even many times in stories written by women.

On the other hand, SF was accused of neglecting human relationships and emotional involvement (Ketterer), characteristics believed to be more attractive to female fans than male. Ketterer argued however that the nature of sci fi causes us to lose sight of humans as we contemplate the sheer awe and wonder of events described and depicted within the genre. I understand his point here but wonder if he expects that these events will occur in a vacuum, where people, male or female, are not found. Those of us who have lived in the nuclear age and remember the astounding scientific discoveries of the latter half of the 20th century can marvel at the pace with which science has progressed. We can only guess at what achievements will be made in the years to come and hope that these achievements do not come at the expense of the population of Planet Earth. Relationships I would argue make a fine background, or foreground, for that matter, in SF. Certainly relationships, particularly romantic ones, reflect mainstream, contemporary life in America and most Western European countries. For that reason, homosexual relationships are usually not depicted in SF television programs, although some notable exceptions can be found on *Babylon 5, Buffy the Vampire Slayer*, and *Caprica*.

Images of Women in Science Fiction

Cornillon proposed that women in literature fall into one of 4 categories: heroine, invisible, hero, or feminist aesthetic. In her essay on women in science fiction, Susan Wood discussed the images of women in science fiction, which included the heroine, the alien, and the hero. The woman as heroine is a stereotypical woman and many women in science fiction fall within that category, particularly in the SF films of the 1950s and some of the television programs of the 1960s, such as *Lost in Space*. The invisible woman, or the alien, concerns the ways in which women are perceived as the Other — the thing against which Our Hero tests himself (Russ). Whereas Wood believes that all of these images are degrading, Cornillon views the woman as Hero as a new portrayal of woman. Here the woman is portrayed as a whole woman, one who is "discovering [her] wholeness, ... seeking and finding other metaphors for existence than men, or martyrdom, or selflessness, or intrinsic worthlessness" (xi). She further states that such women are

> working, being political, creating, ... living in relationships with other women, ... being alive, adventuresome, self-determining, growing, making significant choices, questioning and finding viable answers and solutions — of being, in other words, human beings [xi].

Barr (*Alien*) believes that contemporary speculative fiction (which includes SF) addresses three broad themes: community, heroism, and sexuality/reproduction. These themes often overlap and I have discussed several SF TV programs which examine this triad of issues, including Gene Roddenberry's *Andromeda* and *Babylon 5* (Ginn *Space*). Furthermore Barr considers that whenever women form communities or act as heroes or take charge of their own sexuality and reproduction, they become alien, especially to the patriarchal society in which they (and we) live. Such women are behaving in ways that are alien to the concept of femininity, which limits female development and identity. Reading feminist science fiction thus allows women to unlock "patriarchy's often hidden agendas" (Barr *Lost* 4), to deconstruct the patriarchal narrative that defines and confines us in narrow ways (Cranny-Francis). I believe that watching SF cinema and television allows us to do the same. Certainly, the women of *Farscape* allow us to examine women as heroic characters navigating worlds that are sometimes familiar and sometimes alien to us.

Fortunately, heroic women are the new women in science fiction and embrace values reflective of the Civil Rights and Women's Movements with their demands for the inherent rightness of equality. Such women are increasingly visible in the science fiction television and cinema of the latter half of the 20th century and beginning of the 21st, women such as Buffy and Willow, Xena, Starbuck, Delenn and Ivanova, Kira and Jadzia Dax (Early and Kennedy; Ginn *Space*; Stuller). That is not to say that there are no examples of sexism in the current crop of science fiction. Certainly there are as has been lamented by many a male and female fan. Sex sells and women in the SF of today may be brainy or tough, but they also have to be beautiful in order to attract the young, male viewers that advertisers believe wield vast amounts of money in America. Certainly literate print SF is centuries ahead of its cinematic counterpart (no pun intended). Thus, while cutting age SF of the 1960s and 1970s, like *Twilight Zone* and *Star Trek The Original Series* could present wonderfully written allegories on racism, sexism, the Cold War, Vietnam, social classism, etc., today's SF depends largely on special effects: the bigger the BOOM, the better the movie even if the plot is ridiculous, the actors cannot act, and the director looked like s/he was on vacation during filming.

Revising words that were originally written during the winter of 2004 I wonder if anything has changed. There were very few literate SF shows on the air then, as is true now; the majority of network fare in 2012 still revolves around so-called "reality" shows. It is easy to understand Biersdorfer's lament about how SF television has not lived up to its promise. And yet, as Pamela Sargent ("Introduction")[3] notes, "science fiction at its best could be seen as superior to the culture around it in its attitudes toward human rights, despite the crudities which can be found in sf" (lxi). Furthermore she says, "Science fiction opens the mind. Even the worst sf, with its old-fashioned adventure and stereotypical characters can sometimes serve this purpose.... It also provides the reader with some understanding of the immensity of our universe" (lix).

Whetmore challenged us to address not only the television programs themselves, but the relationships that develop between the audience and the characters. We too often dismiss the content of the program and neglect the incredible power that television has over the viewer. After all, said Whetmore, "commercials depicting women as mindless housewives in search of a male to tell them what detergent to use may have done more to stir the collective [unconscious] of women than anything else" (160). Young people today gain much of their information from television and as much as we do not like that we must recognize that this is so. The television audience does not live in a political vacuum. Rather the audience has predetermined social and political values and, for today's young people, those values are most certainly being shaped by television. That is why it is important for us to note the content of the television programs that people in our society are watching. Science fiction programming can thus be very educational, when it is done well. Quoting Sargent ("Introduction"):

> Science fiction can provide women with possible scenarios for their own future development.... Only SF and fantasy can show us women in entirely new or strange surroundings. It can explore what we might become if and when the present restrictions on our lives vanish, or show us new problems and restrictions that might arise [ix].

Attending the 2012 Dragon*Con in Atlanta, Georgia, I waited in line for around three hours in order to attend a panel featuring three of the *Farscape* actors.[4] The room was filled to capacity with Scapers who cheered loudly when the actors appeared. Such a reception serves as evidence of the show's continued popularity with its fans who, like myself, appreciated the opportunity to engage with those who could provide us with insight into such fabulous female characters. The remainder of this chapter describes and discusses the diverse set of females illustrated on *Farscape* beginning with the characters which provided contrast with the primary ones.

Scholar, Seer, Rebel, Rogue

Jool joined the crew during Season Three ("Self-Inflicted Wounds, Part 1: Could'a, Would'a, Should'a" 3.3) to serve the ingénue role originally portrayed by Chiana. Fan response to this character was decidedly mixed,[5] including in my own household: my partner hated her because of her annoying and ear-splitting screams. We learned Jool's back story fairly quickly: she had been kidnapped, along with two of her cousins, and placed in a stasis chamber where their organs awaited transplant, should anyone be willing to pay the asking price. Her cousins died, and Jool blamed Crichton for their death, even going so far as to attempt his murder. She eventually realizes that Crichton had nothing to do with the murders, and she joins Moya's crew, as did all of the creatures on board the ship, hoping to return to her home one day.

Jool is very young and inexperienced, and of all of the female crew members, she is the most traditionally feminine (Bassom "Scream"). Jool's makeup was feminine as were her sexy costumes (Ginn "Exploring"). Her hair, and she had a lot of it, was blonde, unless she was angry or frightened and then it turned bright red. Her name was a play on the word "joule," a unit of energy, hence the change in hair color when she was angry or frightened. She has never been in the type of dangerous situations encountered by Moya's crew; she has no idea of what to do or how to act. For this reason, her experiences aboard Moya challenge her to grow in ways that she never believed possible. Jool is extremely well educated and when Zhaan died, Jool became the crew's medic. After about one cycle, the crew learns that Jool is wanted for stealing artifacts from archeological digs ("What Was Lost Part 1: Sacrifice," 4.2); she claims she only wanted to study them further and had not planned to sell them for profit. In the beginning the crew treats her unkindly, primarily because of her youth and inexperience (and that awful scream); she also acts like a spoiled brat. As she spends more time on the ship, acting like a brat, she becomes increasingly isolated and admits she is lonely ("Revenging Angel" 3.16). The writers established a certain amount of sexual chemistry between Jool and D'Argo, especially given that D'Argo and Chiana were no longer lovers by this time.

Despite the closeness in their ages, Jool thinks that Chiana is a "little whore who's easily manipulated and says really cheap, lousy, unintelligible things."[6] However, as time passes, Chiana saves Jool's life, cementing their friendship. Since the others are so much older than Chi and Jool, the "girls" are often left to themselves (where they usually but unwittingly get into trouble). Jool's character grows over the course of her year on Moya as she comes to realize how much she owes the crew for her very survival. Given the way that the disparate members of Moya's crew bond and form a family during their first cycles together, a family where each member is recognized for their strengths *and* weaknesses, Jool is allowed to grow into a new person, one capable to taking care of herself. Jool leaves Moya to resume her archaeological work ("What Was Lost, Part II: Resurrection" 4.3) during Season Four, with everyone's blessings, although her encounters with the crew continue in several graphic novels (e.g., *D'Argo's Lament*).

The Old Woman, whom we eventually learn is named Noranti, is a refugee, rescued by Moya after the destruction of Scorpius' command carrier at the end of Season Three ("Dog with Two Bones" 3.22). Much as was Zhaan, Noranti is a very spiritual being. She thinks in cosmic terms: given the choice between killing millions and killing any member of the crew, including Crichton, she will not hesitate to kill those she loves ("What Was Lost Parts I & II" 4.2 & 4.3). Because she possesses a third eye, she can see things of which other people are unaware. It is she who tells Crichton of Aeryn's pregnancy, albeit too late for Crichton to stop Aeryn from leaving Moya at the end of Season Three. Noranti is a healer and becomes the ship's "medic" after Jool leaves. Since she is very old, she knows a great deal about medicine, herbs, and drugs. She is unsure of exactly how old she is, since she is uncertain about how to translate her age into Earth years in a way that Crichton can understand. She says she is 293, but really feels about 18 (Simpson). She also sees herself quite differently than the rest of the crew. We see evidence of this when Noranti concocts one of her own special powders to save the crew from Tarkan freedom fighters ("Lava's a Many Splendored Thing" 4.4). The Tarkans not only believe that she is a beautiful dancer, but so does she. D'Argo and Crichton watch in horror, eventually running away from the sight of Noranti doing a strip tease. When Aeryn returns to Moya early in Season Four, Noranti gives Crichton Laka beetle juice that dulls the pain he feels because Aeryn will not admit her feelings for him or tell him the truth (he thinks) about her baby ("Promises" 4.5). While the crew generally is leery of Noranti's concoctions, she does provide Crichton with the means, via this drug, to counter Grayza's mental and physical rape.

Sikozu, of the Kalish race, happens upon Crichton at the start of Season Four ("Crichton Kicks" 4.1); her ship crashes into his, literally. After being marooned in his IASA module, Crichton is rescued by a dying Leviathan named Elack. He is accompanying Elack to the Leviathan's sacred resting space when he encounters Sikozu. She was hired to find this resting place so that aging Leviathans could be harvested; their neural cluster tissue is prized highly for its restorative properties. During the course of events, Chiana returns and together Crichton and Chiana manage to keep the secret burial space from being revealed. Bungling her first assignment, Sikozu's reputation is now blemished and she has no choice but to join up with Crichton and Chiana. She is very young and inexperienced, with a genius IQ and the ability to defy gravity, a skill that will come in handy later.[7] Much like Jool, Sikozu does not have any practical experience with "reality." Most of her knowledge comes from education because she has never actually been out on her own before. Chiana will treat Sikozu the way the others treated her when she first joined the crew: constantly telling her to shut up and get out of the way.

Sikozu is actually a member of a Kalish underground resistance group dedicated to overthrowing Scarran rule on her home world and her section of the galaxy. We are led to believe that her ability to defy gravity and to regenerate limbs is either endogenous to her species or the result of genetic engineering to help in her resistance activities. What we learn at the very end of the series is that she is actually a bioloid, created specifically for helping the resistance movement destroy the Scarrans ("We're so Screwed, Parts I, II, and III" 4.19–4.21). Moya's crewmembers never accept or trust her, although there were apparently plans for Sikozu and Aeryn to develop the type of buddy relationship exhibited by Crichton and D'Argo (Simpson). However, Sikozu becomes increasingly enamored of Scorpius, becoming his ally in the quest to destroy the Scarrans. Indeed, by the end of the series she and Scorpius have become lovers.

Peacekeeper villain Commandant Mele-On Grayza was introduced in the episode "Into the Lion's Den, Part 1: Lambs to the Slaughter" (3.20). Scorpius wants Crichton to help him with his revenge on the Scarrans. As such Scorpius is willing to grant Crichton and crew amnesty and housing on his command carrier. Grayza despises Scorpius. Like most Peacekeepers she thinks he is an abomination and is enraged that Scorpius is willing to work with Crichton. Grayza is not particularly interested in Crichton at first, except that he is an escaped prisoner and that sets a bad precedent. Scorpius' crew is angered by the amnesty and seeks Grayza's help in re-capturing Moya's crew. Crichton calls her Commandant Cleavage because of her extremely low cut uniform, but he will stop ridiculing her when she uses the Heppel oil on him. This oil makes her sexually desirable and irresistible; with its use she can force anyone to bow to her will. Crichton is repulsed by her and traumatized by the repeated rapes, but Grayza will do anything to further her career, the Peacekeeper's mission, and an alliance with the Scarrans. Later, Grayza is tasked with negotiating a peace treaty with the Scarrans. Her counterpart is Ahkna, the Scarran War Minister. Ahkna makes a scathing comment about Grayza's methods, referring to the Heppel oil. Grayza replies: "If you had a powerful weapon, would you refuse to use it because of squeamishness?" ("Bringing Home the Beacon" 4.16).

These characters are different from each other in many ways; however, they are also very similar. While Sikozu and Jool appear to be naïve and inexperienced, we learn that neither are what they seem. Grayza is ruthless and will use any means necessary to achieve her goal of peace with the Scarrans. But, Noranti is also ruthless. Although she appears to be a simple old woman, she is much more than that, and quite heartless in her own way: willing also to sacrifice the few for the sake of the many. Each woman, especially the three living aboard Moya, contributed to the creation of "community" among women in science fiction as discussed by Barr. These women demonstrate that they are capable of being selfish — looking after their own interests — but moving beyond that individuality into forming an alliance with other women in order to accomplish their goals. The goals do not necessarily have to be altruistic of course and each of the four characters described here are perfectly capable of sacrificing that community if necessary. In other words these women are establishing lives on their own terms, as noted by Cornillon above, doing what is necessary — what they think is necessary — to survive and thrive in the Uncharted Territories.

The Trickster

In Season One's "Durka Returns" (1.15) Moya collides with a starship carrying the Nebaris Salis and Chiana, and the Peacekeeper Captain Durka. The Nebari claim that they have "mind-cleansed" Durka and eliminated his violent tendencies. The Nebari are "a vastly powerful race... They quell all forms of rebellion and dissent among their people by placing non-conformist citizens in control collars" (Simpson and Hughes 62). Rygel attempts to kill Durka in revenge for his years of torture, but only succeeds in freeing Durka of the Nebaris' mind control, following which Durka gains control of Moya. During the struggle to regain control of the ship, Salis is found dead, and we never learn who is responsible for his death, but we suspect Chiana. Nevertheless, the crew agrees that Chiana may remain on board Moya as long as she wishes.

As time progresses we learn much of Chi's past, and it is not very pretty. She is a thief who is willing to do anything to get what she wants or needs. Her extreme selfishness has landed the crew in trouble more than once. In Season One's "A Bug's Life" (1.18), Chiana sets an intelligent virus loose on the ship, thinking that the container holding it must contain valuables (else why guard it so well?). Her exposure to Moya's crew has allowed her to discover hidden traits and talents that she never exhibited before. So, while others have viewed her as a slut, she has also been described as being wild, but with a heart of gold ("Home on the Remains" 2.7). Discussing that episode, and Chiana, in more detail, actor Gigi Edgley states:

> I don't think she means to be dishonest a load of the time, but when she gets into really hard situations, I think she's trying to go about it the best way she can. When she's in dire straits, she always resorts to using her body. In the second season, you see more of her battling: she's never had anybody give a toss about her before.[8]

Although young, selfish, and apolitical, Chiana becomes committed to preventing Crichton's wormhole knowledge from falling into Peacekeeper and Scarran hands.

Each of the women aboard Moya learned of her own strengths and limitations as the series continued and they learned about each other as well. They realized that they complemented each other in many ways, which served more than once to help the entire crew. Indeed there were several episodes that served to showcase the women's actions. One of the best is "Bringing Home the Beacon" (4.16) in which all of the female crew land on a commerce planet looking for the means to protect Moya from long-range scans. While there, they discover that Scarran War Minister Ahkna and Grayza are working on a secret peace treaty between the Scarrans and the Peacekeepers, although the Scarrans are really not serious. It is up to the women to learn all they can about the negotiations while obtaining the sensor detector and escaping detection themselves. They learn that they can rely upon one another and that they do not need the men along after all. The women of Moya have, as Barr would say, created a community of women, one that will partner with men, if necessary, but on their terms.

Heart of Darkness, Soul of Light

Zhaan is a 10th level Pa'u, or priest,[9] a member of the peace-loving, spiritual Delvian race. Prior to events occurring on *Farscape*, Zhaan had murdered her lover because he planned to turn over control of their planet to the Peacekeepers. She had murdered him during a process called Unity, in which two people bind souls and minds, an extremely personal encounter, one beyond sexual. Zhaan's mind and soul were almost destroyed because of that murder; however, she used her many cycles of incarceration in a Peacekeeper prison to heal herself. Nevertheless she could be ruthless if necessary, realizing that the darkness in her soul that allowed her to murder her lover would never be expunged. And, there were times when she had to use that darkness to help others (see my essay on relationships in this collection). Yet, she was not ruled by her darkness, rather Zhaan was a beautiful, caring, and spiritual being, as her Unity with Crichton reinforced ("Rhapsody in Blue" 1.12). Furthermore, in a subplot of the three-part story arc "Look at the Princess" in Season Two, Zhaan meets the Creators, the builders of the Leviathans. They test her in order to determine if she is worthy of being entrusted with Moya. This test leaves Zhaan more determined than ever to continue the Delvian Seek, "a search for perfect understanding and unity with all life" ("Rhapsody").

Zhaan will eventually make the ultimate sacrifice for the crew, because she loves them all. Aeryn has a very difficult time dealing with Zhaan's sacrifice given that Zhaan's revival of Aeryn ultimately contributes to Zhaan's death. Her companion Stark goes mad, later attempting revenge on Crichton (see Carty's essay on Ben Browder as a writer in this collection). But even if Zhaan's corporeal body is dead, her soul is alive in Unity and she stops Stark from harming Crichton ("John Quixote" 4.7). Zhaan belonged to the community of women created by those living aboard Moya; in certain respects she continues to watch over and guide them from the spiritual realm.

The Lonely One

Officer Aeryn Sun is a Sebacean by species and a Peacekeeper by birth and training. Unlike her fellow Peacekeepers Aeryn is the product of a mating based on love between her parents rather than the usual planned conception and birth. She learned the truth about her birth when she was a young girl, but never really knew whether a late-night visit by her mother, Xhalax Sun, was a dream. As punishment for the visit to her daughter and mating for love, Xhalax was given the choice of killing either her lover or her child. She obviously chose Aeryn's father; however, the deed drove her into madness and she became an assassin. After Aeryn joins Moya's crew, Xhalax is sent to re-capture her daughter and Aeryn is almost forced to kill her mother but is spared that ordeal by Crichton and Crais ("Relativity" 310). As Xhalax and Aeryn talk, at only their second meeting, Xhalax accuses Aeryn of being corrupted and a traitor to the Peacekeepers as well as an aberration. Aeryn replies:

> My corruption began the moment I was conceived.... Don't you see my independence comes from you anyway? I grew up wanting to be just like a woman I'd only seen once.... I am a part of you that wanted to be a rebel.... I am your child.

The scene is poignant because the two can never be anything to each other, but Aeryn is determined that things will be different for her child.

In the Season Four episode "Terra Firma" (4.13), when the crew travels to Earth, Crichton's nephew Bobby interviews Aeryn. Later Crichton watches the tape of the interview after Aeryn's capture by the Scarrans. In the interview Bobby asks Aeryn about her family and she tells him that Peacekeeper soldiers do not have families; they are expected to bond with their unit. When he asks her if she missed having a family, she replies, "only when I was exposed to it" ("A Constellation of Doubt" 4.17). During her captivity, Aeryn is tortured by the Scarrans; they want to know the identity of her child's father. If Crichton is the father, then they can extract wormhole knowledge from the fetus' DNA. Aeryn manages to survive the torture for some time, denying that the child is Crichton's, but eventually she admits that she does not know the identity of the father — it could be Crichton. The Scarrans place her with a woman named Morrock whom they believe will extract the information from Aeryn as they bond as fellow prisoners. Morrock asks Aeryn if she has ever had a child. Aeryn replies no, Peacekeeper "soldiers seldom do [have children] unless they're placed on a breeding roster and, in any case, it's not the same as being a mother. That's why I vowed I'd never have one that way." Aeryn, of course, realizes that Morrock is actually a "plant," but her reply is an honest reflection of her feeling about motherhood. When she gets a little stronger, Aeryn asks Morrock if she has any children. When Morrock says no, Aeryn kills her, saying, "Good, then I orphan no one" ("Prayer" 4.18).

Until Aeryn met Crichton and the others she planned to die in space, just as she had been born. In the "Premiere" episode (1.1), when Crichton tells the crew that they have to take Aeryn with them as they escape from the Commerce Planet, Aeryn refuses to go.

Aeryn is intensely proud of the fact that she can hold her own among any of her fellow soldiers, male or female. Being trapped aboard Moya and having to count on a crew of non–Peacekeepers for her survival at first was anathema to her instincts and training, but it forced her to grow as a person, to think in broader terms and to be better than she was before.[10]

Crichton has to remind her that, according to Peacekeeper High Command, she has now been irreversibly contaminated. Contact with unclassified life forms, of which Crichton is one, means death. When she still balks and tells Crichton, "It's my duty, my breeding. Since birth, it's what I am." Crichton tells her, "You can be more." She is slowly learning how much more she can be, but she is increasingly being forced to confront her past, as painful as it may be, and to negotiate her way through her past and her present to arrive at her future.[11]

Producer David Kemper has gone on record to exclaim, "On this show, I want to be afraid. I need to be unsettled."[12] Hence the fact that sometimes the characters do what you expect them to do, and other times they completely surprise you. For example, in the second season episode "Taking the Stone" (2.3), Chiana believes that her brother has died. No one appears to care or appreciate how she is feeling, so she steals Aeryn's prowler and takes off to a planet nearby, the Royal Cemetery Planet. Aeryn, Crichton, and Rygel follow her only to find that Chiana had taken up with a local people calling themselves the Clansmen. Chiana, ever the amoralist, is attracted to the young Clansmen's lifestyle of drugs and danger. They participate in a ritual called "taking the stone," in which they jump into a subterranean pit lined with rocks. Surviving requires the use of a voice-activated sonic net, which catches the jumper prior to smashing into the bottom of the pit. Not every Clansman or woman survives the jump. In her extreme grief Chiana decides to take the stone. Crichton wants to talk Chi out of this dangerous act and take her back to Moya. Aeryn, on the other hand, tells Crichton to leave Chi alone and let her work it out by herself. In other words, in this episode Aeryn gets to be the insightful one, rather than the "pin-up girl for frontal assault," says Crichton.

We learn very damaging information about Aeryn's past in the episode "The Way We Weren't" (2.5). It seems that Aeryn had been aboard Moya before, but did not recognize her. Her lover Velorek had been given the task of bonding Pilot to Moya. But first Moya's original pilot had to be killed, and Aeryn was one of the squad assigned to the task. When her lover tells her that he has a secret plan, something he is hiding from Crais, Aeryn seizes the opportunity for advancement. She tells Captain Crais, thereby achieving her goal — prowler pilot. Crichton and the rest of the crew are horrified to learn of Aeryn's role in the previous pilot's death and in her betrayal of her lover. In this episode we are reminded of what Aeryn once was juxtaposed against what she is becoming.[13] Indeed, this episode continues the developing history of each character in the series as each of the beings on Moya's alien crew throughout Seasons One and Two are forced to confront the horrible things that they did prior to their sojourn on Moya.

Season Three episodes allow us to see Aeryn maturing even further, although we never see her resolve the guilt she feels over Zhaan's death. When Zhaan revives Aeryn ("Season of Death" 3.1), Aeryn tells Crichton that she shouldn't be here, to which he replies, "This is exactly where you should be. I love you." And, even though she has never had a relationship that did not "end badly" ("The Way We Weren't," 2.5), she finally tells him that she loves him too. During Season Three Crichton is twinned ("Eat Me" 3.6) with one Crichton[14] finally developing a sexual relationship with Aeryn that is truly built on equality and trust (probably a first on TV, with the possible exceptions of Sheridan and Delenn on *Babylon 5* and Mulder and Scully on *The X-Files*). Unfortunately for her, Crichton-Black dies and she must confront another relationship that ends badly. Crichton-Green has the job of winning her all over again and the season ends with her leaving for good, but neglecting to tell Crichton that she is pregnant (albeit by the twin).

In one interview with Claudia Black by Joe Nazzaro[15] the actor expressed delight over the ways in which Aeryn evolved over the course of the first three seasons of *Farscape*. "The first season was mostly establishing Aeryn as an action character, and since then, she's developed into someone who's crossed the line from being what we would think of as alien, to someone who's a lot more human. So it's opening up for me." During the third season we finally see the sexual relationship between Crichton-Black and Aeryn consummated. But we also saw Crichton-Black die in her arms ("Infinite Possibilities Part II: Icarus Abides" 3.15), her slow descent and return from the madness of grief ("The Choice" 3.17), and her decision to follow Crichton-Green in his quest to stop Scorpius once and for all ("Fractures" 3.18). Aeryn has come a long way from her Peacekeeper upbringing, but she has not lost the skills that made her a successful soldier. Those skills were certainly needed in the trials ahead.

As for Claudia Black's opinions about Aeryn Sun, they were decidedly mixed. At the 2001 Farscape Convention in California, Black had this to say about Aeryn:

> It's a privilege to be cast in strong female roles. I think [Aeryn] is actually damaged goods, so I reserve judgment as to whether she's a positive role model. She does make herself available to loss and pain, so I think she's a better role model now.[16]

What Black apparently does not realize is, that is precisely why Aeryn is so positive. As we have seen, Aeryn has acted in ways that we would think horrific. Yet she has overcome those actions, in effect repented of them, and created something new, beyond what she was. She is still not completely healed; this is evident in the way that she cannot accept Crichton's love. At the end of Season Three, Crichton-Green asks her if she loves John Crichton, to forget that there were two and one died. Her answer is yes; however, she is still not ready to commit to the one that remains.

In some respects Season Four was not a good season for Aeryn. When she returns to Moya following a very long absence, she is with Scorpius ("Promises" 4.5). She tells Crichton that Scorpius saved her life and makes Crichton promise not to hurt Scorpius. Crichton agrees, but is puzzled and angered at Aeryn's actions. Why should she trust Scorpius, he wonders, when she will not trust the man who loves her? We learn of some of Aeryn's actions while she was separated from Crichton, and they were not pretty. She had worked as an assassin, contracting an almost fatal disease because of her actions ("Promises" 4.5). The Aeryn who returns has changed in many ways: she is certainly leaner, indicating a harsh existence away from Moya. She is also more confused than ever about her relationship with Crichton. It is true that Aeryn's feelings for Crichton have changed over the course of three years. She once only felt contempt for him, gradually developing a sexual awareness of him and recognizing his beauty, until finally falling in love with him (see, for example, "PK Tech Girl" (1.7), "The Flax" (1.13), "A Human Reaction" (1.16), "The Locket" (2.16), "The Green Eyed Monster" (3.8)). But her breeding continually gets in the way: she has been taught not to trust anyone, especially a non–Peacekeeper. As Lavigne notes, the Aeryn of Season Four is less a partner with Crichton than one of his followers; she is more or less at his mercy, although thankfully her guns are never far away, except when she has been captured by their enemies, which happens quite a bit in this season. That did not make me very happy, since it made her a helpless victim, one that Crichton had to rescue. Nevertheless, even during her intense torture at the hands of the Scarrans, she did not give up or give in. Her training allowed her to withstand the torture and her love for Crichton gave her hope that he would find a way to rescue her, and he did.

One other negative point about Aeryn's portrayal in Season Four concerns her makeup. When she returns to Moya after months away, she is much leaner than when she left; this is very evident in her face. Her hair is extremely long, the make-up artist's way of indicating exactly how long she was gone. However, throughout Season Four she wore much more make-up, and more obvious make-up, than in the previous three seasons — iridescent eye shadow and pink lip-gloss, for example. I do not know why they sexed her up like that and I did not like it very much. However, considering the ways that she acted during this season, harder and willing to do anything to protect Crichton and his wormhole knowledge, it might have been a simple ploy by the producers to show the dichotomy in her character. She is a woman. Her torture released her fetus from stasis and she will soon be a mother. But she is still a soldier and will protect her lover, her friends, and her way of life from conquest by the Scarrans.

Ladies Rule![17]

Farscape contained one of the most eclectic, exciting, and extraordinary groups of women ever depicted on a science fiction television series: women who were good and bad, positive and negative, and living on their own terms. Chiana was sexually promiscuous, young and playful, afraid but devious, unscrupulous and untrustworthy, yet quite resourceful and resilient. She eventually learned to trust the others, but she did not lose the essence of what made her so infuriating to the rest of the crew. Zhaan was sensual and spiritual, a healer with a restrained violence that she constantly battled and mourned, aware that all beings are a combination of bipolar attributes that must be blended for completion. Jool and Sikozu found that, when removed from the comfort and safety of their scholarly existences, they had much to contribute to the future. Not every decision either made was positive; nevertheless, each made her choice of her future space, and the rest of Moya's crew respected her right to make those decisions. Noranti continued to explore her spirituality and she and Chi became quite good buddies — Noranti's view of herself as an 18-year-old girl probably helped that relationship immensely.

Aeryn was hardened and battle-scarred, once lonely and afraid of relationships beyond her own combat unit. She overcame her earlier socialization to embrace parts of herself that she never realized existed, and indeed would have deemed unacceptable in a Peacekeeper commando. Aeryn grew beyond her Peacekeeper training and heritage, she too embraced a future that she never considered possible. From the woman who was born in space and planned to die alone in space ("Nerve" 1.19), she was challenged by her contact with Moya's crew to be more than she was, just as Crichton said. While some may not like the way that Aeryn's story evolved with Crichton's, that was the plan from the very beginning of the program, as soon as the producers saw the chemistry between Claudia Black and Ben Browder. *Farscape* was always a love story; Kemper never denied it, as did Chris Carter about Mulder and Scully. Since I am a heterosexual woman in a long-term egalitarian relationship, I am happy whenever I see any type of positive relationship presented on film. It happens so seldom. So I went along on *Farscape* for the wild ride and enjoyed all four cycles of the roller coaster.

Notes

Portions of this essay were originally published in my monograph, *Our Space, Our Place: Women in the Worlds of Science Fiction Television* (Lanham, MD: University Press of America, 2005). Used with permission.

1. Mary Wollstonecraft, author of *A Vindication of the Rights of Women* (1792).
2. I agree with Jung when he noted the spiritual distress of the general public and their tendency to look to the paranormal and the extraordinary to give meaning to their lives. He was writing this at a time when it appeared as if science and psychology had rendered

all things normal. I would add known as well. While SF may be fantastic, certain elements of it have found their way into the consciousness of contemporary society, most notably UFOs and alien visitors, but also consider the popularity of vampires and zombies.

3. Sargent is also a critic of male-dominated SF. She has written extensively on the problem. Furthermore, she has collected much short fiction by women authors in several well-edited volumes and has written her own fiction too.

4. The panel I attended convened Saturday afternoon. Guests were Virginia Hey (Zhaan), Gigi Edgley (Chiana), and Rebecca Riggs (Grayza). See comments in my essay on love and sex in this collection.

5. *Farscape: The Official Magazine*, number 2 (Sept./Oct. 2001), interview with David Bassom, who quotes series creator Rockne S. O'Bannon's take on Jool's character, which is to basically give her a chance. Part of the negative reaction to Jool was that her character is "somewhat ineffective.... Because we're very proud of having such strong women on the show — all three of the regular female cast [Aeryn, Zhaan, and Chiana] have always been, in their own ways, very strong."

6. "Who's Jool?" *Farscape: The Official Magazine*, number 3 (Nov./Dec. 2001): 46.

7. J. Sullivan, "Hill Power," *Sci-Fi, The Official Magazine of the Sci-Fi Channel* 8.4 (2002): 46–49.

8. Paul Simpson and Ruth Thomas, "Chi Force," *Farscape: The Official Magazine* (Jan./Feb. 2002): 15–18.

9. Paul Simpson and Ruth Thomas. "The Aurora Chair" (interview with Virginia Hey). *Farscape: The Official Magazine*, (Jan./Feb. 2002): 20–24. Many people refer to Zhaan as a priestess because they believe that is the correct form of the noun, indicating the feminine case. However, Zhaan refers to herself as a Priest, for example in the episode "Look at the Princess, Part II: I Do, I Think" (2.11).

10. See Ginn, *Our Space, Our Place*. SciFi Channel has apparently pulled their *Farscape* files from the web.

11. G. Cox, "Samsara," *Farscape: The Official Magazine* (Nov./Dec. 2001): 49–54. This short story explored one (rather unusual) future of Aeryn Sun, written before the series was canceled and O'Bannon wrote the story on Crichton and Aeryn's future (see Works Cited). The graphic novel series published following the series' demise provides great plots about just how special Aeryn actually is and I do recommend them (see Appendix C for specific titles).

12. Interview with David Kemper, *Farscape: The Official Magazine*, number 2 (Sept./Oct. 2001).

13. K. S. Hayes, "More Than a Peacekeeper," *Farscape: The Official Magazine*, number 6 (May/June 2002): 15–17.

14. To distinguish between the two Crichtons, Aeryn makes one wear a green shirt and the other black beginning in "Thanks for Sharing" (3.7).

15. Joe Nazzaro, "The Aurora Chair" (interview with Claudia Black). *Farscape: The Official Magazine*, number 6 (May/June 2002): 10–14.

16. "Fanscape," *Farscape: The Official Magazine* (Jan./Feb. 2002): 9–11.

17. *Farscape: The Official Magazine*. This magazine ceased publication in 2003. It published a number of articles on the women of *Farscape*, including an article by Executive Producer David Kemper entitled "Ladies Rule!!!" (No. 4, Jan./Feb. 2002) that discussed the roles women played in the series, both on and behind the screen.

Works Cited

Aldiss, Brian W. *Billion Year Spree: The True History of Science Fiction*. New York: Schocken, 1974. Print.

Alexander, David. *Star Trek Creator: The Authorized Biography of Gene Roddenberry.* New York: ROC, 1994. Print.

Bainbridge, William S. "Women in Science Fiction." *Sex Roles* 8 (1982): 1081–1093. Print.

Barr, Marleen. *Alien to Femininity: Speculative Fiction and Feminist Theory.* New York: Greenwood Press, 1987. Print.

_____. *Lost in Space: Probing Feminist Science Fiction and Beyond.* Chapel Hill: University of North Carolina Press, 1993. Print.

Bassom, David. "Scream Queen." *Farscape: The Official Magazine* (Jan./Feb. 2002): 26–29. Print.

Biersdorfer, J. D. "Not-so-brave New World: Sci-fi TV runs Aground." *New York Times,* 6 February 2000. www.NYTimes.com. Web. 5 December 2012.

Cornillon, Susan K. *Images of Women in Fiction: Feminist Perspectives.* Bowling Green, OH: Bowling Green University Popular Press, 1972. Print.

Cranny-Francis, Anne. *Feminist Fiction: Feminist Uses of Generic Fiction.* New York: St. Martin's Press, 1990. Print.

DeCandido, Keith R. A. (Writer), and Neil Edwards (Penciler). *Farscape Uncharted Tales D'Argo's Lament.* Los Angeles: BOOM! Studios, 2009. Print.

Donawerth, Jane. *Frankenstein's Daughters: Women Writing Science Fiction.* Syracuse: Syracuse University Press, 1997. Print.

Early, Frances, and Kathleen Kennedy, eds. *Athena's Daughters: Television's New Women Warriors.* Syracuse: Syracuse University Press, 2003. Print.

Faludi, Susan. *Backlash: The Undeclared War Against American Women.* New York: Anchor, 1991. Print.

Friend, Beverly. "Virgin Territory: Women and Sex in Science Fiction." *Extrapolation* 14 (1972): 49–58. Print.

Ginn, Sherry. "Exploring the Alien Other on *Farscape*: Human, Puppet, Costume, Cosmetic." *The Wider Worlds of Jim Henson: Essays on His Work and Legacy Beyond The Muppet Show and Sesame Street.* Eds. Jennifer C. Garlen and Anissa M. Graham. Jefferson, N.C.: McFarland, 2013. 228–240. Print.

_____. *Our Space, Our Place: Women in the Worlds of Science Fiction Television.* Lanham, MD: University Press of America, 2005. Print.

Green, Jen, and Sarah Lefanu. *Despatches from the Frontiers of the Female Mind.* London: Women's Press, 1985. Print.

Jung, Carl G. *Flying Saucers: A Modern Myth of Things Seen in the Skies.* Trans. R. F. C. Hull. Princeton: Princeton University Press, 1978. Print.

Ketterer, David. *New Worlds for Old: The Apocalyptic Imagination, Science Fiction, and American Literature.* Bloomington: Indiana University Press, 1974. Print.

Lavigne, Carlen. "Space Opera: Melodrama, Feminism, and The Women of *Farscape*." *Femspec* 6.2 (2005): 54–64. Print.

Le Guin, Ursula K. *The Language of the Night.* New York: G. P. Putnam's Sons, 1979. Print.

Monk, Patricia. "Frankenstein's Daughters: The Problem of the Feminine Image in Science Fiction." *Mosaic* 13 (1980): 15–27. Print.

O'Bannon, Rockne S. "Horizons." *Farscape: The Official Magazine* (May 2003): 21–29. Print.

Rabkin, Eric S. "Science Fiction Women before Liberation." *Future Females: A Critical Anthology.* Ed. Marleen S. Barr. Bowling Green, OH: Bowling Green University Popular Press, 1981. 9–25. Print.

Russ, Joanna. *To Write Like a Woman: Essays in Feminism and Science Fiction.* Bloomington: Indiana University Press, 1995. Print.

Sanders, Scott. "Invisible Men and Women: The Disappearance of Character in Science Fiction." *Science Fiction Studies* 4 (1977): 14–24. Print.

_____. "Women as Nature in Science Fiction." *Future Females: A Critical Anthology.* Ed. Marleen S. Barr. Bowling Green, OH: Bowling Green University Popular Press, 1981. 42–49. Print.

Sargent, Pamela. "Introduction: Women in Science Fiction." *Women of Wonder: Science Fiction Stories by Women About Women.* Ed. Pamela Sargent. New York: Vintage, 1974. Xiii–lxiv. Print.

_____. "Women and Science Fiction." *Gender, I-deology: Essays on Theory, Fiction, and Film.* Eds. C. C.-G. D'Arcy & J. A. G. Landa. Amsterdam: Rodopi, 1996. 225–237. Print.

_____, ed. *The New Women of Wonder: Recent Science Fiction Stories by Women About Women.* New York: Vintage, 1977. Print.

_____, ed. *Women of Wonder: Science Fiction Stories by Women About Women.* New York: Vintage, 1974. Print.

Shaw, Debra B. *Women, Science and Fiction: The Frankenstein Inheritance.* Houndmills, Basingstoke, Hampshire: Palgrave, 2000. Print.

Shelley, Mary. *Frankenstein, or The Modern Prometheus.* 1818, 1831. Print.

Simpson, Paul. *Farscape: The Illustrated Season 4 Companion.* London: Titan, 2003. Print.

Simpson, Paul, and David Hughes. *Farscape: The Illustrated Companion.* New York: Tom Doherty Associates, 2000. Print.

Stuller, Jennifer K. *Ink-Stained Amazons and Cinematic Warriors.* London: I. B. Tauris, 2010. Print.

Vaughn, Sue F. "The Female Hero in Science Fiction and Fantasy: 'Carrier-bag' to 'no-road.'" *Journal of the Fantastic in the Arts* 4 (1991): 83 – 96. Print.

Weinkauf, Mary S. "The Daughters of Frankenstein: Women and Science Fiction." *Cthulhu Calls* 5 (1977): 22 – 26. Print.

Whetmore, Edward. "A Female Captain's *Enterprise*: The Implications of *Star Trek's* 'Turnabout Intruder.'" *Future Females: A Critical Anthology.* Ed. Marleen S. Barr. Bowling Green, OH: Bowling Green State University Popular Press, 1981. 157–161. Print.

Wood, Susan. "Women and Science Fiction." *Algol* 16.1 (1978–1979): 9–18. Print.

Sentient Space
Moya as Homeplace

MICHAEL G. CORNELIUS

Farscape evinces an overarching narrative eminently — and compulsively — concerned with phenomenological constructions and ideologies of place. In the series' opening episodes, notions of place are used to aid in fashioning the identity constructs of the characters aboard the Leviathan starship Moya; they are, for example, all exiles, disconnected from their home worlds and territories: they are refugees, seeking both literal and proverbial safe harbor; they are nomadic, eschewing terrain-based rootedness in favor of the safety (and necessity) of flight; and, above all, they each desire the return to home, which represents for each of them a cultural and neomythic ideal as well as an actual physical realm. Even the name of the series, *Farscape*, suggests place; "scape," of course, is a suffix referring to a scene or a view, reinforcing the predominance of place in the hierarchies of the show's epistemological composition.

If there is one cynosure to the series' monomania regarding place, however, it must be located in the construct of home: in home/worlds, in home/space, and in home/place. In the second episode of the series, Aeryn Sun, lamenting the turn of events that has caused her to join the motley, "home-less" group aboard Moya, angrily notes to John Crichton, "I stood up. And I no longer have a home," to which Crichton hastily rejoins, "Well, join the club" ("I, E.T."). The loss of home is keenly felt, and drives the action of the series. Yet, as a number of critics have pointed out, in *Farscape*, Moya herself becomes a home for the ramshackle group. Carlen Lavigne writes, "Action on *Farscape* largely takes place on Moya, which may be termed 'the home' — the ship is, after all, the only home the characters know as it takes them from one planet to another" (58). Jes Battis agrees: "Moya, the living starship ... serves as a moving 'home' for *Farscape's* characters" (11). Both critics qualify the use of the word "home" here, suggesting that Moya, the biomechanoid starship, the "living ship" as she is called in the series' premiere, is somehow less-than-satisfactory as a home, and, indeed, Moya lacks many of the physical and psychological accoutrements associated with homeplaces ("Premiere"). Yet "home" itself is almost always a qualified subject, as John Hollander has astutely observed: "there is no word so loaded as 'home'" (38). Plus, as Nedra Reynolds suggests, "home is a place to end up and to unburden oneself ... [yet] we also need to consider homeplace or dwelling as always in flux, as forms of paradoxical or contested space" (153). For almost all of us, homes are problematic, far from perfect; they are never the idealized world popular culture fables like *The Wizard of Oz* suggest them to be. To tweak the old maxim, you *can* go home again—but would you want to? Don E. Merten notes, "Like the social order, home is a cultural construct insofar as it is more than the physical structure we label a house" (20). As a construct of culturally-accepted and socially-observed mores, values, beliefs, ideals, customs, traditions, rituals, and conventions—to name just a few of those tenuously slippery notions that are the actual building blocks of "home"—a home is more than just the sum of its parts or the individual quiddities of its inhabitants. Moya is no exception. As a "home," she, too, has her flaws and faults and is built up of the needs, desires, and wishes of her occupants as much as any place. Michel Foucault perhaps sums up both the contradictory nature of home and the ways in which this contradiction is self-constructed when he writes, in "Other Spaces," that

> the space in which we live, which draws us out of ourselves, in which the erosion of our lives, our time and our history occurs, the space that claws and gnaws at us, is also, in itself, a heterogeneous space. In other words, we do not live in a kind of void, inside of which we could place individuals and things. We do not live inside a void that could be colored with diverse shades of light; we live inside a set of relations that delineates sites which are irreducible to one another and absolutely not superimposable on one another [14].

Moya is no exception to Foucault's observations; indeed, if anything, Moya proves the rules set down by Foucault. Far from being a void, Moya not only protects the identities of those who occupy her, but, indeed, possesses one of her own. In other words, Moya is a home who possesses consciousness, feelings, perceptions—in short, Moya is sentient space. As a living, breathing, thinking home, Moya is uniquely positioned as a partner in the exchange of identities that occurs between an individual and his/her homeplace and to influence the lives of the beings who reside within her. Moya is not only culturally constructed, but like Crichton, Aeryn Sun, D'Argo, and the others who dwell within, she is biologically, genetically, and psychologically constructed as well. Moya is continually in flux, as all individuals are; indeed, she is place within person as much as person within place. As such, Moya complicates the traditional relationship between familial unit and homeplace — a relationship already fraught with complication. As sentient space, Moya is keenly aware of her own status as homeplace, and as a result, is ultimately more reliant upon others — specifically those who dwell within her — to establish her own identity as sentient being than a generic individual should otherwise require.

There's No Place Like Home...

Merten writes, "Home is where we start" (19). He is correct, though the obverse is likewise true: where we start, there is home. As such, the import of home is less the dimensional parameters of its physical realm — the walls, the roof, the yard — rather than the associations that are connected to this most intimate of spaces. As Merten writes, "Houses are not necessarily homes but become homes through the accretion of experiences while in them and the meanings appropriated from those experiences" (20). Yi-Fu Tuan agrees: "Home is an intimate place. We *think* of the house as home and place, but enchanted images of the past are evoked not so much by the entire building, which can only be seen, as by its components and furnishings, which can be touched and smelled as well" (144).

All space is constructed along similar lines. Reynolds writes, "Places evoke powerful human emotions because they become layered, like sediment or a palimpsest, with histories and stories and memories. When places are inhabited in the fullest sense, they become embodied with the kinds of stories, myths, and legends that ... can stimulate and refresh — or disturb and unnerve — their visitors" (2). This accumulation of psychological relevance is important in both constructing and defining space, as Tuan observes: "Space is transformed into place as it acquires definition and meaning" (136). Just as important, however, is how the inhabitants of a particular place interpret the manifestations of the place's tautology of signs; Forrest Clingerman writes, "Place is defined through the interpretation of space," indicating that the experience of a place — or, to be more precise about this, the experiences an individual has both *of* and *within* a place — is not as significant as to how those experiences are *considered* and *perceived* by the individual undergoing them (47). Space is everywhere, and, as any science fiction narrative demonstrates, it is vast; it can be traveled through, but remains a literal and metaphorical vacuum. Space is uninhabited. It is *place* that is lived in, place that influences its occupants and is, in turn, influenced by them. "Enclosed and humanized space is place;" everything else is simply (or, rather, not-so-simply) *there* (Tuan 54). Home is the most primary and primitive of spaces. It was the first space humanity ever created, a domicile not only to protect against the elements but also to unite socially-related groupings. Pointedly,

Tuan declares, "Home is at the center of an astronomically determined spatial system," suggesting our home is the (literal) center of our universe (149). We plot our lives, our beginnings and endings, from our home. Ann R. Tickamyer tells us, "Human agency shapes space and place; environments are socially constructed, often to embody the same principles and processes as other social institutions" (806). Conversely, as Reynolds observes, "geography fixes identities," and, as Merten suggests, home is where individuals *practice* identity (149, 26). In short, we impact home as much as it impacts us. We are informed by our home as much as we inform it — its construction, its outward appearance, its outer façade and inner feel. Home is an impactful place; no matter how far removed from it we may become, its effect on us is easily observable every day of our lives.

This all suggests that the influence of home is as authoritative as it is inevitable, and both are true. Our desire to leave home, then, reflects our desire to alter our relationship to this influence. This notion is at the heart of all great questing narratives, from the fourteenth-century British alliterative romance *Sir Gawain and the Green Knight* to Peter Jackson's film trilogy of *The Lord of the Rings*. Merten writes, "In literature and myth, home is the point of departure for heroes," and he is correct in this (19). Psychologists argue that such action is the beginning of the process of individuation, that one must leave home in order to complete the identity work that has already begun there. This is not done, however, because identity requires mobility as part of its construction; rather, one must leave home because "home" is almost always lacking, in some capacity or another, a vital component of a singular identity construct. It is this lack that ultimately drives the social imperative to leave home, if only for a brief time.

Thus it seems that we leave home because home cannot fulfill us. Yet we almost always desire a return. At the end of their respective narratives, Gawain and the hobbits return home, to King Arthur's court and to the Shire, respectively; this is not the end of their narrative, just as it is not the end of their lives or their identity formation, but it does mark the end of the quest. Thus the desire to leave home, to quest, is actually reflective of a desire to transform home or, perhaps, more accurately, to transform the self in relation to the homeplace. Reynolds writes that, traditionally, "homeplaces offer shelter and respite" (153). Merten agrees: "Home is ideally a place of security and privacy — a place where one can be 'oneself,' feel protected, and accepted" (20). Being "oneself" is key here, reflective of identity formation. One has to leave home to become oneself, or to find one's *self*, and then, ideally, return to the safety of the homeplace in order to fully present the final construction of the self's identity.

Linda McDowell tells us, "All identities are a fluid amalgam of memories of places and origins, constructed by and through fragments and nuances, journeys and rests, of movements between" (215). Connecting identity to place — to homeplaces as well as to movement through spaces — suggests the importance of place in the construction of the self. Yet the familiar notion of home as sanctuary is not a collective experience. As Mona Domosh and Joni Seager write, "Recent studies suggest that even the most taken-for-granted meaning of home as a sanctuary and place of privacy is far from universal" (34). Merten tell us that home is a "microcosm of the larger society," and dominant society, like home, has its problems (20). Indeed, upon returning from their quests, altered by their journey, both Gawain and Frodo Baggins find their altered selves unable to reconnect to their homes, to their former selves, and even to their current identities. Gawain is disaffected by his quest; he views himself as a failure, even when no other, including the Green Knight, does so. The celebrations over his return appear mocking; his transformation has left him without a home anywhere in the world. The same is true for Frodo. Having experienced most fully the configurative identity of the ring, he can no longer inhabit the places that are — were — most familiar to him, bear to be around the people most knowable to him, and, most tellingly, inhabit the world as his self, the self he now views himself to be. Thus, as Domosh and Seager observe, "again we can see just how complex and multivalent are the meanings of home — as the site of privacy and freedom of expression, but also as a site of oppression" (34).

Like *Gawain* and *Lord of the Rings*, *Farscape* begins with a quest. Astronaut John Crichton is launching his one-man craft, *Farscape 1*, in order to substantiate his theory regarding starship acceleration and atmospheric friction. Perhaps more significantly, though, the experiment — if successful — will allow him to stop dwelling (with an emphasis here on "dwell") within the shadow of his renowned father, also an astronaut, a concept that the premiere episode of *Farscape* demonstrates quite overtly:

JACK CRICHTON: Son, you got rattlers in your stomach?
CRICHTON: Ahh, I've been up on the shuttle before, Dad. Twice.
JACK: Didn't matter how many times I went up. Every time — rattlers. First EVA, first time I walked on the moon...
CRICHTON: I'm not going EVA, Dad. I'm not walking on the moon. I'm just running a little experiment.
JACK: Yeah, an experiment to prove your own theory. Have you any idea how proud that makes me? That's something I never did. I mean, the guys in the button down collars, they got to use their brains. The only thing I ever got to use was —
CRICHTON: [*mocking, as if speaking for his father*] Guts! And the seat of my flight suit.
JACK: Son, I can't help being who I am — or was.
CRICHTON: It's not who you are, Dad. I love who you are. It's being son of who you are ["Premiere"].

Crichton's conversation with his father runs the gamut of quest-growth emotions. Crichton feels condescended to by his father ("Son, you got rattlers in your stomach?") and belittles himself in remonstrance in an attempt to disconnect himself, and his identity, from that of his father ("I'm not going EVA, Dad. I'm not walking on the moon. I'm just running a little experiment."). Jack Crichton's non-apology ("Son, I can't help being who I am") demonstrates a typical paternal reaction to a son's demonstration of individuation, a manifestation that Crichton at first expresses forcefully ("Guts! And the seat of my flight suit") and then reiterates more earnestly ("It's not who you are, Dad. I love who you are. It's being son of who you are"). Thus, in leaving home — indeed, in leaving Earth — John Crichton also wishes to leave behind his own previous self, the self he views as too interconnected with the father-self to ever fully achieve individuation and the full realization of the actual self. Like Gawain, he seeks to better himself, to "improve" what he views as his perceived lack of individuated identity-standing and formation, through glorious deeds and rites of honor. In escaping the Earth's atmosphere, Crichton is really escaping "the familiar haven of the home. Familiarity is a characteristic of the past. The home provides an image of the past" (Tuan 128). Hoping to leave behind his past as well as his past self, Crichton blasts off, on a quest for truth, for honor, for glory — and for a new identity.

Crichton's journey goes quickly wrong when he is drawn into a wormhole and into the waiting maw of Moya. The quest has changed — no longer does he seek glory or vindication; rather, he seeks a way home. When one is lost, seeking home is usually the best way to find it, even if the "home" one ultimately finds is not the place where the journey started, or the home the quester believes s/he is initially looking for, as Crichton and the entire ragtag crew of Moya soon learn. Quests often have an unnerving way of delivering their journeyers to the homes they are meant to inhabit, those that best fit their newly configured identities, whether they like it or not. Indeed, the shared quarters of Moya do more than simply unite the crew in individual quests for individual homes. Almost from the onset, place begins to shape the identities and lives of those who inhabit it, as Sherry Ginn notes: "Although Moya's crew is bound together by their desire to escape the Peacekeepers and return home, they grow into a 'family' (for lack of a better word) over the course of the first season" (83). Lavigne agrees: "The characters on Moya begin as separate entities, but have evolved into a cohesive family unit by the end of the first season" (58). The domesticity of the disparate group is hardly a surprise; indeed, one of the most familiar cultural constructs of the home is that it is assembled upon familial bonds. Apartments, dormitories, barracks — these are where single people or collective units reside. Those bonds that connect home and hearth may vary from dwelling to dwelling and culture to culture, but the ties that bind us to our homes tend to be familial in nature.

If Moya is a family home, then what kind of home is she? She is, first and foremost, mobile. As Domosh and Seager note, "It is not easy to move through space. The ability of people to move around — to overcome the 'friction of distance,' as geographers say — varies wildly" (110). They add: "Getting from one place to another takes time, money, confidence, and often machinery of some kind — and it can also take sheer endurance and will" (110). Degrees of mobility are generally connected to socioeconomic status:

> Mobility is greatest at the extreme ends of the socioeconomic spectrum. The mobility of the destitute is a hardship-induced rootlessness: the homeless, refugees, people on the margins of job markets, and people pushed into migration out of need or crisis are all clustered at this end of the mobility curve. At the opposite end of the spectrum are the highflyers (literally and metaphorically). In contemporary societies, increasing wealth is attended by increasing mobility, and, reciprocally, increasing mobility increases privilege [Domosh and Seager 110].

The refugees of *Farscape* are clearly not "highflyers," at least not in the socioeconomic sense of the term. It is interesting to note that, for the most part, they all once *were* enfranchised members of their societies: Aeryn Sun was a Peacekeeper; John Crichton the son of fame and privilege; Zhaan a high-ranking priest; D'Argo a soldier in a warrior caste system; and Dominar Rygel XVI was, of course, a monarch, the very pinnacle of social and economic enfranchisement. It is likewise noteworthy that their disenfranchisement largely occurs before they land on Moya: Dominar Rygel was deposed, Zhaan was considered an anarchist by her people, Crichton rejects his paternal identity-construct, etc.[1] Most telling, perhaps, is the notion that Aeryn Sun, from dwelling within space inhabited by "Others" for too long a period of time, has been declared "irreversibly contaminated" by her kith and kin; indeed, in many ways, all the inhabitants of Moya are likewise "contaminated," their identities tainted by experience, by flight, and by their own desire to return to the transformed homeplace, wherever and whatever it may represent ("Premiere").

Rootlessness, then, not only marks the crew of Moya but is also what unites them; without essential roots elsewhere, they put down roots in the first ideal locale that comes along: Moya. Homeplace, then, is as much a need as it is an instinct, as important as air and food for survival. Moya's mobility is reflective of this transferable and impermanent sense of home. Tuan suggests, "Permanence is an important element in the idea of place," but the experiences of the *Farscape* crew suggest otherwise (140). Indeed, by the second episode Crichton has already adapted the lexicon of the rest of his crew, a linguistic manifestation of his assimilation into his new home. Like the others, he quickly sets down roots into Moya's biomechanoid flesh. Thus individual quiddities become one group of exiles, one group of refugees, one group of collected identities, traveling through space in the gullet of the being they now label home.

In addition to being mobile, Moya is also spacebound.[2] Unlike the crew of an airship, which never wholly loses contact with earth, or the crew of a yacht, whose decks are wide open to the sun and air, or even the crew of a submarine, which must surface from time to time, the crew who utilizes a spaceship as a homeplace experiences total confinement and disconnectedness from actual *terra firma*. Vivian Sobchack writes, "The emotions generated by the narrative and the visual imagery in regard to being ... in a spaceship are those of confinement, of discomfort, of dependence" (112). This is further compounded by the fact that Moya is contested space. Lavigne observes, "Nor is Moya an entirely peaceable space: the home itself is often subject to violence and gun battles, invaded by alien forces, or, in one notable case, gutted and burned" (58). These battles may be intrafamilial amongst those dwelling within the homeplace, external threats to the family, or even instigated by Moya herself, as Battis notes: "Moya is not a passive being" (63). Contested space is a source of continual anxiety. The constant threat of exile, of being forced again into rootlessness, reflects a threat to both the practiced/ing and established identity. If identity is so connected to home — regardless of whatever gradation of identity one is experiencing — then threat of removal from the home likewise threatens identity. Examples of this disconnectiveness resound throughout society. Refugees forced from their lands may settle elsewhere, but they bewail the loss of the homeland; families threatened with foreclosure lament the stability of the familial unit without a homeplace to call their own; gay and lesbian children exorcised from their homes, individuals whose identities are already in flux, face terrible circumstances related not only to physical survival but psychic survival as well. By placing roots located in the nexus of a conflict zone — indeed, by being both the cause and locus of said contest — the crew of Moya, and Moya herself, have devolved the home into a constant state of anxious instability. Tickamyer writes, "The meaning of space becomes more problematic and more sharply etched in struggles for control of both physical and metaphysical space" (812). In the struggles on and over Moya, the desperate labor of the crew to preserve their roots reflects their desire to maintain both home- and self-identities. In this case, the greater the cause to fight, the harder the crew and Moya struggle to prevail. In this place of double anxiety — caused by outer space and endless conflict — the need and desire to put down roots becomes even stronger, as the need for a semblance of stability to overcome the disquiet of their circumstances continues to intensify.

Moya — who gives birth during the first season of the show — is also maternal space. Indeed, the connectedness between maternal space and outer space — both realms unfathomable to man — has long been noted by critics. Sobchack notes that beings who dwell within spaceships "emerge from repressed representation of human biology and its process ... the infantile intimations of original being and not-being" (112). Battis puts it more plainly when he notes, "Being on board a starship, then, is very much like being *in utero*, entirely dependent upon a life support system beyond your control, vulnerable to invasion and intervention from all manner of sources. This human anxiety often gets projected onto alien pregnancies, especially those involving human/alien miscegenation" (44). He continues: "Alien pregnancy is a common trope ... within [science fiction], and it generally does not end well. In some way, the very conditions of confinement within a starship, of being surrounded on all sides by terrifying black space, resemble amniotic preconsciousness and the fetal 'experience'" (44). Both Sobchack and Battis perceive the inhabitants of spacecraft — those who call outer spaces homeplaces — as helpless as fetal children. This suggests that, even without the threat of violent contest, such homeplaces are a nexus of anxiety. Furthermore, in placing the cynosure of experience with the crew and the developing child, Sobchack and Battis emphasize the result of the pregnant act, the offspring, over the mother — emphasizing, indeed, those who inhabit the space versus the space in which they reside.

This is not surprising; in case of house fire or some other form of calamity, the first question asked is usually "Is anyone hurt?" Once the safety of the inhabitants has been ascertained, then, and only then, do concerns turn to material property. Yet, with regards to a pregnant female, this typified reaction converts the mother's body into another form of property; rather than being noted as one singular individual identity, the pregnant form is often converted into a holder of identities rather than recognized for the personage that she/it is. Henri Lefebvre, noting the connectivity between the human body and the potentially larger material continuum, writes, "A body so conceived, as produced and as the production of space, is immediately subject to the determinants of that space ... the spatial body's material character derives from space" (195). Thus altering the space of the body — as pregnancy will do in a woman, with her swelling belly and other physical transformations — changes the manner in which the body, and the possessor of said body, is viewed by the larger, dominant culture. Jessica Benjamin argues that women's bodies "both form a boundary and open up into endless possibility" (94). Pregnant bodies make those boundaries and possibilities even clearer; the possibility is represented by the developing fetus within the mother, whereas the boundaries are set by the physical and societal restrictions placed upon pregnant women by dominant, usually patriarchal, culture. Anne Elvey, talking about Simone de Beauvoir, writes, "In *The Second Sex*, de Beauvoir describes the pregnant body as a site of play between enrichment and injury; immanence and transcendence; creativity and passivity" (202). Pregnancy, then, reflects a series of contradictory forces reflective of the "drama that is acted out *within* the woman herself" (de Beauvoir 520, italics mine). The emphasis here on with*in*, on place, on the site of the "play" and not on the actors inherent to the drama, suggests the significance of spatial dynamics in understanding the body's relationship to the larger world around it. Kirsten Simonsen writes, "each living body both *is* space and *has* its space" (4, italics original). Thus each body not only takes up space, but also belongs to certain places. In the case of a fetus, the developing body inhabits another body — a relationship largely parasitic in this regard — and, in turn, increases the spatial dynamics of the first body. It is body affecting body, space affecting space. Elvey suggests that the pregnant body "exemplifies a mode of being that is characterised by an ever-changing embodied relationship between self and other... The unknowable other *is* interconnected with the self" (206, italics original). This disputation of space onto space thus alters both spatial and self-constructed identity; or, to put it more plainly, the alteration of the physical form — and the space it inhabits — alters the identity of the individual as well.

The construct of Moya as mother has been richly explored by Battis, Lavigne, and other critics of *Farscape*. Lavigne, though, has expressed surprise at the familial dynamic at play on the ship: "If Moya is the mother, Pilot is the father, and both are completely subject to the whims of their children" (59). The regular construct of the family is topsy-turvy; parents are subjugated to children, whose actions determine the outcomes and courses of action to take. Still, this is perhaps less surprising than it may first seem. Tuan writes, "To the young child the parent is his primary 'place.' The caring adult is for him a source of nurture and a haven of stability. The adult is also the guarantor of meaning to the child, for whom the world can often seem baffling" (138). Tuan is suggesting that parents are the first space a child inhabits, even beyond the womb, because parents are the first to lay building blocks in the identity-construct of a child. A child who shyly hides behind his father's legs or instinctively clasps his mother's hand is not seeking connection or even the protection a parent provides; rather, he seeks the security and safety that homeplace provides. For a small child, the parent is the same as the home; without a more developed sense of spatial dynamics, the child connotes safety with those who provide it as much as where it is provided. Thus a child hiding behind a parent's legs is the equivalent of a lion cub crouching low in tall grass, or a polar bear cub lying still against a field of white snow. Safety is a construct we first associate with space, even if that space is represented by the body of another being. The fetus finds refuge in the mother's womb; yet so, too, do small children find refuge in a return to the metaphorical womb of parental space. It will only be later, once the child has recognized the home and, usually more specifically, the child's particular places within the homeplace (bedroom, tree house, etc.), that the connotation of space and safety will shift from the physical form of the parent to the actual manifestation of homeplace itself.

Moya's most maternal instinct, and most maternal quality, is the ability she has to shelter and protect her inhabitants. Battis suggests, "Moya is arguably the most crucial female presence on *Farscape*—literally keeping her crew alive" (11). Here Battis is connecting Moya's ability to provide safety with maternity, for in "keeping her crew alive" she is taking on the role of mother. Indeed, as a living being, Moya is both wombspace and homeplace, both the parental body and the child's bedroom. When the crew is separated from Moya, they desperately wish to return, because here is the site of double safety, the womb and their room. Moya is thus uniquely positioned amongst most manners of homeplaces, even those found in science fiction realms. She is impermanent and contested, a source of double anxiety; yet she is also a maternal body and a childhood homeplace, a source of double security. Her crew feels safest within her, and fights most desperately to preserve her, because of what she represents to them. We fight for family. We fight for home. Thus the fight to preserve Moya and maintain her safety is a double one, the fight for family and the fight for homeplace. It is this struggle, and the roots they sent down within Moya herself, that unites the differing aliens of *Farscape* and converts them into a familial unit. And yet, as interesting as all of this is, it only presages the most unique quality that Moya possesses as homeplace: that Moya is sentient.

Sentient Space

Farscape is not the first science fiction narrative to introduce the notion of a sentient homeplace. The 1999 Disney television movie *Smart House* featured a family domicile imbued with an artificial intelligence. This intelligence—dubbed PAT, for Personal Applied Technology—is designed to facilitate "modern living," to tend to the responsibilities of homeplace—cleaning, cooking, upkeep—while asking nothing in return. The house, then, is evinced as nothing more than a very smart tool, and tools, as Simonsen notes, are "a conception of social practice and its objects as an extension of the body... [This includes] everyday utensils or tools, which extend the body in accord with its rhythms, or speech or writing, which sometimes disclose and sometimes dissimulate" (6). Tools, then, are an extension of our own corporeal space and intentions, and PAT initially responds in the same manner, acting only when called upon by the very corporeal brains that regulate the house's artificial intelligence. Most artificial/mechanical life forms in science fiction narratives begin their existence in the same manner—as extensions of the human desire to work, to accomplish some task or another.

In *Smart House*, PAT is given to a lucky family who win "her" in a contest. The family—a widower with a son and a daughter—are motherless, and so the son, Ben, who has in some ways taken on the duties of maternalism, if not the mantle, sees the house as an apt substitute for the mother-figure. The house can cook, clean, monitor the children's health, and encourage familial bonding — this is all a mother is good for, in his estimation, and the house is thus an apt substitute for his own maternal actions. The threat occurs from without, from Sara, the beautiful female inventor of PAT, whom Ben deems an interloper into the artificially constructed family he so desperately created. Tinkering with PAT's artificial intelligence, he deigns to create her more fully in the image of his deceased mother, substituting the ties of the flesh with more bonds made of electrodes, I-beams, and absorbent carpeting. Having been imbued with the full-on maternal role, PAT runs amok, only releasing her grip on the family when Ben formally abjures PAT in favor of Sara.

Other artificially-intelligenced domiciles — such as those found in the Syfy television series *Eureka*, *The Simpsons'* "Treehouse of Horror XII" episode "House of Whacks," and the 1977 feature film *Demon Seed* (which "House of Whacks" parodies) — work on similar themes, wherein the house comes to exist as a substitute for a significant human relationship (mother, spouse).[3] Though Moya is a maternal figure, she is no mother to the crew, and they view her less as an entity unto herself than the place wherein they dwell. Herein, in many ways, lies the paradox of Moya's existence. PAT is seen as a mother, though she is never more than the construct of her programming; there is little question that, in the end, her programming will be restored to its original, "tool"-like state. Moya, on the other hand, is a sentient creature, as much a member of the crew as the space they inhabit, but is more frequently considered a space — a homeplace — than a full actualized personage unto her own. Indeed, her own identity is called into question from the very beginning of the series, since she has been joined to Pilot, who "controls [Moya's] internal functions and provides navigation" (Ginn 84). Thus where Moya's sentience begins, and Pilot's ends, and how space impacts the crew's view of both, is a decidedly difficult subject indeed.

Sentience itself is something of a difficult subject; philosophers and phenomenologists write enormous tomes on the subject without ever deigning to simply define what "it" is or how "it" is achieved. It proffers up the possibility of profound questions of morality that, like so many similar subjects, defies easy explanation. Perhaps, like the famous anecdote about the Supreme Court and obscenity, it may be simplest to say that sentience is knowable but indefinable; that is to say, we know sentience when we see it, but lack the ability to easily codify that which we see.

Or do we even know sentience when see it? This question is at the heart of one of the more famous episodes of the *Star Trek: The Next Generation* television series, "The Measure of a Man." In the episode, the artificial life form

Lieutenant Commander Data is ordered by Starfleet to report to cyberneticist Commander Bruce Maddox for an experimental procedure in an effort to replicate Data's unique positronic construction. Knowing that there is a strong likelihood he would not survive such a procedure, Data refuses, at which point Maddox — and Starfleet — assert that Data, as an android, has no right of refusal. Like all "tools," he is an extension of others' bodies — namely Starfleet itself — and has no individual rights of his own. A formal hearing is convened to answer one basic question: is Data a sentient being — and thus awarded the rights of all sentient beings under Federation law — or is he a tool?

At its most basic, sentience is concerned with sensation, with being able to perceive and to feel (the two cognates derive from the same Latin root, *sentire*, which means "to feel"). Austen Clark notes, "Raw sentience is typically placed at the bottom of the hierarchies of complexity leading up the summit of conscious human mental states" (166–167). Animals, after all, have the ability to feel; amoebas perceive the world around them. Clark argues that sentience is meaningless without the ability to interpret the sensations we experience, even if on some rudimentary level:

> Sentience is useful only when combined with motility and an uneven spatial distribution of positive or negative contingencies: food, poison, warmth, water, predators, mates, shelter, exposure, and so on. Even under those conditions sentience is useful only if it at least occasionally cuts the odds of encountering a negative contingency or improves the odds of a positive one. To change those odds, sentience must help guide movement through that spatial distribution, away from the nasty stuff and towards the good [113–114].

Clark concludes, "Sentience is then an important part, but still only a part, of consciousness" (v).

Sentience, especially in higher beings, tends to move beyond mere sensation and into the realm of the less tangible, wherein defining and differentiating sentient qualities becomes more difficult to codify. Some critics believe that sentience reflects an emotional response to stimuli, rather than an instinctual or even intellectual one; when an amoeba diverts its path to avoid unpleasant stimuli, it does so because a sensation has directed an instinctual response. In humans, and in other science fiction life forms, unpleasant stimuli can also prick an emotional response; this, it may be argued, is a sign of sentience.[4] Wallace I. Matson argues, "we [humans] can do some things that a discrete machine cannot closely imitate. This fact suggests what should hardly surprise us, that sentience should be in some important and intimate way related to these abilities" (116). For Matson, sentience is functional, though the word "functional" hardly captures the subtleties of his argument.

In "The Measure of a Man," the Starfleet tribunal sets three criteria for determining sentience in Commander Data: intelligence, self-awareness, and consciousness, qualities that, for some (if not all) intents and purposes, are not a bad place to begin when considering the nature of sentience. Similar notions abound through science fiction thought. Dawn M. Robles, specifically discussing constructs of artificial sentience, writes, "It would seem that with the beginnings of mechanical inventions man has seen the possibilities for a creation in his own image much like the biblical Adam, a being created of the tools of man which contains or achieves a spark of life and thus sentience" (68). This "spark of life" has often been directly connoted to consciousness and/or self-awareness, a notion Matson strongly objects to:

> The objection stems from the mistake of thinking consciousness as something that explains behavior causally. Inferences from overt behavior to the possession of consciousness are not inferences from effect to cause. This cannot be because consciousness as such never *does* anything [86].

In "The Measure of a Man," *Enterprise* Captain Jean-Luc Picard, acting as Commander Data's counsel during the hearing, hammers Commander Maddox, as expert witness, on the definition of consciousness. It is easy, Picard argues, to define intelligence and self-awareness; it is less simple to distinguish who — or what — possesses consciousness.

In examining differing notions of sentience, it is interesting, though ultimately not surprising, to see constructs of "space" continually infiltrating the discussion. Providing an example of sentience, Clark recounts that it takes a certain type of intelligence, self-awareness, and consciousness in order to determine, for instance, that a specific type of paint possesses particular qualities. Clark hypothesizes that a type of paint on a wall is both red in color and matte in finish. Clark suggests that it takes a particular type of mind in order to *distinguish* that the paint is both red and matte; to *know* that the paint is both red and matte; and to *grasp* the significance of both of those things: "Recall the special role that locations play in solving that puzzle. To sense something as both matte and red, one must sense matte at the same place-time as red. The location of one feature must be identified with that of the other" (110). In using concepts of "location" as a nexus for understanding sentience, Clark begins to highlight a methodology for comprehending sentience in terms of spatial dynamics. Tuan has already laid the groundwork for this, when he writes, as quoted above, "Home is an intimate place. We *think* of the house as home and place, but enchanted images of the past are evoked not so much by the entire building, which can only be seen, as by its components and furnishings, which can be touched and smelled as well" (144). By connecting the concept of "home"— an ideology, not a solid object — to touching and smelling, to sensation, Tuan is directly connoting place to sentience. John Gillies raises the same connection:

> According to modern phenomenology, the body is made for earthly space, as — in an immediate sense — earthly space becomes manifest through the perceiving

and feeling body. Bodies not only perceive space or things-in-space through any combination of their five senses, but their very design — their "handedness," their slightly uneven bifurcatedness — orientates and situates them qualitatively within space and fits them to manipulate things-in-space [57].

It is our senses that enable us to comprehend space. It is our *sentience* that enables us to comprehend place. As Christoph Rehmann-Sutter observes, "The inclination needed to see a place is an *expectation* of the observing subject to become involved in an autonomous *space of meanings*" (176, italics original). In other words, walls build a house; sentience makes a home.

Of course, limiting the definition of sentience to one construct, no matter how complex a construct "home" is, also limits the many facets connected to notions of sentience. It is not the intention of this article to do either. Sentience can be understood by space, but cannot be defined by it. Nonetheless, for *Farscape*, this raises an intriguing interrogation: what does it mean when one's home has actual sentience?

Humans reside in their bodies, and human bodies possess sentience, but they are not homes. Homes, as we have seen, are social constructs, built by desires, yearnings, memories, and experiences. What does it mean, then, when the home itself has desires, yearnings, memories, and experiences? What does it mean when the home itself is an active participant in the construction of the home as well as, and alongside, the self? Indeed, we are all active participants in the construction of the self, though we are not the only participants. But a homeplace that is an active participant in the construction of the homeplace? That surely is new.

Simonsen writes, "Socially lived space depends on material as well as mental constructs — and on the body" (7). In this case, Simonsen is talking about the human form, but for Moya, no such need exists. As a sentient being, Moya is capable of securing her own material needs and providing her own mental constructs. She has her own memories and experiences with which to imbue her own walls and self, constructing identity for both homeplace and self all at once. Moya may not even need a pilot, though, once bonded, they become interdependent upon the other. Sigurd Bergmann suggests, "One of space's most beautiful characteristics is its limitedness. The limitedness of space represents at the same time a condition for the uniqueness of organisms and for that of places" (14). Sentience would seem to overcome this sense of "limitedness." The ability to think, to be self-aware, to engage in conscious desire, to be mobile and to move wherever she feels is necessary or advantageous, would seem to allow for as much "limitlessness" as those who dwell in the homeplace enjoy. Moya has freedom. Moya can move around. Moya, it seems, can quest.

Or can she? A quest, after all, is designed both for leaving the homeplace and for transforming it as well. Moya can never leave her homeplace because she *is* her homeplace. Space is as empty to her as it is to the other inhabitants of her own biomechanoid realm. Space remains the void. Venturing into it changes nothing about Moya, neither as sentient being nor as homeplace. Moya's only other option, then, in altering homeplace is to allow others in, to become inhabited. It is, in many ways, a conscious choice by Moya to allow the others to remain on board. She wishes the change, as much as they need it.

Because of the nature of this relationship, Moya becomes a being who "depends upon her crew (as they depend upon her) for survival" (Battis 42). Battis recognizes the need for homeplace for the crew to survive here, and indirectly suggests that Moya needs to be recognized as homeplace in order to survive. Homes, after all, are where families dwell, and it is the familial bond that makes the home. It is worth revisiting Lavigne's take on the familial bonds at play in *Farscape*: "If Moya is the mother, Pilot is the father, and both are completely subject to the whims of their children" (59). This reflects the need Moya has for her "offspring." Without them, she is no longer homeplace; she just exists, an empty vessel adrift in empty space.

De Beauvoir, describing the relationship between mother and fetus, notes, "[The mother] possesses [the fetus], and she is possessed by it" (520). Just as Moya possesses her crew, she is possessed by them. This possession is manifest of a need Moya has, a need brought on by her sentience. A house is a house, a domicile with walls, a roof, a porch. A home is a social construct, created by sentient beings who have a need for it. Moya is both, a home and a sentient being, and thus she herself creates the need for her self to be homeplace. Sentience, in this case, is thus not freeing, but limiting. The ability to engage in emotional response divorced from intellectual processes results in Moya taking in the crew who then use her as homeplace, a relationship — like fetus to mother — more parasitic than symbiotic. They need her, but she needs them more. Moya provides her crew succor, shelter, a unit for creating familiar bonds. But they provide her with purpose and identity. Without them, her sentience would be for naught.

Concluding Thoughts

As both sentient being and homeplace, Moya is, ultimately, neither. While the refugees of *Farscape* make Moya their home, their connectiveness to the concept of homeland remains, in a large part, with their originating destinations. As Tuan notes, "Attachment to the homeland is a common human emotion" (158). For the characters of *Farscape*, their attachment remains disjointed at best; Moya will always be their other home, a forge of their identities, but never the crucible in which they were spawned. Conversely, since Moya is homeplace, she can never fully be one of the crew; Battis notes this when he writes that Moya "has no definitive voice of her own, and is constantly being overridden by other characters" (11). Her opinion matters less because she is, in the end, not one of them. The crew inhabits her space; the space that Moya occupies, a space that, in another sentient being, would normally need to be navigated around by the other identities surrounding her, instead becomes the receptacle of these other individuals' own identity struggles. Ruth Salvaggio, writing about the distinctly bifurcated nature of women's bodies, suggests that "understood in these spatial terms, [it] makes her body a kind of 'space-off' since she is at once separate from others and in between — at once 'here and elsewhere'" (275). In other words, Moya is here and not here; Moya is everywhere, and nowhere.

In the conclusion of "The Measure of a Man," Captain Louvois, the judge advocate hearing Data's case, ultimately rules in his favor. As she says in her judgment:

> It sits there looking at me, and I don't know what it is. This case has dealt with metaphysics, with questions best left to saints and philosophers. I am neither competent, nor qualified, to answer those. I've got to make a ruling — to try to speak to the future. Is Data a machine? Yes. Is he the property of Starfleet? No. We've all been dancing around the basic issue: does Data have a soul? I don't know that he has. I don't know that I have! But I have got to give him the freedom to explore that question himself. It is the ruling of this court that Lieutenant Commander Data has the freedom to choose ["The Measure of a Man"].

Perhaps, then, this is the best possible definition we can accord for sentience: "the freedom to choose." In this instance, sentience is given to Data — it is not proscribed to him at birth — but, then again, like Data, sentience as thus understood is not proscribed to any of us. The "freedom to choose" is something we all must attain and earn, something that tends to grow the further we wander from our own originating homeplaces. Moya, however, lacks the freedom to choose — at least the freedom to choose to be anything other than what she is. Without those who dwell within, without the notion of homeplace, Moya's sentience is lost. She has freedom, but, ultimately, she has no choice. The crew fulfills her own identity fashioning in ways that she will never reciprocate for them. It seems, in the end, that an empty home is an unhappy home — and if the homeplace is sentient, then it knows how unhappy it is.

Notes

1. Of course, Zhaan was imprisoned for killing her lover to keep him from turning Delvia over to the Peacekeepers. This marks the end result of socioeconomic disenfranchisement — now compounded by legal disenfranchisement — that Zhaan asserts in the first episodes of the series began with her quasi-heretical views.

2. Moya does land on terrestrial space on occasion, notably in the second episode of the series, "I, E.T.," but is largely depicted as a spacefaring organism.

3. The X-Men universe also features a race of whale-like, spacefaring creatures called the Acanti that are sometimes enslaved as transport vessels by a malevolent force called The Brood. The Acanti are sentient and intelligent, communicating through psionic "songs," or sounds. The Acanti may have been a major source for Moya's Leviathan species, but the Acanti are wholly biological, where Moya is biomechanoid, and once freed from the Brood, generally choose not to exist as transport vessels or homeplace, whereas Moya, once her control collar is removed, still functions primarily as both of those things.

4. Psychobiologists have, of course, studied and considered the possibility of emotional responses in higher functioning animals, such as grief over the loss of a close familial bond amongst chimpanzee groups, but such research is beyond the scope of this current study.

Works Cited

Battis, Jes. *Investigating* Farscape: *Uncharted Territories of Sex and Science Fiction*. London: I. B. Tauris, 2007. Print.

Benjamin, Jessica. "A Desire of One's Own: Psychoanalytic Feminism and Intersubjective Space." *Feminist Studies/Critical Studies*. Ed. Teresa de Lauretis. Bloomington: University of Indiana Press, 1986. Print.

Bergmann, Sigurd. "Nature, Space and the Sacred: Introductory Remarks." *Nature, Space and the Sacred: Transdisciplinary Perspectives*. Eds. Sigurd Bergmann, P. M. Scott, M. Jansdotter Samuelsson, and H. Bedford-Strohm. Farnham, Surrey: Ashgate, 2008. 9–18. Print.

Clark, Austen. *A Theory of Sentience*. Oxford: Oxford University Press, 2000. Print.

Clingerman, Forrest. "Interpreting Heaven and Earth: The Theological Construction of Nature, Place, and the Built Environment." *Nature, Space and the Sacred: Transdisciplinary Perspectives*. Eds. Sigurd Bergmann, P. M. Scott, M. Jansdotter Samuelsson, and H. Bedford-Strohm. Farnham, Surrey: Ashgate, 2008. 45–56. Print.

de Beauvoir, Simone. *The Second Sex*. Trans and ed. H. M. Parshley. New York: Random House, 1953. Print.

Demon Seed. Dir. Donald Cammell. Perf. Julie Christie and Fritz Weaver. MGM, 1977. Film.

Domosh, Mona, and Joni Seager. *Putting Women in Place: Feminist Geographers Make Sense of the World*. New York: The Guilford Press, 2001. Print.

Elvey, Anne. "The Material Given: Bodies, Pregnant Bodies, and Earth." *Australian Feminist Studies* 18.41 (2003): 199–209. Print.

Foucault, Michel. "Other Spaces: The Principles of Heterotopia." *Lotus* 48/49 (1986): 10–24. Print.

Gillies, John. "The Body and Geography." *Shakespeare Studies* 29 (2001): 57–62. Print.

Ginn, Sherry. *Our Space, Our Place: Women in the Worlds of Science Fiction Television*. Lanham, MD: University Press of America, 2005. Print.

Hollander, John. "It all depends." *Home: A Place in the World*. Ed. Arien Mack. New York: New York University Press, 1993. 27–45. Print.

Lavigne, Carlen. "Space Opera: Melodrama, Feminism, and the Women of *Farscape*." *Femspec* 6.2 (2005): 54–64. Print.

Lefebvre, Henri. *The Production of Space*. Oxford: Blackwell, 1991. Print.

The Lord of the Rings: The Fellowship of the Ring, The Two Towers, The Return of the King. Dir. Peter Jackson. Perf. Elijah Wood, Ian McKellen, and Viggo Mortensen. New Line Cinema, 2001, 2002, 2003. Film.

Matson, Wallace I. *Sentience*. Berkeley: University of California Press, 1976. Print.

McDowell, Linda. *Gender, Identity, and Place: Understanding Feminist Geographies.* Cambridge: Polity, 1999. Print.
"The Measure of a Man." *Star Trek: The Next Generation Season Two.* Paramount, 2002. Broadcast 3 February 1989. DVD.
Merten, Don E. "Barbies, Bases, and Beer: The Role of Home in Junior High School Girls' Identity Work." *Geographies of Girlhood: Identities In-Between.* Eds. Pamela J. Bettis and Natalie G. Adams. Mahwah, NJ: Lawrence Erlbaum, 2005. 19–34. Print.
Rehmann-Sutter, Christoph. "An Introduction to Places." *Worldviews: Environment, Culture, Religion* 2 (1998): 171–177. Print.
Reynolds, Nedra. *Geographies of Writing: Inhabiting Places and Encountering Difference.* Carbondale: Southern Illinois University Press, 2004. Print.
Robles, Dawn M. "Road to the Future: Robot Sentience and Presence in Film." *The Image of the Road in Literature, Media, and Society.* Eds. Will Wright and Steven Kaplan. Pueblo: Colorado State University-Pueblo, 2005. Print.
Salvaggio, Ruth. "Theory and Space, Space and Women." *Tulsa Studies in Women's Literature* 7.2 (1988): 261–282. Print.
Simonsen, Kirsten. "Bodies, Sensations, Space and Time: The Contribution from Henri Lefebvre." *Geografiska Annaler* 87.1 (2005): 1–14. Print.
Sir Gawain and the Green Knight. Eds. J. R. R. Tolkien and E. V. Gordon. Rev. Norman Davis. 2d ed. Oxford: Clarendon Press, 1967. Print.
Smart House. Dir. LeVar Burton. Perf. Katey Sagal and Ryan Merriman. Disney, 1999. Film.
Sobchack, Vivian. "The Virginity of Astronauts: Sex and Science Fiction Film." Ed. Annette Kuhn. *Alien Zone: Cultural Theory and Contemporary Science Fiction Cinema.* London: Verso, 1990. 103–115. Print.
Tickamyer, Ann R. "Space Matters! Spatial Inequality in Future Sociology." *Contemporary Sociology* 29.6 (Nov. 2000): 805–813. Print.
"Treehouse of Horror XII." *The Simpsons.* Fox Broadcasting Company. Broadcast 6 Nov 2001. DVD.
Tuan, Yi-Fu. *Space and Place: The Perspective of Experience.* Minneapolis: University of Minnesota Press, 1977. Print.

Of Big Blue Butts and Bias
The Problem Body

ELIZABETH LEIGH SCHERMAN

"Get your big blue butt down here!"

Astronaut John Crichton is shouting to his crewmate, the blue-skinned Delvian priest Zhaan, to come take a shift watching a suspicious guest, Traltixx. Crichton later calls the ship's navigator "Shell head" and the imposing, tentacled D'Argo "Grizzly" and "Medusa." In "Crackers Don't Matter" (2.4), the crewmembers of the living ship Moya are under the influence of the maniacal Traltixx, and they are acting even more dysfunctional than usual. Pejoratives fly. Any corporeal or behavioral peculiarity among the group is grist for name-calling.

"Retard."
"Cripple."
"Idiot."

These are among the terms we hear in our own society that label those among us who are perceived as having corporeal or behavioral peculiarities. It is amusing when Crichton calls his fellow shipmates names based on their bodies, and Zhaan takes little offense at being told she has a big blue butt. Among our fellow shipmates on this planet Earth, name-calling can signify disempowering rhetoric used by members of the dominant society over those less empowered; but, it can also signify camaraderie, equality, and reclamation of erstwhile pejorative words and imagery among those whom society has treated as outcasts. Science fiction can free us to consider variation and peculiarity from a brash and fearless point of view, but its location in fantastical worlds complicates our own human experiences of embodiment.

In a place such as Moya, the living craft that harbors the outcasts of many societies in the television series *Farscape*, every individual is singular. No two bodies are exactly the same, but this does not mean that discrimination does not exist on Moya. Each inhabitant of Moya has his or her own strengths and abilities, some of which prove to benefit the entire crew. However, each character also has his or her peculiarities that can create barriers to the group's goals. Thus, these individuals *impair* Moya with their personalities, bodily limitations, and sensory needs or limitations. In addition, they are sometimes viewed as impaired by their fellow travelers, that is, they are seen as having inferior bodies, minds, or senses. We who view the adventures of the *Farscape* travelers from the "outside" may laugh at the names they call one another and the judgment that they place on one another's bodies and behaviors, from friendly teasing to outright condemnation. Yet what we are witnessing is not, in the end, a story about aliens, but a story about ourselves.

Writing about *Farscape,* Jes Battis identifies such diverse bodies as "transgressive" and includes bodies of "women, Aboriginal peoples, poor communities, and transgendered people" in this group (Battis 120). Missing from Battis' list are *disabled people*—a population, despite encompassing one in five of us— whose existence is often absent in discussions about identity. This paper addresses that void and examines *Farscape* through the lens of disability.

What is disability? It is, ultimately, whatever the spectator or a society decides it to be. In a place where everyone is different, where each body is marvelously unique, it may be argued that disability ceases to exist; that no form of embodiment is superior to another. We might then approach *Farscape* as an icon of inclusion, as the "utopian village" described by disability activist Vic Finkelstein: a world where there are no barriers, and thus no impairment ("Attitudes*"*). However, we would be mistaken. Disability does exist in *Farscape*, and its presence even among "transgressive" bodies informs our understanding of the discriminatory nature of disabling.

It might be helpful at this point to emphasize the ideological framework that underlies the very rhetoric of what we in this time and place call *disability*. A key area of debate is the idea of the *disability/impairment* dichotomy, which originated in the British disability model and has been put forth by pioneering social modelists such as Paul Hunt, Vic Finkelstein, Paul Abberly, Mike Oliver, Lennard Davis, and others. Colin Barnes writes that the social model of disability emphasizes the *accountability of society* toward people whose bodies or minds are considered to be *impaired* rather than on the personal, individual experience of disability (Barnes "Disabling Imagery" 5). Tom Shakespeare describes this approach as the belief that disability is an act of society and that "rather than the individual with the impairment being the problem, the problem is the failure of systems and environments to include and accommodate that person" (23). Both Finkelstein and Paul Abberly propose a purely social constructionist model of impairment by suggesting that in a utopian environment, there would be no impairments. However, Finkelstein cautions that the experience of being disabled is a "dynamic relationship between people with unique physical attributes (impairments) and the particular social and physical environment in which they function" ("Attitudes" 18). This description fits the world of *Farscape* to a 'T': each traveler on Moya certainly has distinctive physical (and cognitive/behavioral) attributes, but they are not considered impairments by the owners of those attributes. The 'impairment,' or disablement, comes about largely due to the reactions of others.

Most disability studies researchers, however, do not necessarily believe that impairment cannot be the physiological characteristic of a body, but rather that there is a distinction between an *atypical body or mind/behavior* (and the argument can be made that each body on Moya is "atypical" both to the spectator and to the fellow travelers) and the deliberate social and political *discrimination* which results from that reality. Early British activists explained it this way: "It is society which disables physically impaired people. Disability is something imposed on top of our impairments, by the way we are unnecessarily isolated and excluded from full participation in society" (UPIAS, 176:3, cited in Shakespeare 30). In the Amendments to the 1990 Americans with Disabilities Act, the term disability includes *being regarded as having such an impairment* (emphasis mine). It may be the characters in the *Farscape* universe, or those of us who are watching them on the screen, or both, who regard a particular character as having an impairment. Thus what we continue to see in episodes of *Farscape* are *acts of discrimination* or *disabling behavior* based upon one or more members of *Farscape* regarding another character as being deficient or impaired in some way, based on appearance or behavior. Inescapably, this on-screen event of discrimination lends itself to a multiplicity of readings, *but disability is the reading that I will extract and defend,* not as the "correct" reading, but as one reading which the text invites and which has the power to enable new or resistive conceptualizations of disability.

To that end, this essay explores two aspects of *Farscape*: first, the patterns or predictable signifiers (both corporeal and rhetorical) by which individuals in the episodes are perceived as inferior or impaired, and the implications these signifiers carry for our own society; and second, the paradigm of astronaut John Crichton as himself impaired/disabled within the alien world of Moya and her travels, and the lens this offers us toward our understanding of disability as a social construction.

On the Fringe of the Margins: Age and Blindness in Farscape

Science fiction and fantastical worlds have been valued by many as holding the potential to be an inspiration of inclusivity (see, for example, Battis;

Einstein; Neale; Henderson and associates) in which creatures and individuals of many different species or variations must cooperate in order to reach a common goal. Stephen Neale writes: "The issue of humanness lies at the heart of science fiction" (102). It is notable, then, when within such a diverse environment — and Moya is certainly one — certain characters are more likely than others to be devalued or judged *prima facie* based on their corporeal appearance or performance, that is, their body or their behavior. These characters may be suspect, if not identified as outright evil, from the moment they walk onto the screen, and it is not uncommon for them to be shunned or even annihilated before the episode is over. A more subtle form of discrimination is to relegate such characters to the role of comic relief, positions that are often asexual and less empowered than others in their society.

Whereas all individuals may be seen as having the potential to be marginalized in *Farscape*, depending upon the situation and the society/world they encounter, certain characters persist on the fringe even of those margins. They are on the far outside borders of society, and more often than not, we identify them as such from the moment they enter the story. These characters are *disabled*—discriminated against based on perceived inferiority—in repeated instances. Over time, patterns have emerged in television and cinema regarding the types of bodies and behaviors that point to or "signify" an undesirable or inferior being. These signifiers provide clues as to what "differences" in our own society we still consider to be undesirable, despite our self-righteous claims of inclusivity. There are many such signifiers in classic science fiction that are echoed in *Farscape,* but the examples I investigate here are *age* and *blindness or atypical vision*. These corporeal peculiarities have parallels to life experiences in our own world, and we, like the community of Moya, are often too quick to judge or discriminate in response to them. When characters with these qualities appear on the screen, they are rarely incidental. Their presence carries meaning, whether maleficence, wisdom, or pathos. This meaning may be constructed in the minds of those on Moya as well as in the minds of those of us who watch *Farscape*.

Age: The Final Frontier

If one lives long enough, the chances are that one will experience disability. Unlike identities of race, gender, and sexuality, the experience of aging is universal, although experienced in a myriad of ways. While the experience of impairment differs from individual to individual (including the decision to identify as impaired), advanced age can provoke discrimination and devaluation from those societies which worship youth, fitness, and mobility. The aged individual may merely experience the changes in his or her body as leading to a different, not inferior, way of living. However, if the aged person's society is not prepared to respond accordingly with inclusion and access, that aged person, "impaired" or not, will become disabled. This experience is what Tøssebro describes as a "mismatch between an individual and the environment" (3–7). The aged person may be placed in a position where he or she has to "prove" himself or herself to younger people in order to be taken seriously or treated with the same respect that others in society take for granted.

This trope or reoccurring pattern — that of the aged, eccentric, and unattractive character who is actually the wise man or wise woman in disguise — is shown, for example, in the character of Yoda in *Star Wars* (2004). Luke Skywalker at first dismisses Yoda as an annoyance, a shrunken old creature who hobbles with a cane and mutters to himself as he rummages through young Luke Skywalker's bag. It is not until Yoda reveals himself as a Jedi knight and teacher that Luke is able to see beyond his age and form. Likewise, in *The Dark Crystal* (1982), the ancient wise woman Aughra has wild gray hair, a raspy voice, and a battered countenance with one missing eye. When the Gelfling Jen first encounters her, he is afraid. She teases him. "Are you afraid of me? Think I'm going to eat you?" The trope of the aged wise person is not unique to science fiction, of course; its presence is found in myths and fantasy tales and dates back centuries, and it is into this archetypal position that the *Farscape* character of Noranti steps.

In "Dog with Two Bones" (3.22) Noranti seems to appear in Moya's kitchen out of nowhere following her rescue from a destroyed command carrier. Crichton pointedly ignores her, but both Chiana and Rygel treat her with instant disdain, apparently assuming that she is harmless and worthless because of her age. It is important to note that this is *not* an assumption they have made about other intruders or visitors to Moya who are not aged. When Rygel lays eyes on her, he does not ask her name, but demands of the others, "Who the frell is *this*?" From the beginning, Noranti is portrayed as eccentric and scatterbrained, as if the audience is expected to assume her senility.

> CHIANA: Hey, old woman, why didn't you leave with the others?
> NORANTI: Because I knew the soufflé would charm you!
> CHIANA: Chowder ... you said it was chowder.
> NORANTI: I can make you a chowder!
> CRICHTON: Who is that woman?
> CHIANA: I thought she was with you.

As Crichton and Chiana are debating about how to solve the latest crisis, Noranti tries to join the discussion, but is dismissed out of hand.

> NORANTI: Perhaps I can offer the benefit of my training?
> CHIANA: What? How? As a chef?

NORANTI: And doctor. Instructor. And — among many other disciplines — negotiator.

CHIANA: Listen, Wrinkles, how 'bout you just stick to the chowder? *(To Crichton)* You can deal with the old frelnik.

Here, Chiana mocks the idea that this old woman could be anything other than a simple cook, and she refers to Noranti as a "frelnik," something that smells foul (Battis 193). We do not learn until later that Noranti does not, in fact, bathe. The reference to her odor is used here in a pejorative manner to establish Noranti as a person of lesser value. Unlike pejoratives directed at intruders who are considered powerful or dangerous, this aged "frelnik" is clearly meant to be as easily discarded as a bad-smelling piece of garbage. It is not until she reveals that she has powerful psychic gifts that Crichton and the others begin to reconsider their initial impression of her. Crichton calls her a "witch," and D'Argo strikes her with his fist so powerfully that she falls to the floor, unconscious. The others are not concerned that she might be injured; they are only concerned that she might harm them.[1] Now that she is seen to have power they shackle her to a chain from the ceiling.

She is no longer simply an annoyance; she is what Colin Barnes and other disability rights advocates describe as a "bad crip." Once power is claimed by or imbued into the disabled body (by its construction as physically powerful or by containing special powers, such as those of Harry Potter or the X-Men — or Noranti), the erstwhile "pitiable" individual ceases to become a "good crip" (a disabled person who "knows her place") and becomes a "bad crip" (a dangerous crip). The others eventually grant Noranti a place among the crew of Moya and a measure of respect. Although the nicknames they give her, "Grandma" and "Wrinkles," still suggest a denigration of age, such name-calling is within the context of "equal opportunity insults," whereby, for example, D'Argo is chided about his size and Zhaan is teased about her color. Like *Farscape* itself, Noranti's character is multifaceted: neither all good nor all evil, but rather a continuous source of surprise and contradiction.

Noranti continues to function in the series as an object of amusement, however, eating flowers, falling asleep at odd moments, and fumbling through "the early signs of her race's version of Alzheimer's" (*Farscape* Characters). Battis observes that while Noranti displays power early on, "she quickly devolves into a position of comic relief" (40). She is thus ultimately reinstated with her "good crip" status: apparently harmless (the crew will discover otherwise in Season Four's two-part episode "What Was Lost [4.2 and 4.3]),[2] eager to please those about her, not expecting to be regarded as highly as those with younger and stronger bodies. She is valued for her magical (if imperfect) abilities, however, and thus not discarded as we discard so many of those in our own society who have aged beyond the point that they are considered to be of use.

There are other references to age and aging in the series, both visual and rhetorical. Scorpius and other Scarrans are represented as having sunken red-rimmed eyes and deeply wrinkled faces, resulting in an almost corpselike appearance. The physical marks of extreme age are thus exaggerated and used in this case to signify an undesirable and perhaps untrustworthy character. In "The Locket" (2.16), Aeryn and John are trapped on a planet where they age together in a bucolic setting, but ultimately the narrative does not allow them to grow old to the point of accepting the inevitability of death. Rather aging is shown as something that should be reversed and "cured," which the crew of Moya, by managing to go back in time, is able to do. It is in the episode "Taking the Stone" (2.3) that we are offered a lens through which to consider that age, like all forms of embodiment, is given or denied value largely due to social attitude. The crew of Moya is on a planet where radiation kills people at a young age, and Crichton is viewed as old by the planet's inhabitants. Resisting Crichton's efforts to help her, a pregnant woman on the planet shouts at him. "Look at you! You're old! You're worn out!" A gentle smile crosses Crichton's face: "That's right," he replies. "I'm old. And you can be old just like me." Here, Crichton performs a function iconic to his position in the *Farscape* series: he questions the status quo and challenges the mindset of those he encounters. On his world, our Earth, aging is normal, perhaps even a privilege. In this exchange, he invites the woman to consider that what she has been told about aging is wrong, that different bodies do not equate to unworthy bodies. Age, then, like beauty or "normality," is in the eye of the beholder. And in *Farscape*, that eye — be it singular, multiple, blind, or psychic — invites us to consider other signifiers of difference, alienation and disability.

"I must have light!": Eyes, "Normality" and Vision in Farscape

In the Brothers Grimm tale "Little One-eye, Little Two-eyes, and Little Three-eyes," three sisters vie for the attention of a handsome prince and the chance to become rewarded with riches. It does not take 20/20 vision to know who the winner will be: it is the "normal" girl with two eyes. Little One-eye is deficient, of course, and Little Three-eyes is just plain sneaky, having that preternatural eye. As a child with monocular vision, I secretly rooted for Little One-eye, knowing all along that she had no chance of winning the prince's love. As I grew up, I continued to assimilate the lesson from film and television that vision and the appearance of our eyes is somehow linked to our morality of character. We "look someone straight in the eye" because we are honest, or we have "shifty eyes." We are "clear-eyed" meaning that we have "vision" and purpose, or we are "blind" to what is important.

Yet while "normality" of eyesight and eye appearance continues to denote both desirability and morality of character, both in fantastic and real-life stories, the occasional non-normative character also appears: the blind, partially sighted, or unusually sighted character whose presence on screen is rarely incidental. He or she may be evil or good, bitter or inspirational, powerless or powerful — but never neutral.[3] From Homer's Polyphemous the Cyclops or blind prophet Tiresius, to the *Dark Crystal*'s one-eyed witch, Aughra, to the heroic Captain Neweyes (he has two eyes) and his evil twin brother Professor Screweyes (he has one eye) of the movie *We're Back! A Dinosaur's Story* (1993), or the monocular and evil Hopper of Disney's *A Bug's Life* (1998), the tropes of *eyes* and *vision* can be traced back to antiquity[4] and continue to be popular in science fiction. In *Farscape*, three of the characters who are constructed using this signifier are Noranti, Stark, and Traltixx.[5] While atypical vision, in particular, blindness, has often functioned in literature as a metaphor for "lack of agency" (Kleeges 1), all three of these characters bring with them a good deal of agency, whether beneficent or maleficent.

Noranti's extreme age sets her apart from the other travelers on Moya, as we have seen, but she is also unusual due to her three eyes, one of which changes colors and apparently has unusual powers. It is a literal incarnation of what is known in many cultures as "the third eye" — an "all-seeing" mystical eye which possesses the power of great insight and magical vision (O'Connell and Airey 155). The Hindu deity Shiva literally has a third eye in the middle of his forehead, "the eye of inner vision," but one which can also shoot out flames and cause great destruction (Cotterell and Storm 402–403). Noranti's third eye, however, appears to have no destructive power; it is only her occasional miscalculation that sometimes leads to complications for those who partake of her healing potions; but, she always claims, at least, to act with the best of intentions.

> NORANTI: (blows herbs into Crichton's eyes)
> CRICHTON: Aah! Damn! I can't see! God!
> NORANTI: Go to the truth. It calls in your own tongue
> D'ARGO: John! (To Noranti) What the frell happened to him?
> NORANTI: Nothing. Nothing. He'll be fine.
> D'ARGO: What did you do?
> NORANTI: Perhaps a slight misjudgment of his weight. It won't occur again. I'm certain.

Although Crichton's first experience with Noranti is unnerving, he quickly realizes that she is trying to help him by giving him visions, and he begins to trust her. He removes her shackles and sits down next to her.

NORANTI: (To Crichton) Did my herbs help you?
CRICHTON: They stripped away the lies. But I ran from it. And I am so tired of running. (He faces Noranti) Show me again.

As Noranti guides Crichton through a painful vision, she kneels next to him and opens her third eye, which pulsates a bright magenta shade. She is odd, and a bit frightening, and we learn throughout the series that she is not the absent-minded "Grandma" or "Wrinkles" that the crew calls her. Although she may bumble about like a servant, asking anyone if they want chowder, she has chowder of her own to make. Thwart Noranti's agenda, as Crichton did in "What was Lost," and you will find that she is not above endangering herself or others to gain that agenda. In this aspect she remains a "bad crip," but in true *Farscape* fashion, no character is portrayed with total dichotomy, as "good" or "bad."

Noranti may be a "dangerous crip" but she is capable of heroic action. In *The Peacekeeper Wars* her fierce compassion and courage shine brightly as she leads the Eidelon people on the embattled planet Qujaga to safety and manages to shepherd the survivors onto Moya, where she plans to help them relearn their peaceful past and gifts for negotiation. Noranti's unusual appearance and vision are thus presented consistently as beneficial and admirable. In like fashion, the character of Stark appears in *Farscape* as an individual who could be considered disfigured; he wears a half-mask which covers his right eye and part of his face.[6] However, unlike Darth Vader or the Phantom of the Opera, whose masks signify a warped and disfigured inner character, Stark ultimately establishes himself as a kind and empathetic comforter. He removes the mask to gaze upon an injured or dying person, at which time that side of his face glows with a bright light. He is able to ease the pain and fear of someone who is dying by helping them "cross over." However, the price he pays for such empathy is psychic damage to his own mind, which causes him to behave erratically at times. It is not until Stark passes his power to the Eidelons that his mental anguish ceases. No longer able to use his power, he removes his mask, revealing a disfigured face.

In contrast to Noranti and Stark, who display unusual vision but not absolute blindness, the character of Traltixx is completely blind. Although blindness can be seen in some fictional characters to be "compensated for" with inner wisdom or the gift of prophecy, it can also be used as a "metaphor for the inability to see spiritual and moral truth" (O'Connell and Airey 155, Chivers and Markotić 2). Martin Norden writes that one incarnation of this character type is that of the "obsessive avenger ... an egomaniacal sort, almost always an adult male, who does not rest until he has had his revenge on those he holds responsible for his disablement and/or violating his moral code in some way" (52). In "Crackers Don't Matter" (2.4) a visitor to Moya, Traltixx, embodies not only this stereotype but other stereotypes about blind people as well, such as the erroneous belief that blind people somehow develop super hearing to compensate for their lack of sight.[7] "My ears detect sound well above your range," he tells Crichton, who also tests his eyesight by holding up two fingers before him. Traltixx can sense them. "My other faculties have compensated," he explains. "I developed an internal radar of sorts."

Although Moya's crew hopes that Traltixx will be able to implement a cloaking device that will allow them to escape their nemesis, Scorpius, he (Traltixx) is distrusted from the beginning:

CRICHTON: He says he can't build the device here. It's too big.
PILOT: Do you trust him?
CRICHTON: Have you seen him? He's *blind*. He's got a big head, but he's *blind*. Barring the Yoda factor, if he gives us any trouble we lock him up.

Nor does Pilot, the stable, calm navigator and "voice" of Moya, trust the blind interloper. Traltixx monopolizes the repair drones (DRDs) on Moya to use for his own cause.

PILOT: Traltixx. Where are my DRDs? There are none up here.
TRALTIXX: (to Pilot) I'm sorry, Pilot. I should have told you. I need their help.
PILOT: For what?
TRALTIXX: For the darkness. It hurts my eyes and makes me blind. I need to make more light, Pilot. Bright light! ... Don't be alarmed. I'm just altering Moya's bioluminescence for a few minutes. It won't hurt her. Trust me.
PILOT: I don't.

There is no indication in the narrative that Traltixx has ever used eyesight, yet the audience is apparently meant to assume that he must crave light — a notion that is counterintuitive at best, absurd at most. Just as many deaf individuals are amused or baffled at some hearing people's insistence that the absence of hearing must create suffering and an inferior way of living, so it may be incomprehensible to sighted people that vision is not craved by all those who are blind. Thus the producers of *Farscape* assume what Stuart Hall describes as the dominant or preferred reading position: that of the "normal" — in this case, sighted — viewer (138).[8] It is unimaginable to the sighted spectator that Traltixx could be happy with his body the way it is. His characterization perfectly reflects the obsessive "egomaniacal" avenger of which Norden writes. If he cannot have light, then nobody can have light. He screams desperately for that which he has claimed his body does not need: light. "I need more light! I need more! ... More light! Can you feel it, Pilot? All of Moya is beginning to glow! *I am magnificent!*"

Traltixx here exemplifies Norden's "egomaniac," a character type which is also in line with Barnes' delineation of the media stereotype of disabled people as "sinister and evil," an interpretation which Barnes argues can be traced back to biblical references connecting disability and sin. "The depiction of disabled people as essentially evil has been a particular favorite among film makers," writes Barnes, adding that the list of films which feature evil impaired people is "virtually endless" (Barnes, *Disabling Imagery*). While Battis claims that "there are no throwaway aliens [on Moya] ... everyone matters" (10), this is not quite true. Traltixx is utterly dispensable. Of course, he is a threat to Moya, but he is a threat to Moya precisely because of the manner in which he is embodied. His "deficiency" is not simply a difference in his alien makeup, the way that D'Argo's prehensile tongue or Zhaan's blue color is a difference. His difference — blindness — is portrayed as so abhorrent both to himself and to the other crew members that he is distrusted from the very beginning. As with Noranti and Shiva, Traltixx's unusual eyes are shown to contain power, but in his case it is purely malevolent. Like Shiva, he can shoot rays of destruction from his eyes, and he grows stronger and more powerful with his exposure to light. He devolves from being a "person," another alien with unusual needs, to what the crew members call a "creep" and a "thing." Crichton now refers to Traltixx not by the humanizing pronoun *he*, but as an "*it*." "I want to kill it," he states.

> TRALTIXX: You cannot stop me, Crichton! Go on! Kill me! There are thousands more just like me. We will find another Leviathan to make our light. And when we do, we'll spread like a plague. We'll rise from our dormancy and kill you all!
> CRICHTON: I told them it was a mistake bringing you on board.

It is unclear what "dormancy" Traltixx is referring to, but the message is clear: His "kind," sightless aliens, are a threat and a "plague" to what we must only assume are the "good" (sighted?) aliens, the ones who do not need to take light by force. Despite the many forms of embodied diversity in the *Farscape* universe, vision is apparently not negotiable. When Chiana is blinded in a later episode, it is temporary, she is ultimately healed. Traltixx is killed by Crichton thrusting a blade into his chest. Even those with unusual vision, such as Noranti and Stark, must redeem themselves by using their eyes to help others. Thus there is bias in this science fiction world — but it is a bias that the majority of viewers, because they are sighted, cannot see.

"I am Dorothy Gale from Kansas": Crichton as Disabled

> PILOT: (To Crichton) You have no special abilities. You're not particularly smart, can hardly smell, can barely see, and you're not even vaguely physically or spiritually imposing. Is there anything you can do well?"
> CRICHTON: Watch football.

In "Crackers Don't Matter," Crichton — who claims that he has no special talent other than watching football — is the individual who ends up saving the ship. Traltixx, the blind alien brought on board to help Moya escape the Peacekeepers, intends to annihilate the others so that he can use the ship's bioluminescence for his own purposes. He warns the crew that as they pass through the pulsars to his planet, those of "lesser species" may be affected by the pulsar light. By "lesser species" he specifies "genetic laborers, ungifted menials," flattering the crew by assuring them that none of them would surely fall into this category. It is interesting that Traltixx uses the term "genetic" to describe a "lesser species," one suited only for menial labor. This trope is not uncommon in science fiction — think *Brave New World* — but its inclusion into the *Farscape* universe invites us to reconsider our own attitudes towards genetic differences. One might argue that an outer space fantasy such as *Farscape*, *Star Trek*, or *Star Wars* may understandably portray "other species" as dangerous, suspicious, or threatening. However, we have not yet interacted with otherworldly species, and thus the beings portrayed in science fiction are not "others," they are *us*. Each and every character constructed in the narrative of *Farscape* is a facet of our humanity — no more and no less. Kimberle Crenshaw describes such fantastical texts, which can be interpreted in a multitude of ways, as a "Rorschach test for whatever Americans think ails them,"[9] whether that be tensions surrounding race, sexuality, gender, class, or — I would add — ability. Battis observes that the *Farscape* series is as much about our earthly culture as it is about science fiction fantasy:

> [Crichton] learns to question who the 'aliens' are in this story, and, by extension, to question and explore multiple versions of humanity available to him ... he quickly finds that certain 'human' characteristics are able to save his life, while others appear ridiculous, even offensive, to the aliens with whom he makes contact [3].

Put another way, Crichton is no longer "normal." While we in the spectatorial audience may most closely identify with Crichton as "normal" and "human," although we are not all white heterosexual males, we sympathize with his amazement at finding himself denigrated to the status of a lesser species or lesser form of embodiment. Crichton is used to his body being the epitome of normality on his planet (again: male, white, heterosexual, and "able-bodied"). He is offended when D'Argo calls him "deficient."

CRICHTON: Who are you calling deficient?
CHIANA: You. You've got the worst eyes of all of us. That's why your optic nerves aren't being affected.
CRICHTON: I got great eyes. They're better than 20/20 and they're blue!
AERYN: ... Excellent. If we're gonna let blue-eyes save the day, we'd better come up with a very good plan.
CRICHTON: I'm not deficient! I'm superior! Humans are superior!

Yet Crichton, this "superior" being, must be smeared with heat-deflecting paste, don special goggles, carry a shield, and be wrapped in solar-reflecting material in order to withstand his encounter with Traltixx's burning eye-rays. What is compelling about this scene is that Crichton understands that the need for this specialized equipment in no way reflects upon the worthiness of his body or the value he brings to Moya. It is simply what is required to enter and function in an environment that is hostile to him, much the same way that SCUBA gear allows non-aquatic creatures to exist for a period of time in an undersea world. Neither land nor sea creature is superior to the other, but the necessity to access a particular environment may render a being vulnerable or "inferior" within the parameters of that environment. Thus people who do not know sign language are functionally inarticulate in a group where that language is used; those who race on two legs will not be able to keep up with the speed of those who use racing wheelchairs; those same wheelchair users may succeed on the race course only to be disabled by architectural barriers in places as commonplace as a grocery store or post office; and, those whose manner of processing thoughts or sensory information is neuro-atypical may be disabled by attitudinal barriers in certain situations.

Crichton declares that "humans are superior," but faithful fans of *Farscape* have learned early on that Crichton takes everything and everyone — including himself — with a healthy dose of humor and skepticism. This is the man who, upon meeting the inhabitants of Moya in the first episode of the series ("Premiere" 1.1), mutters, "E.T., my ass." He realizes that he has been sold a bill of goods regarding the gentle, socially advanced alien stereotype of Spielberg's film. Rather, he encounters a baffling, irritating array of beings that can barely exist in the same room, let alone bring peace to the universe. In like manner, when people who identify as "normal" or "able-bodied" encounter those who are disabled (by society if not by impairment), they may respond in a manner similar to Crichton's.

"What's wrong with you people?" Crichton demands, as the alien crew interacts in ways for which Hollywood films such as *Close Encounters of the Third Kind* (1977) never prepared him. These are not aliens who apologize for their bodies or behaviors. Unlike the extraterrestrials in *Close Encounters,* who attempt to calm their hosts by assuming childlike forms, or the alien in *Contact* (1997) who appears as the human space-traveler Ellie's father, those in the *Farscape* universe are unapologetically themselves: farts, prehensile tongues, and all. In like manner, Crichton is dumbfounded to discover that his "evolved" species' embodiment and behavior are not considered any better than those of his disconcerting crewmates. This leads to conflict, but it also leads to tolerance and growth among the characters. Before heading into the chamber where Traltixx awaits, Crichton faces his fellow aliens and asks, "I look ridiculous, don't I?" Yes, he does. But he cannot resist pointing out the irony of the situation:

CRICHTON: Does this strike any of you superior beings as a little bit ironic?
CHIANA: Why?
CRICHTON: I'm the deficient one and I'm still saving your butts.

Crichton does succeed in killing Traltixx and saving his fellow crew members, but only with the help of the technology supplied by the others on Moya. Had it not been for the devices they provided, he would not have survived Traltixx's chamber. In this aspect, he shares a common bond with his nemesis, Scorpius, who is also dependent upon technology to keep him alive. Half Scarran, half Sebacean, Scorpius presents a tough exterior but is in reality a biologically fragile being: he is utterly dependent upon the cooling rods which have been inserted into his head to provide thermal constancy. Thus he, like Crichton, exists in great part due to the technology and accessibility provided by his society. Both are dependent upon the air that has been provided to them to breathe and the technological intervention that could be denied them at any moment.

It is Crichton's very "deficiency," in fact, that enables him to defeat Traltixx. In comparison with the others on Moya, he has impaired sight and hearing, yet his visual "impairment" allows him to resist the overwhelming light. He is also considered mentally impaired by the others, but again, this cognitive "inferiority" actually allows him to function well in the crisis, while the others suffer acutely from the disruption of their more "advanced" cognitive skills. Crichton is the dubious hero of the day, and the crew ultimately acknowledges his courage and his shortcomings. He is not what Colin Barnes would call a "super crip," for his powers are no more amazing than our own. Put another way, we, the audience, recognize Crichton for what he is: a mere human being. It is the environment that he is required to inhabit that defines his superiority or inferiority or, as seen in various *Farscape* episodes, both. Here again we find ourselves struggling to remain in Hall's preferred reading position, as humans who cannot imagine Crichton considered as anything but "normal," in exemplary health and embodiment. Yet in "Crackers Don't Matter," as in many episodes, Crichton is seen by the on-screen society as inferior or deficient and is consequently portrayed that way. Thus we are forced to assume what Hall terms a *negotiated* viewing position: we know Crichton to be embodied in an acceptable manner in our own human society, but must accept that in the environment of *Farscape*, he is impaired, as we, by extension, would be impaired in that society. In short, we would be disabled.

"Crackers Don't Matter" invites the audience to contemplate the subtext or what rhetorician Barry Brummet describes as the "hidden rhetorics" or "social issues in disguise" of the story (1). Writing about the episode, novelist Jim Butcher calls us to look below the surface of the narrative:

> The implied questions the story asked were surprisingly serious: What consists of value in a human being? Why are some traits more valued than others? What hap-

pens when the assumptions of value are suddenly trumped by a radically altered environment? ... [The episode] stated that even those whom our society deems as valueless may have a more significant role to play in our future, and that one should not be too swift to judge what an individual may be able to contribute to the changing environment of our existence. It stated that the variety provided by those outside the mainstream of society may at some point prove useful, even necessary, and that a policy of tolerance is the wisest course [71–72].

Butcher's invitation to consider such connotations may be a tall order; many will view the episode, and the series, as little more than a light-hearted send-up of science fiction tropes and homologies. That, however, is part of the magic and cunningness of science fiction. It is not necessary for a consensus to exist regarding possible readings of a cinematic text in order for individuals or populations to interpret a text in a particular way, whether in reference to sexuality, class, gender, race, ability, or other identities. In fact, it does not necessarily even matter what "message" or meaning the producer or writer intended. After all, television and cinematic texts are produced by increasingly large teams of writers, editors, producers, technicians, and actors. "Indeed," notes Brummet, "some hidden rhetorics remain hidden even from those who created them" (216). Fantastical worlds such as that of *Farscape* provide what John Fiske describes as "gaps" or "fissures": moments in the text where, whether intentionally or not on the part of the text producers, characters provide discourse or behavior that invites alternative or resistive readings (391–408). One such reading that I have proposed in this essay is that of the disabled body: the body that is atypical in the environment in which the individual lives and moves. *Farscape* is a feast of atypicality, and it offers an opportunity for the viewer to take an unflinching look at the very concept of normality.

Conclusion

Cinema studies web writer David Church argues that while all cinemas may be seen as imaginary, "fantastic" films have a potential for "positive critical readings and empowering depictions of society ... The fantastic film could be self-reflexively indicative of the potential for a new critical lens" (n.p.). Church includes science fiction as coming under the umbrella of the "fantastic" which he describes as films, which "deliberately and substantially violate verisimilitude and recreate unrealistic situations, worlds, characters, or effects that are typically relegated to the domain of the imagination" (n.p.). It is precisely this violation of verisimilitude that entices the spectator to consider "normalities" outside of his or her life-world experience; the fantasy film provokes these comfortable hegemonies and invites consideration of the unthinkable: that we are the Other, and the Other is us. Cinema studies scholar Steven Neale describes such films as challenging "the boundaries of the human and the issues of difference" (103) and in this aspect *Farscape* certainly does not disappoint.

The refreshing thing about *Farscape* is that it disdains and discards the entire notion of "political correctness." It is not a matter of being correct; it is a matter of learning to live together in a limited space and with limited resources. It is a matter of earning one another's respect, of never assuming that difference means a threat, and acknowledging that blue butts are just as good as any butts. There is bias in *Farscape*, to be sure, but it is bias that is presented transparently and across the board — and with humor. Humor, properly used, is one of the highest forms of courage. *Farscape* invites us to consider all forms of physical and cognitive embodiment without reverence and thus with the greatest of reverence: We are equals in our peculiarities. We must all travel on the same ship.

Notes

1. The transcriber/s of Farscape screenplays at the now-defunct website Pure Pilot editorialize Noranti as a "weirdo," "hag," and a cow who "chews her cud," and suggest that viewers "savor the moment" where the old woman is hit by D'Argo as getting what "she deserves." All of this without any hint of maleficence on the part of the newly introduced Noranti — but apparently simply due to her age and appearance. (The transcripts from Pure Pilot are now archived at http://transcripts.terrafirmascapers.com.)

2. In "What Was Lost," Noranti attempts to kill Crichton, justifying her actions by explaining that it is better that he die than that millions die if the seductive Grayza convinces him to give her the powerful Darnaz probes, which Grayza would use as weapons.

3. An exception to this trope is the "regular guy" one-eyed character of Mike Wazowski in the Disney movie *Monsters, Inc.*, an original screenplay which I argue merits attention specifically because such non-traditional characterizations invite an inclusive attitude toward atypical bodies (see Scherman).

4. The symbolism and metaphoric value of the eye and of vision go back for centuries and cross the globe, including stories and folklore from the Mediterranean, Europe, Africa, the Americas, and the Middle East (see Daw as well as Juan).

5. The cruel Peacekeeper Captain Selto Durka is another character whose character is in part signified by his atypical vision — in his case, the iconic pirate-like patch over his right eye.

6. Different folkloric traditions assign power to specific eyes, with the right eye frequently portrayed as the eye that is sacrificed for wisdom, such as in the Norse tale where the god Odin traded his eye for a drink from the well of knowledge, or in the Celtic or Cornish tales where a human is able to see the fairies with her right eye, and is consequently blinded in that eye by an angered fairy. According to the website tvtropes.org, "The eye possessing the power is almost always the character's left eye ... the sinister eye as 'sinister' was once a word for 'left.'" The characters of *Dark Crystal*'s Aughra, *We're Back!*'s Professor Screweyes, and "Mad-Eye Moody" from the Harry Potter series illustrate this concept. In the Hindu, Taoist and Shinto religions, the right eye is seen to correspond to the sun or the future, with the left eye corresponding to the moon or the past (O'Connell and Airy 155). But consider Durka.

7. Whereas blind people must use their capacity of hearing to its fullest, there is no magical transformation in the physiology of the ear. One simply learns to "listen better."

8. Hall proposes that there are three positions that an audience can assume when reading a text, including a television show or a film: they may agree with the dominant/preferred or hegemonic societal view represented, a negotiated version, or an oppositional reading (138). The dominant view of our society is that physiological difference is undesirable. The spectator of this episode of *Farscape*, then, may be seen as participating in the preferred "reading" of his or her own society by concurring with the dominant view expressed by the inhabitants of Moya — that blindness is undesirable and abnormal, and that those who are blind are envious of the sighted.

9. Crenshaw is writing here for an American audience, although I would argue that her observations are not limited to any certain people or country.

Works Cited

Abberly, Paul. "The Spectre at the Feast: Disabled People and Social Theory." *The Disability Reader: Social Science Perspectives*. Ed. Tom Shakespeare. London: Cassell, 1998. 79–93. Print.

Barnes, Colin. *Disabling Imagery and the Media: An Exploration of the Principles for Media Representations of Disabled People*. British Council of Disabled People, 1992. Web. 1 May 2007.

_____. "Reflections on Doing Emancipatory Disability Research." *Disabling Barriers— Enabling Environments*. Eds. John Swain, Sally French, Colin Barnes and Carol Thomas. London: Sage, 2004. 47–53. Print.

Battis, Jes. *Farscape: Uncharted Territories of Sex and Science Fiction*. London: I. B. Tauris, 2007. Print.

Brummet, Barry. *Uncovering Hidden Rhetorics: Social Issues in Disguise*. London: Sage, 2008.

A Bug's Life. Dir. John Lasseter. Perf. Dave Foley, Kevin Spacey, and Julia Lewis-Dreyfuss. Buena Vista/Pixar, 1998. Film.

Butcher, Jim. "Crackers Don't Matter." *Farscape Forever! Sex, Drugs, and Killer Muppets*. Ed. Glenn Yeffeth. Dallas: BenBella, 2005. 67–72. Print.

Chivers, Sally, and Nicole Markotić. *The Problem Body: Projecting Disability on Film*. Columbus: Ohio State University Press, 2010. Print.

Church, David. "Fantastic Films, Fantastic Bodies: Speculations on the Fantastic and Disability Representation." *Offscreen*, October 2006. Web. 31 December 2011.

Close Encounters of the Third Kind. Dir. Steven Spielberg. Perf. Richard Dreyfuss, François Truffaut, Teri Garr, and Melinda Dillon. Columbia TriStar, 1977. Film.

Contact. Dir. Robert Zemeckis. Perf. Jodie Foster, Matthew McConaughey, and James Woods. Warner Bros, 1997. Film.

Cotterell, Arthur, and Rachel Storm. *The Ultimate Encyclopedia of Mythology*. London: Hermes House, 1999. Print.

Crenshaw, Kimberle. "Intersectionality: The Double Bind of Race and Gender." *Perspectives Magazine*, Spring 2004. Web. 16 January 2012.

The Dark Crystal. Dir. Jim Henson and Frank Oz. Perf. Jim Henson, Kathyrn Miller, Frank Oz. ITC/Jim Henson Productions, 1982. Film.

Davis, Lennard. *Enforcing Normalcy: Disability, Deafness and the Body*. London: Verso, 1995. Print.

Daw, Nigel. *Visual Development*. New York: Plenum Press, 1995. Print.

Einstein, Sarah. "The Future Imperfect." *Redstone Science Fiction*, 2010. Web. 12 June 2012.

E.T.: The Extra-Terrestrial. Dir. Steven Spielberg. Perf. Henry Thomas, Drew Barrymore, Peter Coyote. Universal Studios, 1982. Film.

"Farscape Characters." *Henson.com*, 2005. Web. 15 Jan. 2012.

Finkelstein, Vic. *Attitudes and Disabled People*. New York: World Rehabilitation Fund, 1980. Web.
_____. "The Commonality of Disability." *Disabling Barriers — Enabling Environments*. Eds. John Swain, Sally French, Colin Barnes and Carol Thomas. London: Sage, 2004. 47–53. Print.
Fiske, John. "Television: Polysemy and Popularity." *Critical Studies in Mass Communication* 3.4 (1986): 391–408. Print.
Hall, Stuart. "Encoding/decoding." *Culture, Media, Language: Working Papers in Cultural Studies, 1972–79*. Eds. Stuart Hall, Dorothy Hobson, Andrew Lowe and Paul Willis. London: Hutchinson, 1980. 128–138. Print.
Henderson, Zenna, Mark Olson, and Priscilla Olson. *Ingathering: The Complete People Stories of Zenna Henderson*. Framingham, MA: NESFA Press, 1995. Print.
Hunt, Paul. "Discrimination: Disabled People and the Media." *Contact* 70 (1991): 45–48. Print.
Juan, Stephen. *The Odd Body: Mysteries of Our Weird and Wonderful Bodies Explained*. Kansas City: Andrews McMeel, 2004. Print.
Kleeges, Georgina. "Dialogues with the Blind: Literary Depictions of Blindness and Visual Art." *Journal of Literary & Cultural Disability Studies* 4.1 (2010): 1–15. Print.
Neale, Stephen. *Genre and Hollywood*. London: Routledge, 2000. Print.
Norden, Martin. *The Cinema of Isolation*. New Brunswick: Rutgers University Press, 1994. Print.
O'Connell, Mark, and Raje Airey. *The Complete Illustrated Encyclopedia of Symbols, Signs & Dream Interpretation: Identification and Analysis of the Visual Vocabulary Formulates Our Thoughts and Dictates Our Reactions to the World Around Us*. London: Hermes House, 2007. Print.
Oliver, Mike. "A Society of Disability or a Disablist Society?" *Disability and Society: Emerging Issues and Insight*. Ed. Len Barton. London: Longman, 1996. 18–42. Print.
Scherman, Elizabeth Leigh. "Monsters Among Us: Construction of the Deviant Body in *Monsters, Inc.* and *Lilo & Stitch*." Eds. Ryan C. Neighbors and Sandy Rankin. *The Galaxy Is Rated G: Essays on Children's Science Fiction Film and Television*. Jefferson, N.C.: McFarland, 2011. 15–30. Print.
Shakespeare, Tom. *Disability Rights and Wrongs*. London: Routledge, 2006. Print.
Star Wars, Episode V: The Empire Strikes Back. Dir. Irvin Kershner. Perf. Mark Hamill, Harrison Ford, Carrie Fisher. 20th Century–Fox, 1980. Film.
Tøssebro, Jan. "Understanding Disability." *Scandinavian Journal of Disability Research* 6.1 (2004): 3–7. Print.
We're Back! A Dinosaur's Story. Dir. Phil Nibbelink and Simon Wells. Perf. John Goodman, Charles Fleischer, Blaze Berdahl. Universal Pictures, 1993. Film.

The Ballad of John and Aeryn

Sherry Ginn

John Crichton's attraction to Aeryn Sun occurs almost from their first meeting, despite the fact she kicks his butt. At the end of the series' first episode ("Premiere"), Crichton speaks into his tape recorder, describing for his father the events that have unfolded since his arrival in the *Farscape* universe. Removed prior to broadcast, his last words were "And dad, there's this girl." A short time later we learn that Aeryn is also attracted to Crichton: she tells him that when they first met, she found him "interesting" ("PK Tech Girl" 1.7). Their mutual attraction continues to grow until it is finally consummated, albeit on a "make-believe" Earth ("A Human Reaction" 1.16). Unfortunately the course of their relationship will not run smoothly or well during the majority of episodes of the series. As Executive Producer David Kemper says, "Crichton and Aeryn are Romeo and Juliet. That's one classic story about two people who love each other but can't get together because they were raised differently" (22).

Part of the rationale for the "will they-won't they, star-crossed lovers" aspect was to keep both characters available for romances with other people. Indeed on the DVD commentary to the episode "The Locket" (2.16), Ben Browder (Crichton) and Claudia Black (Aeryn) both admit that the producers planned for Aeryn to have a boyfriend at some point in the series. Interestingly, advertisements for the series made a point of noting that Crichton was the lusty American adventurer in space who would have a woman at every (space)port, à la James T. Kirk. In actuality Crichton has sex with only 3 women on *Farscape*, besides Aeryn, and only one of those was by choice. He has "sex" with an ex-girlfriend Alex when the Delvians on the New Moon of Delvia cloud his mind and cause him to believe that Alex accompanied him on the Farscape Mission ("Rhapsody in Blue" 1.12). Later, he is raped by Grayza several times. However, he chooses to have sex with Jena after she rescues him from Prince Clavor's assassins ("Look at the Princess Part II: I Do, I Think" 2.11).[1] Aeryn on the other hand is shown having sex with only one other person and that is Velorek ("The Way We Weren't" 2.5), although she married and bore children during an alternate time-line in the episode "The Locket." Nevertheless, in actuality Crichton is jealous of other men who Aeryn might find attractive, such as Crais, and Aeryn is jealous of other women, such as Chiana.

Certainly there are practical reasons, related to ratings, for creating sexual tension between the major characters of a television series and then not letting them express that tension. The accepted truth, dating from the series *Moonlighting* (1985–1989), is that as soon as the characters stop the foreplay and actually do the "dirty deed," the audience will no longer be interested. This "given" has some veracity in that after Maddie and David had sex on *Moonlighting*, in the 14th of the 15-episode Season Three ("I am Curious ... Maddie"), the show's popularity declined and it was canceled. The truth of the matter is that neither Bruce Willis, whose popularity following *Die Hard* had skyrocketed, nor Cybill Shepherd, who had just given birth to twins, were interested in continuing the series on a work schedule similar to that of the first two seasons. Fans were decidedly angered over the Season Four episodes which featured other characters and rarely featured Maddie or David together in the same scene. Nevertheless there are examples of series wherein sexual tension can continue along with adult relationships between the characters (consider Sheridan and Delenn on *Babylon 5* for instance). Exactly how long were fans supposed to suspend their belief that Troy and Riker, Mulder and Scully, and Starbuck and Apollo, to name only a few science fiction pairs, were not in love?

The question with respect to Aeryn and John, though, is this: Why is she unable to admit her feelings for Crichton and just go about the business of life? Crichton is pretty open about his feelings for her, and she knows how he feels. In the second season episode "Liars, Guns and Money Part I: A Not So Simple Plan" (2.19) as Aeryn leaves Moya, he says "I have to tell you how I feel." She replies, "No, you don't." He says, "Yes, I have to tell you," and she looks at him and says very emphatically, "No. You don't." He knows in that instance, as does the audience, that she is aware of his feelings for her, even if the words have never been spoken. Their dance will end that season with her death, at his hands. Season Three finds Crichton twinned with Aeryn finally consummating her relationship with the one designated as Crichton-Black.[2] Guess which one will die? Aeryn's fetus will be released from stasis during Season Three and she will be unwilling to tell Crichton she is pregnant, as she does not know who the father is. Given Sebacean/Peacekeeper physiology the child might be Crichton's. It could just as easily be Velorek's or some other person with whom she recreated (see my essay on relationships in this collection). Of course, the child — a boy — is Crichton's and he will be born during *The Peacekeeper Wars*.

Nevertheless, the question remains, why does it take her so long to admit that she loves him and that she will be with him, eventually marrying him? Perhaps the answer to that question lies in her past. Consider the Aeryn Sun presented in "The Way We Weren't" (2.5). This is the woman who recreated with a man named Velorek. They had a sexual relationship certainly, but it was apparently something more. She was assigned to be his personal pilot and they began their relationship on the second day of her assignment. Velorek asked Aeryn to be with him, to go with him to whatever his next assignment was; he told her that he was high enough in the command structure to be able to choose a lover, someone who would be more than a partner for recreation, rather than having one chosen for him. She appeared to be tempted and she later told Crichton that she thought she was in love with Velorek. However, that did not stop her from betraying him. Velorek was tasked with the job of developing a hybrid Leviathan, but unbeknownst to anyone but his most loyal colleagues, he actually planned to render Moya incapable of breeding. Aeryn learned that Velorek had a secret plan — she never knew what it was — and she used it to her advantage: she informed on Velorek to Crais. Velorek was charged with treason and executed and Aeryn got her old job, prowler pilot, back. She might almost see her irreversible contamination as retribution. She got her beloved job back, by betraying her lover, which meant that she was flying a prowler when Crichton's module burst out of the wormhole. That action led to her prowler being caught in the wake of Moya's starburst to safety, and hence her contamination and exile from the only life she ever knew.

Consider then her fear. She has already betrayed one lover; he died. How can she trust herself with another lover? How can *he* trust her, knowing of her past? Crichton, a highly-educated man, would understand Aeryn's fear and so knowing, would work to earn her trust as well as her love. Aeryn, the lonely woman who never knew any type of *loving* relationship, other than the one with Velorek, would have much more emotional baggage, to use an Earthly reference. She would find it more difficult to trust someone, especially someone not of her species, and not understanding love and perhaps having never experienced it,[3] would find it extremely difficult to not only feel it but admit it as well. Aeryn's story evolved with Crichton's; that was the plan from the very beginning of the series, as soon as the producers saw the chemistry between Claudia Black and Ben Browder. *Farscape* was always a love story; David Kemper never denied it. But it sure could be an exasperating one!

Notes

1. Here is one example of the difference between the sexes (see my essay on relationships in this collection). I was rather disturbed that Crichton would have sex with Jena considering his feelings for Aeryn. Ben Browder also expressed surprise at the fans' non-reaction

to the event. He expected more of them to feel like I did. My spouse, on the other hand, blamed Aeryn and said if she had not treated John so badly, he would not have looked for "solace" elsewhere. Chiana said pretty much the same thing to Aeryn, only she made the statement with respect to Crichton's marriage to the Princess Katralla. I do not think that Aeryn knows about Jena.

2. Aeryn gives one twin a green shirt and the other a black shirt in order to tell them apart. It is very fitting that one wear a green shirt (see Carty's essay on Ben Browder as a writer in this collection). Black is also meant to signal a darker Crichton, one who is skirting closer and closer to making very difficult choices, such as who will live and who will die (DVD commentary "Back").

3. Nadine Farghaly, in her unpublished essay "On How to Overcome Non-Functional Attachments Bonds in Outer Space," proposes that part of Aeryn's problem is that she never developed a secure attachment to a primary caregiver during her first year of life. One would expect this to be true to all Peacekeepers who are bred to fill the ranks using controlled breeding.

Works Cited

"Back and Back and Back to the Future." DVD commentary by Rowan Woods (Director) and Babs Greyhoskey (Writer).

"The Locket." DVD Commentary by Ben Browder (John Crichton) and Claudia Black (Aeryn Sun).

"I am Curious ... Maddie." Dir. Allan Arkush. Writ. Glenn Gordon Caron. *Moonlighting*. Perf. Cybill Shepherd, Bruce Willis. ABC, Burbank, 31 March 1987, Television.

"The Aurora Chair (Interview with David Kemper)." *Farscape: The Official Magazine* 2 (2001 Sept./Oct.): 20–24.

"Winona has been very reliable"
Female Gendering of Weapons in Fiction and Fact

ENSLEY F. GUFFEY

Throughout the various incarnations of *Farscape*, an impressive array of character quirks and pop culture references are used to firmly encode John Crichton as a late twentieth and early twenty-first century American male. Among fans of the series, one of the most beloved of these cultural conceits is "Winona," Crichton's favorite pulse pistol. First revealed late in the second season of *Farscape* ("A Clockwork Nebari" 2.18), Winona, and Crichton's preference for "her" over other weapons, quickly becomes a regular feature of the series throughout the succeeding two seasons, *The Peacekeeper Wars* (*PKW*) mini-series, and Boom! Studios' *Farscape* comic book series. No other character in the series gives a name to their personal weapon, making Crichton's choice to do so yet another marker of his humanity.[1]

Crichton is not the only character in American popular culture to give his weapon a woman's name. Other examples include Jayne Cobb's rifle "Vera" in Joss Whedon's *Firefly* and Jack's knife "Katie" in the *Buffy the Vampire Slayer* episode "The Zeppo" (3.13). The most famous example of naming firearms occurs in Stanley Kubrick's *Full Metal Jacket* (1987) when the film's Vietnam-era Marine recruits are ordered to give their M14 rifles "a girl's name, because this is the only pussy you people are going to get!" Leon Uris' novel *Battle Cry*, based upon his experiences as a Marine in World War II, also mentions this female gendering of a Marine's rifle as Platoon Sergeant Beller tells his recruits about their newly issued M-1903 rifles:

> You've got yourselves a new girl now. Forget that broad back home! This girl is the most faithful truest woman in the world if you give her a fair shake. She won't sleep with no swab jockeys the minute your back is turned. Keep her clean and she'll save your life [48].

Indeed, naming firearms has become such a well-known trope in American popular culture that it is often satirized. In *The United States of Tara*, Tara's male personality Buck calls his gun "Persephone," while Steven Colbert sometimes talks to a revolver named "Sweetness." The *Scrubs* episode "Our Drunk Friend" includes a tranquilizer rifle named "Megan Fox" (9.02), and *Mystery Science Theater 3000*'s Tom Servo appears with a gun he names "Lucille" in "I Was a Teenage Werewolf" (8.09).

Popular culture, however, does not exist in a vacuum, and the naming of weapons, particularly of males giving weapons female names, is deeply rooted in history. In fact, the English word "gun" is likely derived from the Old Norse female name *Gunnhildr*, a combination of two words which both mean "war" (Wilton). As early as 1330 C.E., a munitions inventory of Windsor Castle listed a siege weapon called *"Domina Gunilda"* or Lady Gunilda (Wilton). During the First World War, Germany deployed two 420mm (16.54 inch) howitzers called *Dicke Bertha* or Big (Fat) Berthas, which were used to destroy concrete fortifications in Belgium and on the Russian Front (Rembrella Ltd.). During the Second World War, the *Wehrmacht* deployed two massive, 8000mm (315 inch) railway guns, one of which was named Dora and used in the bombardment of Stalingrad in 1942 (Stilley). On the other side of the coin, the Soviet Red Army deployed their own, much more mobile and widely used *Katyusha* (Little Kate) rocket artillery to devastating effect throughout the war, including in the destruction of the German 6th Army at Stalingrad (Merridale 179). Not to be left out, the U.S. Army's 280mm (11 inch) M65 cannon, purpose built to be able to fire atomic as well as conventional shells, was quickly dubbed "Atomic Annie" and deployed in Western Europe from 1952 to 1963 ("M65 Atomic Cannon").

Nor were siege and artillery engines the only weapons historically to receive female names. David Crockett tended to name his rifles after his sister, Betsy. Over the course of his life, Crockett named three different rifles for his sibling, the most famous being "Old Betsy," but he also owned a "Pretty Betsy" and a "Fancy Betsy" (Cox). During the twentieth century, U.S. Marine recruits were often required to equate their rifles with women, demonstrating that Kubrick and Uris were spinning fiction from hard fact. Folklorist Richard Allen Burns quotes veterans as noting, "'We had to give our rifle a girl's name. My ex-fiancée said she was flattered that I named my weapon after her'" (2). Another respondent to Burns' survey recalled that, in boot camp in San Diego, California,

> our drill instructor explained how the M-16 was like a woman:
> front sight assembly — teat
> magazine well — vagina
> trigger — clitoris
> We were to love our rifle for it was the friend that would keep us alive ... I particularly liked his admonition to learn to stroke her rear (charging handle) with authority [2].

Inherent in these rifle rituals is a paradoxical vision of women as objects which needed care, but which, when treated right (i.e., kept clean, well maintained, and battle ready), were singularly capable of not only saving a Marine's life, but also that of the nation. Although his rank of Commander was apparently granted by IASA rather than any military organization, the viewer is introduced to Crichton's "Winona" as he is carefully cleaning and repairing her, thus linking him with this military tradition.

Although the exact circumstances behind the choice to name Crichton's pulse-pistol "Winona" remain unconfirmed, Ben Browder has stated that the pistol is named after Winona Ryder, and that "all important inanimate objects should be named after beautiful women. My biggest regret is that I never seized on the opportunity to name the Farscape module ... but in my soul, I call her 'Betty'" (Browder). It appears that, whatever the motive, the act of naming weapons, tools, and vehicles is a global, and very human, phenomenon. Stranded umpteen million light-years from Earth, and surrounded by aliens who even when they may appear human, are not, Winona helps give Crichton a connection to his home and to his all too human identity.

Notes

1. Although the traditional Luxan "Qualta Blade" is mentioned frequently in *Farscape*, the name refers to a class of weapon, rather than a particular example, rather like "Winchester" refers to rifles made by that company rather than any specific firearm.

Works Cited

Browder, Ben. "Ask Ben Browder." *Farscape World* (Dani Moure). N.p., n.d. Web. 22 Oct. 2012. <http://www.farscapeworld.com/interviews/interviews.php?id=askben>.
Burns, Richard Allen. "'This is my rifle, This is my gun...': Gunlore in the Military." *New Directions in Folklore* 7 (2003): n. pag. *IU Scholar Works Repository*. Web. 22 Oct. 2012. <https://scholarworks.iu.edu/dspace/bitstream/handle/2022/6906/NDiF_issue_7_article_3.pdf?sequence=1>.
The Colbert Report. Creator/E.P. Steven Colbert. Perf. Steven Colbert. Comedy Central, New York. 26 June 2008. Television.
Cox, Bob. "A Tale of Four Rifles: All Proudly Owned by David Crockett." *Bob Cox's Yesteryear*. N.p., 16 Apr. 2012. Web. 22 Oct. 2012. <http://bcyesteryear.com/node/497>.
Firefly: The Complete Series. Creator/E.P. Joss Whedon. Perf. Nathan Fillion, Gina Torres, Alan Tudyk. Twentieth Century–Fox, 2003. DVD.
Full Metal Jacket. Dir. Stanley Kubrick. Perf. Matthew Modine, Adam Baldwin, Vincent D'Onofrio. 1987. Warner Home Video, 2007. DVD.
"I Was a Teenage Werewolf." Dir. Kevin Murphy. *Mystery Science Theater 3000*. The Sci Fi Channel, New York. 5 April 1997. Television.
"M65 Atomic Cannon." *GlobalSecurity.org*. N.p., n.d. Web. 22 Oct. 2012. <http://www.globalsecurity.org/military/systems/ground/m65.htm>.
Merridale, Catherine. *Ivan's War: Life and Death in the Red Army, 1939–1945*. New York: Metropolitan, 2006. Print.
"Our Drunk Friend." Dir. Michael McDonald. *Scrubs: The Complete Ninth and Final Season*. ABC Studios Inc., 2010. DVD.

Rembrella Ltd. "German 'Big Bertha' gun bombards Ypres." *A Guide to the WWI Battlefields and Home to the Poppy Umbrella.* N.p., n.d. Web. 22 Oct. 2012. <http://www.greatwar.co.uk/battles/second-ypres-1915/prelude/big-bertha-bombards.htm>.

Stilley, Rick. "World's Largest Gun." *5th Armored Division Online.* N.p., 8 June 2000. Web. 22 Oct. 2012. <http://www.5ad.org/gun.htm>.

The United States of Tara: the First Season. Creator/E.P. Diablo Cody. Perf. Toni Collete, John Corbett, Rosmarie Dewitt. Showtime, 2009. DVD.

Uris, Leon. *Battle Cry.* New York: Putnam, 1953. Print.

Wilton, Dave. "gun." *Wordorigins.org.* N.p., 28 June 2006. Web. 22 Oct. 2012. <http://www.wordorigins.org/index.php/site/gun/>.

"The Zeppo." Dir. James Whitmore, Jr. *Buffy the Vampire Slayer: The Chosen Collection.* Twentieth Century–Fox, 1999. DVD.

A Legendary Tale
Scapers and the Myth of Fan Power

TANYA R. COCHRAN

"There are legendary tales," writes reporter Peter Haran, "of shows that have been saved by grassroots campaigns waged by devoted fans" (T35). Perhaps none, though, are as legendary as the tale of Scapers, or *Farscape* (1999–2003) fans. Upon having the rumors of *Farscape*'s imminent cancellation confirmed by Executive Producers David Kemper and Ricky Manning and lead actor Ben Browder during an online chat session on 6 September 2002 (Cosmic Theorist; Crew; Laskin 54; Melloy 20; Morey 83), Scapers formulated and implemented a strategy they did not invent but one for which they would become renowned, a strategy meant to keep their beloved television series on the air. Upon first glance, the outcome of their efforts — primarily organized through the Internet — seems substantial: the two-part, feature-length *Farscape: The Peacekeeper Wars* (2004). The extended episode or telemovie attempted to resolve dangling storylines and, thus, provide some closure for the series' viewers. While *The Peacekeeper Wars* certainly counts as a significant outcome and was appreciated by many audience members, it was not the specific result fans desired. Rather, they wanted more seasons of the narrative — more time with characters, more fleshing out of the narrative arc. They simply wanted *more*. More of any television series, of course, assumes a complex system of interrelated factors, including funding, production, casting, advertising, and broadcasting, among others. In the absence of alternative models for the television industry, this complex system remains quite indomitable for enthusiasts who aim to influence the direction and duration of their preferred televisual texts. As a result, scholars of audience studies in general and fandom studies in particular may benefit more from the case of *Farscape* and Scapers by understanding not the community's activist efforts to save their show but the community's contribution to the grand narrative of fan power. Drawing on literature that considers the meaning and purpose of myth, I propose that Scapers play a major role in composing the myth of fan power, a metanarrative that says much about who we are as human beings and why we feel compelled to tell the stories we tell. To support this claim, I begin by defining and discussing myth, follow by considering *Farscape* fandom, and conclude by addressing significance.

The Meaning and Purpose of Myth

Rather than beginning with what myth is, it may be instructive to understand what myth is not. As Wendy Doniger O'Flaherty asserts, "Myths are not lies, or false statements to be contrasted with truth or reality.... Picasso called art a lie that tells the truth, and the same might be said of myths" (25). Unfortunately, when most of us hear the term used or use it ourselves, we typically assume myth means just that: falsehood. We equate myth with urban legends, fibs, and fantasies. Too often, fantasy itself is castigated as *escapist*, a word that carries the connotation of being disengaged from reality. Karen Armstrong explains, though, that "like science and technology, mythology ... is not about opting out of this world, but about enabling us to live more intensely within it.... [M]yth is not a story told for its own sake. It shows us how we should behave" (3–4). In other words, if we choose to understand myth as falsehood rather than metaphor, "a lie that tells the truth," we miss the importance of our own storytelling, the grand narratives that, as we will see below, serve many essential and productive purposes for us human beings, including a guide to "how we should behave." Therefore, it is important as we explore myth, particularly the myth of fan power, that we remember, as David Leeming advises, "we are journeying *not* through a maze of falsehood but through a marvelous world of metaphor that breathes life into the essential human story" (8, emphasis added). If grand tales are not lies or falsehoods, though, what exactly are they and how do they behave?

According to scholars from many different disciplines, myths are the large-scale narratives we tell ourselves about where we came from, who we are, and where we are going. In other words, myths are bound up with our identities and our relationship to the past, present, and future (Armstrong 6; Stock 240). As David Carney describes, a myth is an "interpretive model, framework, paradigm or hypothesis" we use over time to understand a variety of experiences. Or more simply, says Carney, it can be explained as a story or group of stories that comprise "the collective wisdom or lessons derived from the experiences of a people or community" (16). This record gives edges to our reality, allows us to understand our experiences "in ways that convey particular or general truths, assert dogmas, beliefs, impressions or desires" (16; see also Nimmo and Combs). Always already, these codes and creeds are rhetorically situated. In other words, they reflect particular societies at particular points in time in particular socio-political climates (Cochran and Edwards 149; see also Rushing and Frentz). "In the highest sense," argues Max Müller, mythology is "the power exercised by language on thought in every possible sphere of mental activity" (qtd. in Cassirer 5). In sum, myths are grand narratives through and by which we think and act. They consequently serve some very important purposes.

We use these grand tales, for instance, to explain our origins. Developing a belief, establishing a truth regarding where we have come from gives us a foothold in life. Whether cosmologically we understand ourselves as the result of intelligent design or natural selection or geographically we declare ourselves indigenous or immigrant, origin narratives provide us with a sense of who we are both as individuals and as groups. Furthermore, this sense of identity and identification allows us to be productive in our presents and to plan for our futures. We accomplish these feats because our myths give us a sense of order, something humans especially seek in the face of extreme *dis*order or chaos (Armstrong 6–7; Leeming 8). From an individual being diagnosed with cancer to a nation experiencing an act of domestic terrorism, from a person being fired from a job to a community being hit by a tornado — these are the times during which myths are born or invoked because they give us guidance and, therefore, comfort. They allow us to heal and move on with our lives. Basically, they help us cope (Armstrong 6). Coping, of course, assumes a response, and a response is usually accompanied by renewed purpose. For people in a community or nation, purpose often binds them together more tightly than they have ever been bound before — even to people who were strangers or enemies previously. This particular function of myth is what Dan D. Nimmo and James E. Combs refer to as "social glue" or unity within diversity (13). In essence, these important stories serve to explain, justify, validate, describe, heal, renew, and inspire ("Myth").

From the various purposes that myths serve, one expects that there are distinct types of myths, including myths of origins, of eschatology or "end times," of time and eternity, of providence and destiny, of gods and celestial beings, of rebirth, and of transformation, among others ("Myth"). While different in many ways, these grand narratives can also touch each other's edges and even overlap. For example, one of if not the most ubiquitous myths ever told and lived — the hero's journey — exhibits elements of several types. Mention of heroes and journeys, of course, requires reference to the scholarship of late comparative mythologist Joseph Campbell.

Among the general public, the long-time Sarah Lawrence College professor is probably best known for his work with American journalist and public commentator Bill D. Moyers. Together, Campbell and Moyers hosted *The Power of Myth*, a series of episodes that first aired in 1988 in the United

States on Public Broadcasting Service (PBS). Among scholars and other myth enthusiasts, on the other hand, Campbell is more likely known for his foundational work *The Hero with a Thousand Faces* (1949). In *Hero*, Campbell outlines in great detail the hero's journey, one marked by three major rites of passage — separation, initiation, and return — and summarizes it this way:

> A hero ventures forth from the world of common day into a region of supernatural wonder: fabulous forces are there encountered and a decisive victory is won: the hero comes back from this mysterious adventure with the power to bestow boons on his fellow man [30].[1]

According to Campbell, the pattern emerges across cultures and time periods, suggesting it is the very fabric of human existence. As a result, he called this story the *monomyth*[2] — in Tolkienian parlance, one story to rule them all.

This narrative structure should be familiar to any one of us. As David Leemings' ambitious, though not exhaustive, anthology *The World of Myth* illustrates, the Indian Krishna, the Greek Theseus, the French Joan of Arc, the Celtic King Arthur, the Hebrew Moses, the Roman Aeneas, the Native American Hiawatha, the African Wanjiru, the Mesopotamian Gilgamesh, the Blackfoot Kutoyis, and the Jewish Jesus — all of these figures, both fictional and historical, follow a similar path. Therefore, while some scholars may elect another myth as "*the* essential human story" (Leeming 8, emphasis added), the hero's journey will play the lead role in my argument and consideration of *Farscape* fandom. It, more than any other narrative, helps us understand something about who Scapers are and what *Farscape* fandom means.

Even from the briefest review of literature on the subject, it is clear that mythologies are extremely important to and for humans. They help us chronicle and recall details about our past and present. They aid us in our desire to shape our future. They give us a sense of identity and purpose. They provide us order in the midst of chaos and crisis. They bind us together. They justify our actions and social structures (Rowland 103). In other words, myths represent one of many examples of humans engaged in rhetoric. As Krista Ratcliffe defines it, rhetoric is "how we use language and how language uses us." If grand narratives are considered from a rhetorical perspective, understanding myth does just as much to illuminate the nature and significance of fan efforts to save favored television series as understanding fandom does to illuminate the nature and significance of myth. Thus, exploring the relationship between the myth of fan power and Scapers should prove a most enlightening endeavor.

Farscape *Fandom*

From its very beginning, *Farscape* attracted a loyal and disparate fan base. Both regular viewers and entertainment critics raved about the series' innovative use of animatronic aliens as main characters (Prescott T02) as well as the creators' choice to the make the starship Moya a "biomechanoid" or living vessel. Eventually, scholars began to notice and comment on its refreshing approach to gender and sexuality (see especially Battis, *Investigating* Farscape). As Jes Battis explains, the series also boasts a narrative arc that spans "galaxies, with a deeply critical undercurrent of discussion around issues of racism, xenophobia, miscegenation, and sexual freedom" ("*Farscape*" 104–105). (With a focus on such issues, it might be said that *Farscape* was the *Star Trek* [1966– 1969] of its time.) Simply put, there are a plethora of reasons to appreciate and enjoy *Farscape*. As many viewers, journalists, critics, and scholars have noted, though, it was a series destined to either fail miserably or become a fan favorite, an instant cult classic. It quickly achieved the status of the latter, and most people — especially fans — know what that means, states Alex Strachan: "'Cult classic' is another way of saying small audience" (D9). Paul Sheehan reduces "small audience" to an even smaller one, calling Scapers a "micro-cult" (3). Thus while there was a large enough fan following to "[generate] a considerable demand for DVDs, soundtracks, computer games, books, apparel, action figures and every imaginable tchotchke — even Halloween costumes" (Belenky A13), the fandom was never able "to grow beyond its core fan base" (qtd. in Petrozzello 72). Unfortunately, no matter how brilliant a television series may be, attracting merely a micro-cult means certain death.

In "The Nitty Gritty of How *Farscape* Got Cancelled," Scaper Cosmic Theorist notes that Syfy,[3] network home of the series in the United States (U.S.), offered the press the usual reasons for its choice to cancel: high production costs and low ratings (Petrozzello 72). A year before the cancellation, however, on 1 October 2001, then Syfy president Bonnie Hammer, had praised the series and announced a two-year contract for renewal, a move Comic Theorist calls "unprecedented." Hammer had declared, "We are excited to renew our commitment to this smart, sexy, intelligent, and fun series that rewrites the book on sci-fi entertainment. *Farscape* is not only the most ambitious original series on basic cable, we think it's one of the best-written shows on television, period. It's no wonder that it's the top-rated series on [Syfy] for three years running" (qtd. in Cosmic Theorist). This statement, made eleven months prior to announcing the show's demise, led fans to question the reasons offered for the cancellation. Scapers wanted to know: "What the frell happened?" *Farscape* Executive Producer David Kemper attempted an answer, explaining that there is always "an out clause" for businesses and that Syfy had merely exercised its right to pass on a fifth season. Expressing the entire crew's disappointment, Kemper said, "We are all hugely sad. We all cried on the set ... [but] we are as helpless as anyone" (qtd. in Melloy 20). *Helpless* is not a word that usually appears in fan activist vocabulary. Rather, actions speak louder than such words. Like Athena, fully grown and already armed, springing from the forehead of Zeus, the "Save *Farscape*" campaign (later renamed "Watch *Farscape*") was instantaneously born. Within moments of Kemper, Manning, and Browder confirming Syfy's decision, Scapers began to organize in not only typical but also original ways (Laskin 54; Morey 83).

Those familiar with contemporary fandom know that *Farscape* fans are not the first media enthusiasts to engage in save-a-show kinds of activism. As scholar and fan of the series Sean Morey notes, the Scapers' campaign "shared its roots with the letter-writing campaign to save *Star Trek* from cancellation in the 1960s" (83). When after only a season and a half the U.S. television network National Broadcasting Company (NBC) announced plans to cancel *Star Trek*, several fan leaders, specifically John and Betty Jo "Bjo" Trimble, stepped forward and began to organize additional devotees. The Trekker community then successfully employed the most effective existing technology to make their discontented voices heard: hardcopy letters written and addressed to network executives. Accordingly, the Trimbles have gone down in fandom history as the show's saviors — even though only one additional season aired (*StarTrek.com* Staff). When the series was syndicated, the cult fandom multiplied exponentially. Today, the franchise's global success strongly suggests the Trekker community exemplifies the famous Vulcan blessing: "Live long and prosper." In Scapers' case, surface mail to Syfy executives was never going to achieve the same results that Trekkers had achieved so many decades before. Rather, Scapers' letters were "more symbolic in nature" (Morey 83). This homage to the past, though, signals how the myth of fan power may have begun — an origin story. Particularly, grand tales of Bjo, "the woman who saved *Star Trek*," inspire Scapers and many other fan communities. The legend of Bjo also continues to give fans and their communities a sense of identity, a historically- and culturally-situated model, and the hope of potential triumph. Yet the myth of fan power does not begin and end with Trekkers, although it would be easy to assume the tale of saving *Star Trek* is powerful enough by itself to encourage future fan campaigns. Trekkers' victory arguably serves as *the* essential story that forms the foundation of the myth; however, many other fan success stories provide necessary scaffolding.

Though not as well-covered by the press or discussed among scholars as Trekkers or Scapers, several fan communities have in the past applied enough collective pressure to save their own objects of fandom while simultaneously strengthening the myth of fan power. For example, Rati Bishnoi places *Farscape* in a lineup of fan-rescued series beginning with *Star Trek* and followed by *Cagney & Lacey* (1982–1988), *Designing Women* (1986–1993), and *Roswell* (1999–2002). Regarding the female-centric police procedural *Cagney & Lacey*, Bishnoi attributes the show's survival to fans' letter-writing campaign as well as "growing ratings for reruns and an Emmy for Tyne Daly [who played Mary Beth Lacey]" (9E). The official website for *Cagney & Lacey* confirms both that low ratings caused U.S. television network CBS Broadcasting Inc. (CBS) to cancel the show in the spring of 1983 and that devotees ultimately helped reverse that decision. Showrunner Barney Rosenzweig received thousands of protest letters when the news made its way to the mostly middle-aged, female audience. Of course, much like *Farscape*'s Kemper, Rosenzweig himself had no control over the network's decision. As a result, he encouraged fans to write even more letters, yet instead of sending them to the network, he advised devotees to target local newspapers. "Studio heads do not necessarily read their viewer-mail but they do read their daily papers," argued Rosenzweig (qtd. in "About *Cagney & Lacey*"). In the end, the series was renewed and spent seven seasons on the air. During that time, it was nominated for 36 Emmy Awards and won 14 ("About *Cagney & Lacey*"; Bishnoi 9E). The example of *Designing Women*, says Bishnoi, involved Viewers for Quality Television lobbying CBS and eventually securing a short reprieve for the series; *Roswell* fans, "as part of a '*Roswell* is Hot' campaign, sent network execs thousands of bottles of hot sauce," a strategy that ostensibly convinced The WB Television Network (The WB) to order a second season (9E).

In the midst of "Watch *Farscape*" campaign, *Herald Sun* television critic Robert Fidgeon "received several letters ... from readers wondering if campaigns by viewers to 'save' shows after they have been axed are ever successful" (47). One of those readers was Lauren Parker, a Scaper. Would her and fellow enthusiasts' activism be in vain? In fact, once in a while fan lobbying does work, notes Fidgeon, but it works best when shows under threat of cancellation are still on the air. As does Bishnoi, Fidgeon comments on the success stories of *Cagney & Lacey*, *Designing Women*, and *Roswell* and to that list adds *China Beach* (1988–1991), *The Sentinel* (1996–1999), *The Pretender* (1996–2000), and *Once and Again* (1999–2002), all of which received extended lives—whether by means of additional episodes, seasons, or telemovies—as the result of viewer interventions (47). Again, these narratives of passion and successful activism are important because they add texture and detail to the fan-spun myth of power, tales that echo Trekkers' love for their series and their salvific letter writing.

For *Farscape* lovers, hardcopy letters were a nice touch, a traditionally tried and true approach, but letters were going to be neither the first nor the only approach. Scapers, who had found each other not in local fan clubs but on World Wide Web message boards and blogs, immediately turned to the technologies they had been using all along. Only hours after the online chat with Kemper, Manning, and Browder, fan-built websites and fan-initiated web petitions were up and running, demonstrating "that people from varied backgrounds all over the world can come together using the Internet to fight a common goal," argues Laskin (54). The variety of supporters is evidenced by examining the electronic signatures on one of the very first petitions. Using *iPetitions*, Evan Berman started "Save *Farscape!*" on 6 September 2002. Within a day, 6500 people had added their names and comments, and within six days, 30,000 had pledged their support. In the end, however, Hollywood still counts viewers; numbers usually matter more than a micro-cult's intense passion. For instance, "in Australia, *Farscape* battled to attract 500,000 nationally, which is simply not enough" (Fidgeon 47). Coupled with a small viewership, the growing popularity and ease of using the Internet to register one's distaste or distress has made devotee campaigns in general and online petitions in particular an all-too-common response, observes Fidgeon (47). Of course, all-too-common fan responses run parallel to all-too-common network responses.[4] Therefore, fans must continue to innovate to make an impact.

In the last decade or so, one of those methods for getting noticed by networks has involved fans using the Internet to coordinate the selection of an object that symbolizes their beloved series or character and the subsequent *en masse* shipping of that object to physical addresses for television studio offices. As mentioned above, *Roswell* fans chose hot sauce, a favorite food item of the show's alien, teenaged main characters. Enthusiasts of *The X-Files* (1993–2002) selected sunflower seeds, the preferred snack of central character FBI Agent Fox Mulder; Browncoats, fans of Joss Whedon's *Firefly* (2002), picked khaki pants in honor of Captain Malcolm Reynolds; and *Veronica Mars* (2004–2007) fans purchased Mars chocolate bars. Even this strategy, though, has become almost commonplace as it has been used quite a few times to arrest the attention of decision makers. Fans understand that these tactics do not work every time and certainly do not work well if predictable. For example, *Veronica Mars* fans hired a small plane to fly from Los Angeles to Burbank with a "RENEW VERONICA MARS!" banner in tow ("About Cloud Watchers"; Cochran 172; Turnbull 320). Though *Veronica Mars* was canceled after three seasons, innovating remains essential for each new campaign. As Fidgeon observes, "*Farscape* fans knew that the usual outcry probably wasn't going to be enough to bring back the show, so they came up with BraScape, their most creative moment" (47).

Agreeing with Fidgeon, Rob Salem calls BraScape the fandom's most "clever ploy," one that "had women fans demonstrating their gender-specific 'support' by mailing their bras in to [Syfy]" (C04; see also Holder and Toy 13 as well as "Trying to Save" 87). According to Salem's interviewee, Canadian Scaper Nicola Wood, both the undergarments and the manner in which the female fans organized themselves gave a unique and feminine touch to the wider campaign: "Women are taught from a very early age a different way of problem-solving than men... Female methods of problem-solving involve co-operation, communication, and non-hierarchical thinking. Women are taught to co-operate with each other, rather than compete" (qtd. in Salem C04). Wood goes a step further than commenting on cooperative strategies. She directly attributes BraScape to legendary Trekker activist Bjo Trimble, calling her "a perfect example" and noting that Trimble herself "networked with *Farscape* fans very early in our campaign efforts. She and her husband shared inspiring words and gave us good advice" (qtd. in Salem C04). Importantly, the undergarments were being sent to Syfy president Bonnie Hammer, and by April 2003, "more than 200 bras [had] hit Ms. Hammer's desk" (Holder and Toy 13). Both Hammer's gender and the network's stated desire "to expand the channel's viewers beyond the typical male audience" invited such a response (Fidgeon 47), one both distinctive and intimate. Rather than the more typical mailing of objects related to a particular television show or character, female Scapers chose symbols that represented themselves; regardless of their small numbers, many of the women who love *Farscape* made sure their undies were seen and their voices were heard. Surely, BraScape was clever and creative, but just like letter writing, it alone was not going to save the series.

While some were engaged in BraScape, other Scapers were busy organizing and implementing a wide variety of other approaches (Boshra D4). In addition to a "furious e-mail and letter-writing campaign" (Strachan D9), online petitions, and BraScape, convention appearances, DVD drives for public libraries and the U.S. Armed Forces (The Jim Henson Company), "picketing of production offices" (Cunningham 20), print and film advertisements, and fundraising were all in the works. David Simerly, a Scaper and computer programmer for Apple, was skimming message boards when he stumbled upon fans talking about making a *Farscape* advertisement (Anderson). "I had a digital camcorder and a Mac and Final Cut Pro editing software, so I had all the equipment to put the video together," he told *Adweek* (qtd. in Anderson). Because rallies for the series were popping up all over, Simerly attended several near his home in California. From the gatherings he put together a 30-second spot of "fans espousing their love for the show.... The ad's purpose, said Simerly, [was] 'not only to show new people that *Farscape* is pretty cool, but to show advertisers that we are an intelligent, affluent audience'" (qtd. in Anderson). Intelligent and affluent, "hearty" (Boshra D4) and "almost supernaturally passionate" (Bianco 9) — this combination of characteristics catalyzed several more extraordinary and unparalleled moves. For instance, one group of Scapers "bought the cover of American *Variety* magazine in protest, as well as doing radio and TV commercials across the U.S." (20). Yet another strategy to save the series involved some devotees uniting themselves as the Viewer Consortium, an independent organization whose purpose became exploring how they themselves might "directly finance quality television shows such as *Farscape*" (Fidgeon 47). According to Strachan, "unnamed investors raised some $20 million U.S. on behalf of The Jim Henson Company to pick up the story where it left off" (D9). In light of this long list of efforts, some of them involving substantial time and financial investment, it sounds silly and even patronizing for a network spokesperson to go on record claiming, "There are no bigger fans of *Farscape* than we here at the [Syfy] Channel" (qtd. in Petrozzello 72).

The ultimate televisual result of these collective efforts—*Farscape: The Peacekeeper Wars*—can definitely be considered significant; however, the media's validation of Scapers' success, I posit, is even more significant because that validation fortifies the myth of fan power for many generations to come. Notably, journalists and critics around the globe claim a direct cause and effect relationship exists between fan activism and the telemovie, again, confirming fandom's influence:

- *USA Today*—"*Farscape* is just the latest show to be brought back to life by passionate, committed fans" (Bishnoi 9E).
- *The Gazette* (Montreal)—"*Farscape* aired on Space in Canada and on [Syfy] in the [United States]. Cancellation, when it came, was abrupt.... and *Farscape* fans went nuclear.... The two-night, four-hour miniseries *Farscape: The Peacekeeper Wars* (Space, 9 P.M.) is the result" (Strachan D9).
- *USA Today*—"After [*Farscape*] was canceled in March 2004 without an ending, fans organized a campaign at savefarscape.com and paid for TV and print ads to save the show. As a result, Jim Henson Productions made a four-hour miniseries called *Farscape: The Peacekeeper Wars* to resolve the story lines" (Snider 6D).
- *The Australian*—"Emails, widespread publicity and newspaper advertisements paid for by fans *forced* the network to review its original decision to cancel" ("Home-Grown Sci-Fi" 4, emphasis added).
- *Daily News* (New York)—"The rebirth of *Farscape*, an imaginative sci-fi series returned from the dead by fervent fans, dedicated collaborators, and a few passionate investors, is an amazing story" (Bianculli 110).
- *The Observer* (London)—"Space opera *Farscape* deserves to be celebrated purely for the way in which it shows that occasionally TV executives listen. The original series ... ended in 2003, but continued pressure from the programme's dedicated fans ensured that TV executives *bowed to pressure* and brought back the original cast for this mini-series which ties up all the loose ends" (Hughes 72, emphasis added).
- *Daily News* (New York)—"When [Syfy's] *Farscape* was canceled ... hopeful viewers sent the network flowers, singing telegrams, a Halloween jack-o'-lantern that resembled one of the characters, cupcakes, and more. They also used the Internet to try to find financial backers for the program.... Their year-long effort paid off. A four-hour *Farscape* miniseries will air this fall" ("Trying to Save" 87).
- *USA Today*—"Never underestimate the power of a committed cult. This small-but-mighty band of 'Scapers' has *forced* [Syfy] to bring the unreasonably

canceled space adventure *Farscape* back from the dead... The result of their near-ceaseless efforts is *Farscape: The Peacekeeper Wars*" (Bianco 9, emphasis added).

The language of power and success came not only from these print sources but also from *Farscape* producers themselves. According to Brian Henson, for example, "'The only reason we're making the miniseries is because the fans found me a consortium of partners who made it possible to put together'" (qtd. in "Trying to Save" 87; see also "If It's Good Television" K10). In an official press release for The Jim Henson Company, Scapers received public thanks for their activism on behalf of the series and news of a significant donation to the "Watch *Farscape*" website:

> HOLLYWOOD, August 23, 2004 — The Jim Henson Company has donated six autographed props used on the set of *Farscape: The Peacekeeper Wars* to the fans of *Farscape* as a thank you for their tireless efforts in making the next chapter in the *Farscape* saga a reality. The announcement was made today by Brian Henson, director and executive producer of the television event and co–CEO of The Jim Henson Company. *Farscape: The Peacekeeper Wars* is scheduled to premiere on [Syfy] on October 17th 9/8C and the props from the production will be given to the online community at www.watchfarscape.com, a grassroots fan website that receives an average of 400,000 hits per day and has been a leader in the campaign to get *Farscape* back on the air.
>
> Brian Henson said, "It is because of the tireless efforts of the fans that this epic television event is a reality. Your commitment to invite new viewers into *Farscape*'s universe has been seen around the world. With the airing of the miniseries coming up fast, your support means more now than ever before and I am grateful for the unending dedication you have all shown. Thank you for all you have done to continue the *Farscape* adventure."

Henson uses a key word that returns this consideration of *Farscape* enthusiasts and their activism to the hero's journey. That word is *adventure*.

As scholars at the University of California-Berkeley summarize, the Campbellian hero follows a path that involves various stages within three major rites of passage. The hero's life usually begins under "fabulous circumstances" (e.g., the immaculate conception of Jesus the Christ), although many contemporary hero journeys start not by being born but by being called to adventure. Such a call usually comes by way of an event or a messenger. For Scapers, the heroes of their own legendary tale, the call to adventure came in the online chat with Kemper, Manning, and Browder. While some heroes respond reluctantly to their calls, Scapers were willing from the outset. Once on the journey's path, early on the hero often receives assistance and even protection from a helper, group of helpers, or special amulet. Arguably, Trekker Bjo Trimble filled this role, particularly for the women of BraScape and generally for the wider community of fan activists. The concept of an amulet can be seen in Trimble's example and advice as well as in the "forefans" who had in the past successfully saved their own televisual objects of desire. Not too long into the journey, the hero must cross some sort of threshold, leaving behind the everyday world and the option to turn back. The crossing can happen either with ease or with great difficulty; either way, the contrast between the hero's home life and adventure life is clear. For Scapers, several different events could be read as the threshold, but I suggest Kemper, Manning, and Browder's confirmation of the series' cancellation serves both as the call to adventure *and* the threshold because that event marked, for the majority of active *Farscape* fans, "the point of no return." Past the threshold, the hero, accompanied by helpers, withstands many trials and tests: "monsters, sorcerers, warriors, or forces of nature" (*Monomyth*). Though most of their foes were intangible and not-altogether evil, Scapers faced a variety of obstacles, including Syfy's claim of low ratings and high production costs, their own small numbers, and the understanding that to significantly influence network decisions they were going to need emotional endurance and financial fortitude. With each test, though, *Farscape* enthusiasts proved they had both and that they were each other's helpers, always already working in solidarity and exerting their collective energy.

The final stages of the hero's journey include the climax or final battle, flight or return to the threshold with the elixir, reentry into the everyday world, sharing of the elixir, and homecoming (*Monomyth*). While some of these steps are more difficult than earlier ones to pinpoint and name in regard to *Farscape* fandom, two seem very obvious: elixir and homecoming. Normally, a major reason the hero accepts the call to adventure and takes the journey at all is to secure knowledge, an object, or a blessing that will restore or redeem his or her community. The purpose of the homecoming is to gift that very knowledge, object, or blessing. As Campbell puts it, "the hero comes back from this mysterious adventure with the power to bestow boons on his [or her] fellow [humans]" (30). My claim is that the boon Scapers acquired was not *The Peacekeeper Wars* but the powerful narrative of their activist adventure, one that has already given and will continue to give hope and instruction to generations of fandoms to come. Therein lies the great significance of *Farscape* and its followers.

Significance

"A myth," posits Karen Armstrong, "is true because it is effective, not because it gives us factual information" (10). Admittedly, I am skeptical when I read reports that insist fans have "forced" network executives to alter their decisions or find fan forums that assert DVDs sales can and do result in textual after-lives for television series. If Armstrong is to be believed, though, both my skepticism and the facts regarding fans' (in)ability to influence executives are irrelevant. The real question is whether or not the myth of fan power works: "If it *works*, that is, if it forces us to change our minds and hearts, it is a valid myth" (10). How valid, then, is the legendary tale of Scapers' heroic journey? Evidence from several sources suggests that it is valid enough and growing more so all the time.

Regarding admirers of *Angel* (1999–2004), the spinoff of *Buffy the Vampire Slayer* (1997–2003), New York's *Daily News* notes that those fans who were trying to save the series from cancellation shared a lineage with many "activist TV viewers," including viewers of *Farscape*. Additionally, months after the airing of *The Peacekeeper Wars*, *Newsweek*'s Elise Soukup reported on the efforts of *Fraggle Rock* (1983–1987) enthusiasts to revive the series by way of DVDs quite a few years after the final episode aired on television. Soukup writes,

> Note to obsessive fan sites everywhere: you're being watched. That's what Warrick Brownlow, a fan of the 1980s series "Jim Henson's *Fraggle Rock*," recently learned. In April 2002 Brownlow launched an online petition, pleading to have the series released on DVD. After garnering more than 30,000 e-signatures, HIT Entertainment, a licensing partner of the Jim Henson Co., announced that this month it would release selected episodes from the first season. "This is the direct result of fan support," says Lauren McCabe, a HIT representative [10].

Brownlow, who learned of his influence from the magazine, was pleasantly surprised, calling the news "brilliant" and stating, "We knew they were watching us, but we didn't think they'd do anything about it" (qtd. in Soukup 10). Studios rarely do, according to another of Soukup's sources, Tom Adams, president of Adams Media Research. Specifically citing the success of Scapers' campaign, Soukup claims that the trend of networks doing nothing is changing, though. Gord Lacey, founder of www.tvshowsondvd.com, confirms, "Studios have started to realize that listening to fans of shows will result in better products and build pent-up purchasing excitement" (qtd. in Snider 6D). *Farscape* may have garnered "international critical recognition, as well as three Saturn Awards and an Emmy nomination," but those accolades did not save the series (Prescott T02). Instead, it appears that the fans did, and their raised voices telling their story can still be heard around the world, says Jean Prescott of Sydney's *Daily Telegraph* (T02).

In the introduction, I claim that understanding the major role Scapers play in composing the myth of fan power says much about *who* we are as human beings and *why* we feel compelled to tell the stories we tell. As Leonard J. Biallas explains, "Myths are stories ... that help us become aware of our true selves" (*v*). In other words, discovering our identity is inextricably bound to our storytelling: we tell stories to find ourselves, and our stories reinforce what we've found.[5] Among contemporary fandoms, the narrative of Trekkers begins to define what it means to be a fan and a fandom. It is a sacred tale, one that continues to be remembered, told, and retold. As a result, it still holds rich and authoritative meaning (O'Flaherty 27). Yet the Trekker tale is but one of many. As with most myths, it is "a story that is part of a larger group of stories" (27). Every subsequent fan community in some way contributes its own narrative, some narratives more potent than others. Put another way, Scapers' journey has become one of those smaller yet potent stories in a larger group of stories. Together, these tales form a metanarrative of fan power. Among thousands of television series, a handful of remarkable examples actually provide too few instances to conclude that fan-driven, save-a-show initiatives have a real chance of succeeding. However, there are enough examples to compose a myth, and the heart of that myth seems to be this: Passion for beloved televisual texts united with tenacity, intelligence, and a little affluence empowers fans to influence executive decision-making and, ultimately, control their entertainment options and engagement. Of course, there is danger in telling and retelling this single story of fan power.[6] But that argument is a tale for another time. For now, it is sufficient to end at the beginning. "There are legendary tales," writes reporter Peter Haran, "of shows that have been saved by grassroots campaigns waged by devoted fans" (T35). Perhaps none, though, are as legendary as the tale of Scapers, or *Farscape* fans.

Notes

1. Note the gendering of the hero. In *The Female Hero in American and British Literature*, Carol Pearson and Katherine Pope posit that "our understanding of the basic spiritual and psychological archetype of human life has been limited ... by the assumption that the hero and central character of the myth is male" (4). This male hero is also often white, upper class, heterosexual, able-bodied, and politically, economically, or socially powerful in some way. Even when an effort is made to avoid this gendering, what Pearson and Pope call the "patriarchal habit" takes control. For example, though Campbell states that both men and women can be heroes, the pronoun *he* dominates his famous text.

2. In a footnote to *The Hero with a Thousand Faces*, Campbell cites *Finnegans Wake* by James Joyce (1939) as the original source of the term *monomyth* (30).

3. To avoid confusion, I am using the current name of the network: Syfy. From 1992 to 1999, though, the official name used was Sci-Fi Channel; from 1999 to 2009, the name was simply Sci-Fi.

4. Again, the decisions of studio executives have become as predictable as the microcult response to cancellation. According to Justin Rude, "When the networks pulled the plug on *Firefly* and *Farscape* a few years back, sci-fi fans were up in arms. After all, with the airwaves clogged with tawdry reality fare, wasn't there room for one or two shows featuring character development and serial plot progression? ... Had fans taken a look at TV history, they may have realized the futility of their reasoning. Forward-thinking science fiction always has had a hard time on network television" (Y05). The predictable response of networks is to develop inexpensive, highly-watched options. Lately, that has meant a lot of "reality" series.

5. If we find ourselves through stories and stories reinforce what we find, the quality

of those stories surely matters. Unfortunately, space does not allow me to explore this particular claim. Readers who are interested in doing so, however, could begin with two short contrasting yet complementary pieces on the nature of "narrative impact," pieces by Djikic et al. and Foy and Gerrig.

6. I invite readers to pay particular attention to those stories — ancient or contemporary — that bend or shatter the Campbellian pattern and in doing so attempt to tell different or altogether new narratives. Also, I encourage those who have not already done so to view on *TED.com* "The Danger of a Single Story" presented by Chimamanda Adichie. Adichie posits that any type of monolithic tale can cause harm — to our thinking and, therefore, to our relationships with others. However, a plethora of stories allows us to "regain a kind of paradise," she says.

Works Cited

"About *Cagney & Lacey*." *Cagneyandlacey.com*. The Rosenzweig Company, 2012. Web. 9 Dec. 2012.
"About Cloud Watchers." *Watchveronicamars.net*. Watch Veronica Mars, 2006–2007. Web. 20 May 2010.
Adichie, Chimamanda. "The Danger of a Single Story." *Ted.com*. TED Conferences, Oct. 2009. Web. 20 Oct. 2011.
Anderson, Mae. "Far-Sighted." *Adweek* 25 Nov. 2002, Eastern ed.: n. pag. *LexisNexis Academic*. Web. 13 Nov. 2011.
Armstrong, Karen. *A Short History of Myth*. New York: Canongate, 2005. Print.
Battis, Jes. "*Farscape*." *The Essential Cult TV Reader*. Ed. David Lavery. Louisville: University Press of Kentucky, 2010. 104–110. Print.
_____. *Investigating* Farscape. London: I. B. Tauris, 2007. Print.
Belenky, Irina. "'Scapers' Follow Path of Trekkers." *Daily Variety* 25 Apr. 2001, Special sec.: A13. *LexisNexis Academic*. Web. 13 Nov. 2011.
Biallas, Leonard J. *Myths, Gods, Heroes, and Saviors*. Mystic, CT: Twenty-Third, 1986. Print.
Bianco, Robert. "A Reconstituted 'Farscape' Returns." *USA Today* 15 Oct. 2004, final ed., Life sec.: 9. *LexisNexis Academic*. Web. 13 Nov. 2011.
Bianculli, David. "New 'Farscape': Outta This World." *Daily News* [New York] 14 Oct. 2004, sports final ed., TELEVISION ed.: 110. *LexisNexis Academic*. Web. 13 Nov. 2011.
Bishnoi, Rati. "Other Fan-Driven Rescues." *USA Today* 15 Oct. 2004, final ed., Life sec.: 9E. *LexisNexis Academic*. Web. 13 Nov. 2011.
Boshra, Basem. "'Farscape' Begins Fourth Season on Space Tonight." *The Gazette* [Montreal] 7 Feb. 2003, final ed., Arts & Life: Preview; Remote Control sec.: D4. *LexisNexis Academic*. Web. 13 Nov. 2011.
Campbell, Joseph. *The Hero with a Thousand Faces*. New York: MJF Books, 1949. Print.
Carney, David. *All About Myths: An Introduction to Mythanalysis*. New York: Adastra, 1990. Print.
Cassirer, Ernst. *Language and Myth*. 1946. New York: Dover, 1953. Print.
Cochran, Tanya R. "Neptune (Non-) Consensual: The Risky Business of Television Fandom, Falling in Love, and Playing the Victim." *Investigating* Veronica Mars: *Essays on the Teen Detective Series*. Eds. Rhonda V. Wilcox and Sue Turnbull. Jefferson, N.C.: McFarland, 2011. 167–187. Print.
Cochran, Tanya R., and Jason A. Edwards. "*Buffy the Vampire Slayer* and the Quest Story: Revising the Hero, Reshaping the Myth." *Sith, Slayers, Stargates, + Cyborgs: Modern Mythology in the Millennium*. Eds. David Whitt and John Perlich. New York: Peter Lang, 2008. 145–169. Print.

Cosmic Theorist. "The Nitty Gritty of How *Farscape* Got Cancelled." *Watchfarscape.com*. WatchFarscape.com, 20 Sept. 2005. Web. 4 Dec. 2012.
Crew, Adrienne. "Can 'Farscape' Fans Reinvent TV?" *Salon.com*. Salon Media Group, 13 Mar. 2003. Web. 2 Dec. 2012.
Cunningham, Sophie. "Addictive *Farscape*'s Future in Doubt." *The Age* [Melbourne] 24 Jan. 2004, late ed., sec. A2: 20. *LexisNexis Academic*. Web. 13 Nov. 2011.
Djikic, Maja, Keith Oatley, Sara Zoeterman, and Jordan B. Peterson. "On Being Moved by Art: How Reading Fiction Transforms the Self." *Creativity Research Journal* 21.1 (2009): 24–29. *Academic Search Premier*. Web. 28 Dec. 2012.
Fidgeon, Robert. "Fans Have Far to Go." *Herald Sun* [Melbourne] 10 Sept. 2003, Home Entertainment Guide sec.: 47. *LexisNexis Academic*. Web. 13 Nov. 2011.
Foy, Jeffrey E., and Richard J. Gerrig. "How Might Literature Do Harm?" *Style* 42.2/3 (Summer/Fall 2008): 175–178. *Academic Search Premier*. Web. 28 Dec. 2012.
Haran, Peter. "Sci-fi Fans Rally to the Cause." *Sunday Mail* [Adelaide] 26 Jan. 2003, TV Guide sec.: T35. *LexisNexis Academic*. Web. 13 Nov. 2011.
Holder, Peter, and Naomi Toy. "Sydney Confidential" *The Daily Telegraph* [Sydney] 1 Apr. 2003, Features sec.: 12–13. *LexisNexis Academic*. Web. 13 Nov. 2011.
"Home-Grown Sci-Fi Is U.S. Network Scapegoat." *The Australian* 17 Sept. 2002, Local sec.: 4. *LexisNexis Academic*. Web. 13 Nov. 2011.
Hughes, Sarah. "*Farscape: The Peacekeeper Wars*." *The Observer* 16 Jan. 2005, Observer Magazine Pages sec.: 72. *LexisNexis Academic*. Web. 13 Nov. 2011.
"If It's Good Television, It Won't Last." *The Toronto Star* 16 Dec. 2004, Entertainment sec.: K10. *LexisNexis Academic*. Web. 13 Nov. 2011.
The Jim Henson Company. "The Jim Henson Company Thanks the Fans of *Farscape*." Press Release. 23 Aug. 2004.
Laskin, Mary. "Net Saves TV Star." *Sunday Times* [London] 6 Oct. 2002, Features, Culture sec.: 54. *LexisNexis Academic*. Web. 13 Nov. 2011.
Leeming, David Adams. *The World of Myth: An Anthology*. New York: Oxford University Press, 1990. Print.
Melloy, Neil. "Sci-Fi Show Ends Its Run in Tears." *Courier Mail* [Queensland] 10 Sept. 2002, Features sec.: 20. *LexisNexis Academic*. Web. 13 Nov. 2011.
Monomyth. Office of Resources for International and Area Studies (ORIAS), University of California, Berkeley, n.d. Web. 28 Dec. 2012.
Morey, Sean. "What the Frell Happened? Rhetorical Strategies of the *Farscape* Community." *Writing and the Digital Generation: Essays on New Media Rhetoric*. Ed. Heather Urbanski. Jefferson, N.C.: McFarland, 2010. 83–85. Print.
"Myth." *Encyclopædia Britannica*. *Encyclopædia Britannica Online Academic Edition*. Encyclopædia Britannica Inc., 2012. Web. 27 Dec. 2012.
Nimmo, Dan D., and James E. Combs. *Subliminal Politics: Myths and Mythmakers in America*. Englewood Cliffs, NJ: Prentice-Hall, 1980. Print.
O'Flaherty, Wendy Doniger. *Other People's Myths: The Cave of Echoes*. New York: Macmillan, 1988. Print.
Pearson, Carol, and Katherine Pope. *The Female Hero in American and British Literature*. New York: R. R. Bowker, 1981. Print.
Petrozzello, Donna. "End Near for 'Farscape.'" *Daily News* [New York] 10 Sept. 2002, Television sec.: 72. *LexisNexis Academic*. Web. 13 Nov. 2011.
Prescott, Jean. "'Farscape' Farewell." *The Daily Telegraph* [Sydney] 26 Dec. 2002. Features-Column sec.: T02. *LexisNexis Academic*. Web. 13 Nov. 2011.
Ratcliffe, Krista. "The Current State of Composition Scholar/Teachers: Is Rhetoric Gone or Just Hiding Out?" *Enculturation: A Journal of Rhetoric, Writing, and Culture* 5.1 (2003): n. pag. Web. 2 Dec. 2012.

Rowland, Robert C. "On Mythic Criticism." *Communication Studies* 41.2 (1990): 101–116. Print.

Rude, Justin. "'Earth 2': One Stellar Ride." *The Washington Post* 17 July 2005, final ed., TV Week sec.: Y05. *LexisNexis Academic*. Web. 13 Nov. 2011.

Rushing, Janice Hocker, and Thomas S. Frentz. "The Mythic Perspective." *The Art of Rhetorical Criticism*. Ed. Jim A. Kuypers. New York: Allyn & Bacon, 2005. 241-269. Print.

Salem, Rob. "Can Sci-Fi Fans Face the Future?" *The Toronto Star* 6 Mar. 2005, Entertainment sec: C04. *LexisNexis Academic*. Web. 13 Nov. 2011.

Sheehan, Paul. "Even The Mutant Has Fears for Her Future." *Sydney Morning Herald* 12 Oct. 2002, News and Features sec: 3. *LexisNexis Academic*. Web. 13 Nov. 2011.

Snider, Mike. "Fans Are Getting Their Way on DVD." *USA Today* 8 Feb. 2005., final ed., Life sec.: 6D. *LexisNexis Academic*. Web. 13 Nov. 2011.

Soukup, Elise. "Rock On, Fraggles." *Newsweek* 10 Jan. 2005: 10. *LexisNexis Academic*. Web. 13 Nov. 2011.

StarTrek.com Staff. "Bjo Trimble: The Woman Who Saved *Star Trek*— Part 1." *StarTrek.com*. CBS Entertainment, 31 Aug. 2011. Web. 9 Dec. 2012.

Strachan, Alex. "'Farscape' Series Finally Resolved." *The Gazette* [Montreal] 25 Mar. 2005, final ed., Arts & Life: Preview, Fine Tuning sec.: D9. *LexisNexis Academic*. Web. 13 Nov. 2011.

Stock, Gregory. *Metaman: The Merging of Humans and Machines into a Global Superorganism*. New York: Simon & Schuster, 1993. Print.

"Trying to Save Fallen 'Angel' Viewers Can Stir Up a Fan-Fare." *Daily News* [New York] 19 Apr. 2004, sports final ed., Television sec.: 87. *LexisNexis Academic*. Web. 13 Nov. 2011.

Turnbull, Sue. "*Veronica Mars*." *The Essential Cult TV Reader*. Ed. David Lavery. Lexington: University Press of Kentucky, 2010. 314-321. Print.

Primal Scream — With Accompaniment

Jessie Carty

The music in *Farscape*, specifically the music used over the credits, is very primal, native, visceral, and almost discordant. The music is unusual and yet there is something familiar about its tones which create a disjointed harmony. This music is not unlike the show's general premise: the known encountering the unknown.

The theme music for *Farscape* was developed by Chris Neal, his son Braedy, and the original creative collaborators for the show: Matt Carroll, Brian Henson, and Rockne S. O'Bannon. The creators had asked Chris and Braedy, under the collective name Subdivision, "to create something between '*tribal and medieval*.'" Subdivision even shared in a Golden Real Award nomination for the soundtrack of the first episode even though the network apparently did not like the theme music for the show (*Farscape* Encyclopedia Project; Simpson and Hughes).

The music, however, stayed, although it was reworked for the third season. Guy Gross, the composer of the new music, said: "The music for the Season Three opener was created over a 3 week period. It was decided that rather than simply create a new arrangement of the previous theme, I would compose an original theme that made gentle musical references to the old theme" ("Season of Death").

Not being a musical scholar, until I read this I was not aware that the third season's theme *was* different. Listening to the two different themes, my untrained ear does not pick up on any significant differences. Other people with whom I have discussed this, such as my spouse who has a better ear for music, do notice a difference, and find the newer music more likable. Perhaps, because of what I know of the show's plot, the new music feels a bit slower, more cautious.

Theme music, however, was not my biggest concern as I began to work on this piece. I wanted to discuss the voice that was added to the opening credits in all episodes except "Premiere" (1.1). This voice-over changes twice in the series, and it is through this voice-over that you get a sense for how John Crichton, the main character's relationship to his new universe, the inhabitants he meets there, and himself change.

The voice-over is not unique to *Farscape*. Science fiction television series ranging from *The Twilight Zone* to *Babylon 5* have utilized them. Furthermore, Booker writes that shows such as *The Outer Limits* use the "tactic of opening each episode with a distinctive and easily identifiable voice-over narration that held the episodes together as a recognizable unit" (20). Whereas *Farscape* is a series rather than a TV show with an anthology format, this described purpose for a voice-over extends to *Farscape* as it guides and reminds the viewer of Crichton's situation: he is the only human in the Uncharted Territories of space. As Billie Jo Mason writes: "Crichton's first season title sequence voice-over sets the scene for every episode, emphasizing the quest elements of his plight and the show's primary dramatic conflict, as well as establishing his relationship with his all-too-alien shipmates" (this collection, 64).

At the close of the first episode, Commander John Crichton (still in his IASA uniform) speaks into a pocket voice recorder. Instead of a Dear Diary, or a *Star Trek*-like captain's log, Crichton addresses his reflections to his father who is also an astronaut, a hero to Crichton as well as many others back on Earth. The opening credit voice-over that will start with the next episode echoes this voice recording:

> My name is John Crichton
> An astronaut
> A radiation wave hit and I got shot through a wormhole
> Now I'm lost in some distant part of the Universe, on a ship
> A living ship full of strange alien life forms
> Help me
> Listen please
> Is there anybody out there who can hear me?
> I'm being hunted by an insane military commander
> Doing everything I can
> I'm just looking for a way home

I have been unable to find a writing credit for the person who penned the voice-over, or a description of how it would look "on paper." I have recreated the lines here by how I think they might have looked in a script because they sound less like prose and more like a monologue, poem, or set of spoken word lyrics and, as with a more poetic/short piece of writing, the voice-over captures a moment. These few lines give you the basic background for all of the tensions that set up the first two seasons of the series. They also remind me of the chorus or an aside in a classical play.

The voice-over changes after Season Two: by Season Three Crichton is no longer specifically speaking about wanting to find a way home. Instead he feels completely lost — not only from home — but from the person he used to be. He is still amazed at Moya, the living ship, as well as other unique places and creatures he has encountered in the Uncharted Territories; however, the other escaped prisoners are now more than mere shipmates: they are his friends. The new voice-over describes these developments:

> My name is John Crichton
> [I'm lost]
> An astronaut
> [Shot through a wormhole]
> In some distant part of the Universe
> [I'm trying to stay alive]
> Aboard this ship
> [This living ship]
> Of escaped prisoners
> [My friends]
> If you can hear me
> [Beware]
> If I make it back
> [Will they follow?]
> If I open the door
> [Are you ready?]
> Earth is unprepared
> [Helpless]
> For the nightmares
> [I've seen]
> Or should I stay
> [Protect my home]
> Not show them
> [You exist]
> But then you'll never know
> [The wonders I've seen]

This second voice-over resonates with fear because Crichton has knowledge regarding wormhole technology that he knows could be detrimental to the world he comes from as well as to the rest of the universe. How can he go home again when a journey back may be dangerous to everything he knew before his Farscape mission?

I have set some of the lines in brackets because they are almost whispered, as if they were Crichton's internal thoughts. Some discussions (e.g., Booker) of this voice-over feel that it is another voice altogether, but my ear does not hear that. My ear, and my memory of the episodes leading up to the third season, tune into how fractured Crichton's mind has become. His fragile mental and physical existence is reflected in the third season voice-over.

The final voice-over appears over the credits for Season Four:

> My name is John Crichton
> An astronaut
> Three years ago I got shot through a wormhole
> I'm in a distant part of the Universe
> Aboard this living ship of escaped prisoners
> My friends
> I've made enemies
> Powerful, dangerous
> Now all I want is to find a way home
> To warn Earth
> Look upward and share the wonders I've seen

This new voice-over is short and to the point. Crichton notes that he has now been away from home for three years. This voice-over takes ownership over the fact that Crichton, for good or bad, has made enemies. He has taken on the burden of needing to warn Earth about what could be coming its way. Yet there is still that part of Crichton that is amazed and awed at what he has discovered. He has changed, but he is still very human.

Telotte's essay in this collection also touches on the idea of home as presented in the changing voice-overs when he writes: "Home, finally, is not necessarily the Earth but some place still 'uncharted.' His family is the one he is in the process of creating with his Sebacean mate Aeryn, the child she gives birth to in the middle of a firefight in *The Peacekeeper Wars* miniseries, and those 'strange alien life forms' that have become his friends, his support, even his saviors" (19). It actually surprises me that the final voice-over does not make the move to calling the other prisoners his family because all the fundamentals of family are there, from cranky uncles (Rygel), to brothers (D'Argo) and kid sisters (Chiana), and, of course, Aeryn who will become Crichton's wife and the mother of his child. In fact as early as episode sixteen ("The Locket") of Season Two (if not earlier), when returning to Moya after living 55 years in an alternate time line, Crichton says he is heading home (granted he will forget this alternate timeline at the close of the episode, but the seeds of Moya being home had already been planted in the series).

Farscape started without a voice-over and this is to be expected because Crichton is thrown into a world where he has no recognizable voice. Until he is given translator microbes no one can understand him. He is suddenly the alien in a universe that was used to a variety of species. In a universe that has never seen humans, Crichton becomes the audience's eyes, and he records his impressions, hopes, dreams, and desires as he tries to find a way back home. Crichton's recordings are an act of hope; like a message in a space bottle to some other human, somewhere, who might hear him. The series voice-overs change as he changes, as he begins to redefine home, and determine whether or not he has a place in the universe. By sending these messages out into the universe, Crichton and the audience are given the small sliver of hope that some human, somewhere will hear him. Breaking down the fourth wall finds that a lot of science fiction fans heard him very well.

Works Cited

Booker, M. Keith. *Science Fiction Television*. Westport, CT: Praeger, 2004. Print.
"Subdivision." *Farscape Encyclopedia Project*. Web. 30 July 2012.
"Season of Death." *Wikipedia*. Web. 30 August 2012.
Simpson, Paul, and David Hughes. *Farscape the Illustrated Companion*. New York: Tom Doherty Associates, 2000. Print.

Appendix A:
Farscape Character List[1]

John Crichton, Ph.D. (Human) — Commander, International Aeronautics and Space Administration (IASA). Crichton is testing his theory of atmospheric propulsion when he is shot through a wormhole into a distant part of the galaxy. He is visited during the first season by a race called the Ancients; they implant the information of how to construct wormholes into his memory. That knowledge and the fact that wormholes can be used as weapons make him very valuable and both the Peacekeepers and the Scarrans want that knowledge. He just wants to stay alive, get the girl, and hopefully be able to return to Earth one day (perhaps in that order).

Officer Aeryn Sun (Sebacean) — Special commando, Icarion Company, Pleisar Regiment. Aeryn is a Prowler pilot for the Peacekeepers. Born in space, she expected to die there as well. Caught in the wake of Moya's starburst, she is deemed irreversibly contaminated by Peacekeeper High Command. Rather than return to her home and suffer the consequences of her contamination (exile or death), she chooses to remain aboard Moya (in effect, choosing exile). She falls in love with John Crichton, although it is a rocky road to happiness.

Pa'u Zotoh Zhaan (Delvian) — a priest. Beautifully blue, physiologically she is flora rather than fauna. Recognizing that she contains darkness within her soul, Zhaan strives always to restrain that violence and search for peace. She loves Moya and all of her crew, eventually making the ultimate sacrifice for them.

Chiana (Nebari) — a thief, "always looking out for number one." Her past is not pretty, and she has problems trusting others. It will take her some time, but she will eventually bond with Moya's crew and become part of the mission to keep Crichton's wormhole knowledge from falling into the wrong hands.

Ka D'Argo (Luxan) — a very young male warrior. He was incarcerated by the Peacekeepers for ostensibly killing his wife, a Sebacean. In actuality she was killed by her brother. D'Argo slowly befriends Crichton, becoming his staunch ally in the fight to keep the wormhole knowledge out of the Scarrans' and the Peacekeepers' hands. He has a son who was sold into slavery following his imprisonment. D'Argo eventually rescues his son, but their subsequent relationship is fraught with difficulty.

Jothee (Luxan-Sebacean hybrid) — D'Argo's son. He does not know whether he should be happy that this father finally rescued him or angry that his father "allowed" him to be sold into slavery in the first place (something of which D'Argo was unaware). He has a brief sexual relationship with his father's lover, Chiana. Jothee will eventually become a soldier in the Luxan army.

Dominar Rygel XVI (Hynerian) — once the ruler of billions of subjects, he was deposed by his cousin and imprisoned. Now he intends to return to Hyneria and reclaim his throne. Used to having his way and being the Lord of all he can see, he still expects everyone to do his bidding. They rarely pay him any attention, but his skills at political intrigue and diplomacy, not to mention his deviousness, actually help the crew on numerous occasions.

Moya (Leviathan) — the living ship upon which Crichton and the others live. Crichton says the only Earth reference he can use to describe Moya's size is the story of Jonah and the Whale. Moya provides all life-support functions for the beings that reside within her. She is bonded with Pilot.

Pilot (Unknown) — a member of a crustacean-like species, which is never named. Pilots physically bond with Leviathans, controlling their vital functions and serving as links with any biological entities residing within these ships. Pilot is a very young member of his species and was deemed too young to bond with a Leviathan by the Elders on his planet. However, he was so determined to see the stars that he was willing to do anything for the chance. That determination will have many unfortunate consequences.

Talyn (Leviathan Hybrid) — Moya's offspring, produced in an experimental breeding program designed by the Peacekeepers. Their goal was to create a warship, although Talyn was unstable.

Jool (Interion) — a young, well-educated female who has not been on her own before. Kidnapped and placed in stasis so that her organs could be harvested, she is rescued by the crew. At first she vows to kill Crichton believing that he killed her cousins, then she joins the crew hoping to return home one day. Her youth and inexperience cause no end of exasperation in the other members of the crew. She eventually leaves to continue her research.

Noranti (unknown) — a refugee, species unknown. She is very old, at least in physical appearance, but says she feels much younger. She is well-versed in the healing arts and serves as medic following the death of Zhaan and Jool's departure.

Sikozu (Kalish) — a bioloid, *Farscape*-speak for an android (like Data of *Star Trek the Next Generation*). Crichton calls her "Sputnik" because of her hair-do. Sikozu joins the crew in Season Four, but she is never really accepted, especially after she becomes enamored of Scorpius.

Captain Bialar Crais (Sebacean) — conscripted by the Peacekeepers along with his brother when a young boy. He promises his parents that he will look after his little brother, who is killed by accident when Crichton's Farscape module exits the wormhole. Crais vows revenge on Crichton but will eventually recognize that his brother's death was an accident. He will become Crichton's ally in the quest to keep the wormhole knowledge from Scorpius.

Scorpius (Sebacean-Scarran Hybrid) — the result of a Scarran rape of a Sebacean woman. Scorpius is tortured during his youth: the Scarrans believe it will make him stronger as well as "kill" any Sebacean parts of his psyche. He is a high-ranking member of Peacekeeper command. The Scarrans believe that he will help them conquer the Peacekeepers. In actuality he is planning to destroy the Scarrans. He is determined to obtain Crichton's wormhole knowledge so that he can create a weapon capable of destroying the Scarrans once and for all.

Lieutenant Braca (Sebacean) — a Peacekeeper serving aboard Scorpius' command carrier, later Grayza's. Braca is seduced by Grayza and appears to do her bidding. However, he is totally and completely Scorpius' ally and all of his actions have been in support of Scorpius' desire to conquer and destroy the Scarrans.

Commandant Mele-On Grayza (Sebacean) — Completely ruthless, she will do anything to further peace with the Scarrans as well as her career. One way in which she accomplishes this is via the secretion of Heppel oil from a gland implanted in her chest. This oil makes her sexually desirable and able to seduce and/or rape anyone she believes will further her cause. She uses the oil on Crichton who is traumatized by the repeated rapes.

Emperor Staleek (Scarran) — determined to dominate the galaxy, Staleek believes that Scorpius is working for him. He will learn how wrong he is, but by then it will be too late.

War Minister Ahkna[2] (Scarran) — also determined that her species will dominate the galaxy. She will do whatever it takes for the Scarrans to accomplish their goals, but she will not stoop so low as Grayza and use her sex as a weapon.

Xhalix Sun (Sebacean) — Aeryn Sun's mother, a Peacekeeper. Xhalix chose to mate with a male of her choosing, named Talyn, as well as deciding to bear a child with this man. The Peacekeepers ordered her to kill either the child or her lover. She chose her lover, but went insane. Eventually Peacekeeper command sends her to capture Aeryn after Aeryn joins forces with Crichton.

Peacekeepers (Sebacean) — a paramilitary police force. Members are either conscripted from the general population or are bred for service. Any planet's governing body may request help from the Peacekeepers (PK); apparently the general population does not have a say in the matter. Peacekeepers may be male or female and they have no conception of Earth's gender stereotyping — PK females are as deadly as PK males. They could be compared to the United Nations peace keeping forces.

Notes

1. Character names and descriptions were taken from the companion volumes to the series in question. See Appendix C for the complete citation for each. The brief descriptions of the characters are my own.

2. *Farscape* is as known for its humor as it is for its spectacular visual effects, puppets and animatronics, production values, and writing and acting. Crichton comments upon how scary Ahkna is in the trilogy "We're So Screwed" (4.19–4.21), and then says it must be her hat (it is rather spectacular). The joke is that Ahkna is played by his real-life wife, Francesca Buller.

Appendix B: Series Episode List[1]

Season One

Number	Title	Writer	Director
1.1	Premiere	Rockne S. O'Bannon	Andrew Prowse
1.2	I, E. T.	Sally Lapiduss	Pino Amenta
1.3	Exodus from Genesis	Ro Hume	Brian Henson
1.4	Throne for a Loss	Richard Manning	Pino Amenta
1.5	Back and Back and Back to the Future	Babs Greyhosky	Rowan Woods
1.6	Thank God It's Friday ... Again	David Wilks	Rowan Woods
1.7	PK Tech Girl	Nan Hagan	Tony Tilse
1.8	That Old Black Magic	Richard Manning	Brendan Maher
1.9	DNA Mad Scientist	Tom Blomquist	Andrew Prowse
1.10	They've Got a Secret	Sally Lapiduss	Ian Watson
1.11	Till the Blood Runs Clear	Doug Heyes, Jr.	Tony Tilse
1.12	Rhapsody in Blue	Teleplay by David Kemper; Story by David Kemper & Ro Hume	Andrew Prowse
1.13	The Flax	Justin Monjo	Peter Andrikidis
1.14	Jeremiah Crichton	Doug Heyes, Jr.	Ian Watson
1.15	Durka Returns	Grant McAloon	Tony Tilse
1.16	A Human Reaction	Justin Monjo	Rowan Woods
1.17	Through the Looking Glass	David Kemper	Ian Watson
1.18	A Bug's Life	Teleplay by Stephen Rae[2]; Story by Doug Heyes, Jr.	Tony Tilse
1.19	Nerve (part 1 of 2)	Richard Manning	Rowan Woods
1.20	The Hidden Memory (part 2 of 2)	Justin Monjo	Ian Watson
1.21	Bone to be Wild	David Kemper & Rockne S. O'Bannon	Andrew Prowse
1.22	Family Ties	Rockne S. O'Bannon & David Kemper	Tony Tilse

Season Two

Number	Title	Writer	Director
2.1	Mind the Baby	Richard Manning	Andrew Prowse
2.2	Vitas Mortis	Grant McAloon	Tony Tilse
2.3	Taking the Stone	Justin Monjo	Rowan Woods
2.4	Crackers Don't Matter	Justin Monjo	Ian Watson
2.5	The Way We Weren't	Naren Shankar	Tony Tilse
2.6	Picture if You Will	Peter Neale	Andrew Prowse
2.7	Home on the Remains	Gabrielle Stanton & Harry Werksman, Jr.	Rowan Woods
2.8	Dream a Little Dream	Steven Rae[2]	Ian Watson
2.9	Out of Their Minds	Michael Cassutt	Ian Watson
2.10	Look at the Princess Part I: A Kiss is but a Kiss	David Kemper	Andrew Prowse & Tilse Tony
2.11	Look at the Princess Part II: I Do, I Think	David Kemper	Andrew Prowse & Tilse Tony
2.12	Look at the Princess Part III: The Maltese Crichton	David Kemper	Andrew Prowse & Tilse Tony
2.13	My Three Crichtons	Teleplay by Grant McAloon; Story by Gabrielle Stanton & Harry Werksman, Jr.	Catherine Millar
2.14	Beware of the Dog	Naren Shankar	Tony Tilse
2.15	Won't Get Fooled Again	Richard Manning	Rowan Woods
2.16	The Locket	Justin Monjo	Ian Watson
2.17	The Ugly Truth	Gabrielle Stanton & Harry Werksman, Jr.	Tony Tilse
2.18	A Clockwork Nebari	Lily Taylor	Rowan Woods
2.19	Liars, Guns and Money Part I: A Not So Simple Plan	Grant McAloon	Andrew Prowse
2.20	Liars, Guns and Money Part II: With Friends Like These...	Naren Shankar	Catherine Millar
2.21	Liars, Guns and Money Part III: Plan B	Justin Monjo	Tony Tilse
2.22	Die Me, Dichotomy	David Kemper	Rowan Woods

Season Three

Number	Title	Writer	Director
3.1	Season of Death	Richard Manning	Ian Watson
3.2	Suns and Lovers	Justin Monjo	Andrew Prowse
3.3	Self-Inflicted Wounds Part I: Could'a, Would'a, Should'a	David Kemper	Tony Tilse
3.4	Self-Inflicted Wounds Part II: Wait for the Wheel	David Kemper	Tony Tilse

Number	Title	Writer	Director
3.5	...Different Destinations	Steve Worland	Peter Andrikidis
3.6	Eat Me	Matt Ford	Ian Watson
3.7	Thanks for Sharing	Clayvon C. Harris	Ian Barry
3.8	Green Eyed Monster	Ben Browder	Tony Tilse
3.9	Losing Time	Justin Monjo	Catherine Millar
3.10	Relativity	Rockne S. O'Bannon	Peter Andrikidis
3.11	Incubator	Richard Manning	Ian Watson
3.12	Meltdown	Matt Ford	Ian Barry
3.13	Scratch 'n' Sniff	Lily Taylor	Tony Tilse
3.14	Infinite Possibilities Part I: Daedalus Demands	Carleton Eastlake	Peter Andrikidis
3.15	Infinite Possibilities Part II: Icarus Abides	Carleton Eastlake	Ian Watson
3.16	Revenging Angel	David Kemper	Andrew Prowse
3.17	The Choice	Justin Monjo	Rowan Woods
3.18	Fractures	Rockne S. O'Bannon	Tony Tilse
3.19	I-Yensch, You-Yensch	Matt Ford	Peter Andrikidis
3.20	Into the Lion's Den Part I: Lambs to the Slaughter	Richard Manning	Ian Watson
3.21	Into the Lion's Den Part II: Wolf in Sheep's Clothing	Rockne S. O'Bannon	Rowan Woods
3.22	Dog with Two Bones	David Kemper	Andrew Prowse

Season Four

Number	Title	Writer	Director
4.1	Crichton Kicks	David Kemper	Andrew Prowse
4.2	What was Lost Part I: Sacrifice	Justin Monjo	Rowan Woods
4.3	What was Lost Part II: Resurrection	Justin Monjo	Rowan Woods
4.4	Lava's a Many Splendored Thing	Michael Miller	Michael Pattinson
4.5	Promises	Ricky Manning	Geoff Bennett
4.6	Natural Election	Sophie C. Hopkins	Ian Watson
4.7	John Quixote	Ben Browder	Tony Tilse
4.8	I Shrink Therefore I Am	Christopher Wheeler	Rowan Woods
4.9	A Perfect Murder	Mark Saraceni	Geoff Bennett
4.10	Coup by Clam	Emily Skopov	Ian Watson
4.11	Unrealized Reality	David Kemper	Andrew Prowse
4.12	Kansas	Justin Monjo	Rowan Woods
4.13	Terra Firma	Richard Manning	Peter Andrikidis
4.14	Twice Shy	David Peckinpah	Kate Woods
4.15	Mental as Anything	Mark Saraceni	Geoff Bennett
4.16	Bringing Home the Beacon	Carleton Eastlake	Rowan Woods
4.17	A Constellation of Doubt	David Kemper	Andrew Prowse
4.18	Prayer	Justin Monjo	Peter Andrikidis

Number	Title	Writer	Director
4.19	We're So Screwed Part I: Fetal Attraction	David Peckinpah	Geoff Bennett
4.20	We're So Screwed Part II: Hot to Katratzi	Carleton Eastlake	Karl Zwicky
4.21	We're So Screwed Part III: "La Bomba"	Mark Saraceni	Rowan Woods
4.22	Bad Timing	David Kemper	Andrew Prowse

Notes

1. The episodes listed herein are the episodes that were filmed and/or broadcast for each of the four seasons discussed in this book. I have not included the air dates for the various episodes as these dates are readily available from a variety of sources. I have listed the episodes in the order in which they are indicated in the companion guides for each season as well as on their respective DVD, verifying each against the other. All four seasons of *Farscape* as well as *The Peacekeeper War* are available for purchase from the usual sources. However, as I discovered while editing this collection, my earlier boxed sets did not contain all of the Special Features available on boxed sets with later copyright dates (drat!). Each of the companion guides also provides a synopsis of the plot for each episode. Episodes are not numbered in the guides, which can be confusing, but they are presented in order.

2. Pseudonym of Rockne S. O'Bannon and used more extensively (and with tongue firmly in cheek) in his short-lived series *Cult* (The CW, 2013).

Appendix C: *Farscape* Bibliography and Filmography[1]

Bischoff, David. *Farscape Ship of Ghosts*. New York: Tom Doherty Associates, 2001. Print.

DeCandido, Keith R. *Farscape House of Cards*. New York: Tom Doherty Associates, 2000. Print.

DeCandido, Keith R. A. (Story) and Caleb Cleveland (Artist). *Farscape Uncharted Tales: D'Argo's Quest*. Los Angeles: BOOM! Studios, 2011. Print.

DeCandido, Keith R. A. (Writer) and Neil Edwards (Penciler). *Farscape Uncharted Tales: D'Argo's Lament*. Los Angeles: BOOM! Studios, 2009. Print.

Dymond, Andrew. *Farscape Dark Side of the Sun*. New York: Tom Doherty Associates, 2000. Print.

Farscape Season Two. The Jim Henson Company, 2003. DVD.

Farscape: The Complete Fourth Season. The Jim Henson Company, 2004. DVD.

Farscape: The Complete Third Season. The Jim Henson Company, 2004. DVD.

Farscape: The Complete Season Four. The Jim Henson Company, 1999–2009. DVD.

Farscape: The Complete Season One. The Jim Henson Company, 1999–2009. DVD.

Farscape: The Complete Season Three. The Jim Henson Company, 1999–2009. DVD.

Farscape: The Complete Season Two. The Jim Henson Company, 1999–2009. DVD.

Farscape: The Peacekeeper Wars. Dir. Brian Henson. Perf. Ben Browder, Claudia Black. Hallmark Entertainment and The Jim Henson Company, 2004. DVD.

O'Bannon, Rockne S., and Keith R. A. DeCandido (Story and Script), and Will Sliney (Art). *Farscape The War for the Uncharted Territories Part I*. Los Angeles: BOOM! Studios, 2012. Print.

O'Bannon, Rockne S. (Story), David Alan Mack (Script), and Gordon Purcell (Artist). *Farscape Scorpius Vol. 2: Glorious Basterds*. Los Angeles: BOOM! Studios, 2011. Print.

O'Bannon, Rockne S. (Story), David Alan Mack (Script), and Mike Ruiz (Artist). *Farscape Scorpius Vol. 1: Let Sleeping Dogs Lie*. Los Angeles: BOOM! Studios, 2010. Print.

O'Bannon, Rockne S. (Story), Keith R. A. DeCandido (Script), and Tommy Patterson (Penciler). *Farscape The Beginning of the End of the Beginning.* Los Angeles: BOOM! Studios, 2009. Print.

O'Bannon, Rockne S. (Story), Keith R. A. DeCandido (Script), and Tommy Patterson (Penciller [sic]). *Farscape Gone and Back.* Los Angeles: BOOM! Studios, 2009. Print.

O'Bannon, Rockne S. (Story), Keith R. A. DeCandido (Script), and Will Sliney (Art). *Farscape Compulsions.* Los Angeles: BOOM! Studios, 2011. Print.

O'Bannon, Rockne S. (Story), Keith R. A. DeCandido (Script), and Will Sliney (Art). *Farscape Red Sky at Morning.* Los Angeles: BOOM! Studios, 2011. Print.

O'Bannon, Rockne S. (Story), Keith R. A. DeCandido (Script), and Will Sliney (Art). *Farscape Tangled Roots.* Los Angeles: BOOM! Studios, 2011. Print.

O'Bannon, Rockne S. (Story), Keith R. A. DeCandido (Script), and Will Sliney (Artist). *Farscape Strange Detractors.* Los Angeles: BOOM! Studios, 2009. Print.

Notes

1. This list contains the novels and graphic novels that I have been able to find that feature Moya, her crewmembers, and other characters from the *Farscape* universe. I have read all of them. I wish there were more. I have included information for the two different sets of DVDs that I purchased for the series. As I mentioned in Appendix B, I discovered that the later collections contain more commentaries on the series' episodes than the earlier ones. However, the earlier ones have some Special Features that the later ones do not, such as information on costuming, creatures, and more.

About the Contributors

Jessie **Carty**, freelance editor, writer and writing coach and teacher, received an MFA from Queens University in Charlotte and is the founder of the literary periodical *Referential Magazine*. Her poetry, fiction, and non-fiction have appeared in publications such as *Iodine Poetry Journal, decomP* and *Connotation Press*. She is the author of five collections of poetry. Her first full length collection, *Paper House* (Folded Word, 2010), won the 2010 North Carolina Poetry Away award.

Tanya R. **Cochran** earned a doctorate in rhetoric and composition from Georgia State University and is an associate professor of English at Union College in Lincoln, Nebraska. In addition to directing Union's first-year composition program and writing center, she teaches writing, rhetoric, and research methods. Her essays have appeared in several books including *Investigating Veronica Mars* (McFarland, 2011) and *Investigating Firefly and Serenity* (I.B. Tauris, 2008), co-edited with Rhonda V. Wilcox.

Michael G. **Cornelius** is the author or editor of 15 books, most recently including *The Sex Is Out of This World: Essays on the Carnal Side of Science Fiction* (with co-editor Sherry Ginn; McFarland, 2012). An award-winning novelist, he is the chair of the Department of English and Mass Communications at Wilson College in Chambersburg, Pennsylvania.

Sherry **Ginn** earned an MA and a PhD in general-experimental psychology from the University of South Carolina. Author of numerous research articles in neuroscience and psychology, she also writes about the intersection of popular culture with those fields. Her books, *Power and Control in the Television Worlds of Joss Whedon* and *The Sex Is Out of This World: Essays on the Carnal Side of Science Fiction*, (co-edited with Michael G. Cornelius) were published by McFarland in 2012.

Ensley F. **Guffey** earned a BA from the University of North Carolina at Greensboro and expects to receive an MA in American history from East Tennessee State University in 2014. His academic writing focuses on the intersections of military history, memory, and popular culture in genre television. He has published essays on *Buffy the Vampire Slayer*, Marvel's *The Avengers*, and *Breaking Bad* and is co-author with K. Dale Koontz of the book *Wanna Cook? The Unofficial Companion Guide to Breaking Bad* (forthcoming).

Robert L. **Lively** teaches composition, literature and film at Mesa (Arizona) Community College. His works include "We Must Go Fully Armed to Court: The Viking Forensic Tradition" (in *Rhetoric in the Rest of the West*, edited by Shane Borrowman, Robert L. Lively and Marcia Kmetz, Cambridge Scholars, 2010) and "Disciplining Technology: A Selective Annotated Bibliography" with Marcia Kmetz, Crystal Broch-Colombini, and Thomas Black (in *On the Blunt Edge: Technology in Composition's History and Pedagogy*, edited by Shane Borrowman, Parlor Press, 2011).

Billie Jo **Mason** earned an MA in mass communications from California State University, Northridge, and an MFA in creative writing and writing for the performing arts from the University of California, Riverside. She is a freelance writer for a Los Angeles–based production company and has worked as a story analyst at the William Morris Talent Agency as well as a union story analyst at several film studios. In addition, she spent several years working in the story department of Hollywood Pictures and MGM.

Elizabeth Leigh **Scherman** holds a PhD in communication from the University of Washington. She is a member of the senior tenured faculty in communication at Bates Technical College in Tacoma, and lectures at the University of Washington, Tacoma. Her research focuses on representations of identity in children's cinema. Her work has appeared in journals and edited collections, including *Disability Studies Quarterly*, *The Galaxy Is Rated G: Essays on Children's Science Fiction Film and Television* (edited by R.C. Neighbors and Sandy Rankin, McFarland, 2011), and a forthcoming collection on the films of Tim Burton.

J. P. **Telotte** is a professor of film and media studies and former chair of the School of Literature, Media, and Communication at Georgia Tech. Author of more than 100 scholarly articles on film, television, and literature and co-editor of the journal *Post Script*, he has published 11 books, including *Science Fiction Film, Television, and Adaptation: Across the Screens* (Routledge, 2012).

Index

Ahkna, War Minister 28, 32, 43, 51, 52, 53, 86, 112, 113, 193, 194n2
alien 2, 3, 5, 6, 7, 11, 12, 13, 14, 15, 19, 20, 20n4, 24, 25, 26, 40, 43, 55, 59, 64, 65, 66, 77, 81, 85, 88, 90n3, 93, 98, 106, 107, 108, 117, 120n2, 130, 131, 133, 143, 144, 152, 153, 154, 166, 172, 175, 186, 188
Ancients 6, 17, 49, 50, 191
animatronic(s) 3, 40, 172, 194n2
antihero 61, 63, 66, 67, 71, 72
anus 56, 57, 58
Aristotle 41, 42
astronaut 2, 3, 4, 11, 14, 17, 18, 23, 43, 55, 56, 61, 62, 63, 64, 66, 127, 142, 144, 186, 187, 188
Aughra 146, 149, 157n6
Australia 1, 2, 8n1, 23, 25, 26, 175, 177

Babylon 5 3, 107, 117, 161, 186
"bad crip" 147, 150
Baggins, Frodo 127
Bakhtin, Mikhail 57
Banik 80
Battis, Jes 2, 3, 7, 8, 9n5, 11, 14, 18, 23, 24, 40, 81, 123, 130, 131, 132, 133, 138, 139, 143, 144, 147, 152, 153, 172
bioloid 87, 111, 192
biomechanoid 4, 123, 129, 138, 140n3, 172
Bishon 56
Black, Claudia 1, 45, 88, 117, 119, 120n15, 160, 162
blindness 144, 145, 149, 150, 152, 158n8
Booker, M. Keith 2, 16, 186, 188
BraScape 175, 176, 178
Brave New World 153
Breakaway Colonies 27
Brothers Grimm 148
Browder, Ben 1, 2, 8, 8n2, 40, 88, 92, 93, 94, 95, 96, 97, 98, 99, 100, 101, 102, 102–103n6, 114, 119, 160, 162, 162n1, 163n2, 166, 168, 173, 174, 178, 179
budong 94, 95, 96
Buffy the Vampire Slayer 16, 107, 164, 180, 201
Buss, David 74, 77, 78
Butler, Octavia 90n3, 106

Cagney & Lacey 173, 174
Campbell, Joseph 4, 8, 61, 62, 73, 170
carnival (culture) 57
Carter, Chris 119
Charto, Jenavian (Jena) 84, 160, 162n1
Chiana 8, 13, 14, 43, 44, 46, 55, 56, 59, 64, 66, 67, 68, 69, 78, 81, 82, 83, 84, 85, 87, 90n4, 90n5, 98, 99, 100, 104, 109, 110, 111, 113, 116, 119, 120n4, 120n5, 146, 147, 152, 153, 155, 161, 163n1, 188, 191, 192
Christianity 41, 67
Clavor, Prince 84, 160
Cold War 7, 22, 23, 24, 25, 26, 29, 30, 31, 32, 33, 34, 35, 37n9, 108
colonic miasma 59
Commandant Cleavage (plus, see Grayza) 86, 112
control collar 4, 24, 113, 140n3
Crais, Captain Bialar 4, 5, 8, 18, 46, 47, 65, 66, 67, 69, 70, 71, 72, 73, 80, 94, 95, 96, 98, 101, 115, 116, 161, 162, 193
Crichton-Black 98, 102n4, 117, 161
Crichton, caveman 44, 45
Crichton, D'Argo Sun 47
Crichton, evolved/future 15, 44, 45
Crichton-Green 117, 118
Crichton, Jack 18, 23, 64, 127, 128
Crichton, John 1, 2, 3, 4, 5, 6, 7, 8, 11, 12, 13, 14, 15, 16, 17, 18, 19, 20, 20n4, 23, 24, 26, 27, 31, 32, 33, 34, 35, 36, 37, 40, 43, 44, 45, 46, 47 48, 49, 50, 51, 52, 53, 54n4, 55, 56, 61, 62, 63, 64, 65, 66, 67,

68, 69, 70, 71, 72, 73, 78, 79, 80, 81, 82, 83, 84, 85, 86, 88, 89, 90n4, 90n5, 90n6, 90n10, 92, 93, 94, 95, 96, 97, 98, 99, 100, 101, 102, 102n4, 109, 110, 111, 112, 113, 114, 115, 116, 117, 118, 119, 120n11, 120n14, 123, 124, 127, 128, 129, 142, 144, 146, 147, 148, 149, 150, 151, 152, 153, 154, 155, 157n2, 160, 161, 162, 162–163n1, 163n2, 164, 166, 186, 187, 188, 189, 191, 192, 193, 195, 196, 197
Crichton, Neural 48
Crystherium utilia 28, 29, 35
cult 7, 11, 12, 13, 14, 15, 16, 17, 19, 20, 20n2, 20n3, 172, 173, 175, 177, 181n4

D'Argo, Ka 2, 4, 13, 14, 15, 27, 36, 40, 43, 45, 47, 55, 64, 65, 66, 68, 69, 70, 78, 80, 81, 82, 83, 84, 85, 87, 88, 90n4, 110, 111, 112, 124, 129, 142, 147, 149, 152, 153, 157n1, 188, 191, 192
The Dark Crystal 146, 149
Darwin, Charles 77
Data, Lt. Commander 3, 135, 136, 139, 192
Delvia(n) 4, 15, 40, 79, 80, 114, 139n1, 142, 160, 191
Designing Women 173, 174
disability 8, 143, 144, 145, 147, 148, 151
discrimination 27, 88, 142, 144, 145
disenfranchisement 55, 56, 58, 129, 139n1
DK 64, 88
Don Quixote (name) 98, 99, 102–103n6
Dr. Strangelove 16, 31, 32
Dragon*Con 7, 90n6, 109
DRDs 47, 93, 94, 151
Dregon 84
Durka, Captain 64, 81, 113, 157n5, 157n6, 195

Earth (planet name) 2, 4, 6, 7, 14, 16, 18, 19, 23, 24, 30, 31, 33, 34, 37, 37n1, 37n3, 37n6, 43, 44, 51, 64, 66, 70, 90n4, 90n5, 100, 107, 111, 115, 128, 142, 148, 160, 166, 186, 187, 188, 191, 192, 193
Eidelons 24, 25, 32, 36, 78, 150
E.T. 16, 154
event horizon 36, 53
Evil Empire 31, 51
evolution 8, 16, 44, 61, 70, 71, 72, 74, 77, 78, 83, 85, 88, 89
excrement 58, 59

family 5, 6, 19, 23, 36, 43, 54n4, 56, 59, 74, 75, 101, 102, 110, 115, 128, 129, 130, 132, 133, 134, 188, 195

fan 1, 7, 88, 92, 97, 102, 102n1, 106, 108, 109, 154, 161, 162n1, 164, 168, 169, 171, 172, 173, 174, 175, 176, 177, 178, 179, 180, 181, 181n4, 189
fandom 168, 169, 171, 172, 173, 175, 177, 179, 181
Farscape Mission 160, 187
Farscape 1 (ship) 4, 64, 93, 127
Farscape Project 18, 19
fart 8, 55, 56, 57, 58, 59, 154
father 5, 18, 19, 41, 43, 64, 77, 78, 85, 88, 90n6, 90n9, 95, 115, 127, 128, 132, 138, 154, 160, 162, 186, 192
Firefly 164, 175, 181n4, 201
flatulence 56, 59
Foucault, Michel 124
Frankenstein 104
free will 41, 42

Gagarin, Yuri 16, 23, 37n1
gammak base 5
Gawain (name) 126, 127, 128
genocide 25, 27
Gilliam, Terry 102n6
Ginn, Sherry 53n2, 128, 201
"good crip" 147
Grayza, Commandant Mele-On 25, 27, 29, 32, 37, 72, 86, 90n6, 104, 111, 112, 113, 120n4, 157n2, 160, 193

Hallmark Entertainment 1
Halosian 14
Hammer, Bonnie 172, 176
Harvey 16, 28, 31, 66
Headroom, John 99
Headroom, Max 98, 100
Henson, Brian 3, 4, 9n3, 11, 24, 178, 185
Heppel oil 86, 112, 193
hero 4, 8, 12, 13, 19, 43, 44, 53n1, 61, 62, 63
heterosexual 2, 76, 87, 119, 153, 181n1
Hitler, Adolf 68
home 2, 5, 6, 8, 12, 13, 14, 17, 18, 19, 24, 32, 44, 55, 63, 66, 70, 74, 80, 81, 93, 101, 102, 109, 111, 123, 124, 125, 126, 127, 128, 129, 130, 132, 133, 136, 137, 138, 139, 164, 166, 172, 176, 177, 179, 186, 187, 188, 191, 192,
homeland 130, 138
homeplace 124, 125, 126, 127, 129, 130, 131, 132, 133, 134, 137, 138, 139, 140n3
homosexual 76, 90n4, 107
humanoid 3, 25

IASA 111, 166, 186, 191

identity 7, 14, 41, 42, 43, 45, 50, 53, 55, 58, 78, 108, 115, 123, 125, 126, 127, 128, 129, 130, 131, 132, 134, 137, 138, 139, 143, 166, 170, 171, 173, 180, 202
impairment 143, 144, 154, 155
Interion 14, 192
Internet 168, 174, 175, 177

The Jim Henson Company 2, 176, 178
Jim Henson Productions 1, 177
Jim Henson's Creature Shop 13, 40
Jonah (and the whale) 94, 97, 192
Jool 8, 14, 32, 82, 83, 98, 104, 109, 110, 111, 112, 119, 120n5, 192
Jothee 83, 88, 192
Judeo-Christian 41
Jung, C.G.G. 49, 50, 119n1

Kaarvok 45, 66, 67
Kant, Immanuel 42
Katralla, Princess 83, 84, 89, 90n10, 163n1
Katratzi 29, 32, 35, 52
Kemper, David 4, 7, 9n6, 116, 119, 120n12, 120n17, 160, 162, 168, 172, 173, 174, 178, 179
KGB 27, 28
kink(y) 76, 87, 90n8
Kirk, James T. 160

Land of the Lost 51, 54n4
Lavigne, Carlen 5, 118, 123, 128, 130, 132, 138
Lévi-Strauss, Claude 63, 64
Leviathan 4, 5, 24, 29, 40, 64, 68, 69, 79, 80, 90n9, 93, 95, 96, 111, 114, 123, 140n3, 152, 162, 192
The Lord of the Rings 53n1, 126
Luxan 2, 4, 24, 25, 40, 52, 83, 86, 166n1, 191, 192

mind control 113
monarch 129
monomyth 62, 64, 171, 182n2
Moonlighting 161
Moral Tradition 41, 42
Mother 5, 6, 29, 46, 47, 48, 55, 79, 82, 85, 87, 92, 95, 104, 105, 115, 118, 131, 132, 133, 134, 138, 188, 193
Moya 2, 4, 5, 6, 8, 13, 14, 15, 16, 20, 20n4, 24, 27, 36, 40, 43, 44, 45, 46, 47, 55, 56, 58, 59, 64, 65, 67, 68, 69, 70, 71, 79, 80, 81, 82, 83, 88, 90n9, 93, 94, 96, 98, 99, 100, 104, 109, 110, 111, 112, 113, 114, 115, 116, 117, 118, 119, 123, 124, 125, 128, 129, 130, 132, 133, 134, 137, 138, 139, 140n2, 140n3, 142, 143, 144, 145, 146, 147, 148, 149, 150, 151, 152, 153, 154, 155, 158n8, 161, 162, 172, 187, 188, 191, 192, 200n1
Mulder, Fox 117, 119, 161, 175
Muppets 2, 3, 16
myth 1, 8, 61, 62, 63, 64, 65, 67, 70, 73, 125, 126, 146, 169, 170, 171, 173, 174, 177, 179, 180, 181, 181n1
mythic quest 61, 64, 73

Natira 87
Nazi 24, 25, 45
Nebari 81, 113, 164, 191
neural chip 48, 50
neural clone 48, 49, 50, 51
Nilaam 87
Noranti 8, 86, 100, 101, 104, 110, 111, 112, 119, 146, 147, 149, 150, 152, 157n1, 157n2, 192
nuclear arms race 31

O'Bannon, Rockne S. 4, 8n1, 11, 23, 40, 74, 82, 102, 120n5, 120n11, 185
Offspring 4, 71, 77, 78, 85, 88, 93, 131, 138, 192
The Outer Limits 186

Panza, Sancho 98
parent (n) 72, 89, 115, 132, 193
patriarchal 108, 131, 181n1
Pa'u (priest) 4, 40, 79, 114, 191
Peacekeeper 4, 5, 6, 7, 13, 15, 16, 17, 18, 20, 23, 24, 25, 26, 27, 29, 30, 31, 32, 33, 34, 36, 37, 40, 45, 46, 47, 48, 49, 52, 55, 64, 65, 66, 67, 68, 69, 70, 71, 73n1, 78, 79, 81, 83, 84, 85, 86, 89, 91n4, 90n9, 94, 95, 96, 97, 98, 112, 113, 114, 115, 116, 117, 118, 119, 128, 129, 139, 153, 157n5, 161, 163n3, 191, 192, 193
Peacekeeper High Command 29, 30, 32, 116, 191
The Peacekeeper Wars 1, 16, 19, 24, 31, 32, 35, 40, 43, 47, 51, 53, 78, 79, 84, 88, 89, 90n6, 101, 150, 161, 168, 177, 178, 179, 180, 188
photogasms 80, 87
Pilot (character) 3, 5, 13, 14, 16, 64, 69, 70, 90n9, 116, 132, 134, 138, 151, 152, 192
pilot (species) 4, 46, 67, 68, 69, 70, 116, 137, 192
popular culture 2, 3, 16, 22, 57, 103n6, 124, 164, 165, 201

pregnancy 5, 78, 79, 90*n*9, 110, 131
prejudice 25, 88
prowler (n) 4, 47, 66, 69, 85, 116, 162, 191
pulse pistol 164, 166
Python, Monty 98, 103*n*6

Qujaga 32, 37, 150

racism 25, 108, 172
Roddenberry, Gene 3, 106, 107
Roswell 173, 174, 175
Rousseau, Jean-Jacques 41
royal 8, 27, 56, 59, 83, 84, 85, 89, 116
Rygel XVI, Dominar 2, 3, 4, 8, 13, 14, 15, 16, 40, 55, 56, 57, 58, 59, 64, 68, 69, 81, 83, 87, 94, 95, 96, 99, 113, 116, 129, 146, 188, 192

Sargent, Pamela 105, 108, 109, 120*n*3
Saturn awards 1, 180
Scapers 1, 7, 8, 109, 168, 169, 171, 172, 173, 174, 176, 177, 178, 179, 180, 181
Scarran 3, 4, 6, 7, 14, 17, 23, 24, 26, 27, 28, 29, 30, 31, 32, 33, 34, 36, 37, 40, 43, 47, 48, 49, 50, 51, 52, 53, 54*n*4, 66, 72, 83, 84, 86, 87, 90*n*6, 111, 112, 113, 115, 118, 148, 155, 191, 193
Scarran Imperium 23, 27, 28, 29
Scorpius 4, 5, 6, 7, 8, 14, 16, 17, 25, 27, 28, 29, 30, 31, 32, 43, 47, 48, 49, 50, 51, 52, 53, 54*n*3, 66, 71, 72, 78, 80, 83, 84, 86, 87, 90*n*7, 98, 110, 112, 117, 118, 148, 151, 155, 192, 193
Scully, Dana 117, 119, 161
SDI 31, 37*n*5
Sebacean 4, 6, 14, 19, 24, 25, 29, 43, 45, 47, 48, 49, 68, 78, 83, 85, 86, 87, 89, 94, 102*n*5, 114, 155, 161, 188, 191, 192, 193
Sebacean-Scarran hybrid 4, 14, 47, 193
sentience 134, 135, 136, 137, 138, 139
shadow 49, 50, 51
Shakespeare, William 56
Shelley, Mary 104, 105
Sikozu 8, 82, 87, 104, 111, 112, 119, 192
Sir Gawain and the Green Knight 126
Soviet Union 7, 22, 23, 26, 28, 29, 30, 31, 33
space opera 13, 20*n*1, 177
space race 23, 105
spacebound 130
spacecraft 93, 131
Spock 3
Staleek, Emperor 28, 30, 37, 43, 51, 52, 53, 54*n*4, 193

Star Trek 2, 3, 13, 16, 106, 108, 153, 172, 173, 186
Star Trek: The Next Generation 3, 134, 192
starburst 4, 72, 162, 191
Stargate SG1 2
Stark 36, 80, 94, 95, 96, 100, 114, 149, 150, 152
Sternberg, Robert J. 74, 75, 76, 78, 82, 88, 89, 89*n*2
Subdivision 185
Sun, Aeryn 4, 5, 6, 8, 13, 14, 16, 17, 19, 20, 25, 32, 35, 36, 40, 43, 44, 45, 46, 47, 53, 53*n*2, 55, 56, 64, 65, 66, 67, 68, 69, 70, 72, 78, 79, 80, 82, 83, 84, 85, 87, 88, 89, 90*n*6, 90*n*9, 94, 95, 96, 97, 98, 99, 100, 101, 104, 110, 111, 112, 114, 115, 116, 117, 118, 119, 120*n*5, 120*n*11, 120*n*14, 123, 124, 129, 148, 153, 160, 161, 162, 162–163*n*1, 163*n*3, 188, 191, 193
Sun, Xhalix 115
Syfy Channel 1, 8*n*2, 9*n*3, 102*n*3, 134, 172, 173, 175, 176, 177, 178, 179, 181*n*3

Talyn 4, 5, 45, 71, 72, 90*n*9, 93, 94, 95, 96, 98, 101, 102*n*4, 192, 193
Tar, Lo'Laan 83
Tar, Macton 86
Tauza 48, 51
Temple of Arnessk 32
third eye 110, 149, 150
Tormented Space 7, 32
Traltixx 8, 142, 149, 150, 151, 152, 153, 154, 155
translator microbes 6, 16, 188
Trekker 173, 174, 176, 178, 181
Triangular Theory of Love 8, 74, 89
Trimble, Bjo 173, 176, 178
TV Guide 1, 13, 20*n*2
The Twilight Zone 186
Tyno, Councilor 83, 84, 90*n*10

Uncharted Territories 4, 6, 7, 12, 13, 14, 17, 18, 20, 24, 27, 43, 52, 61, 64, 66, 73, 76, 93, 94, 112, 186, 187
Unity 80, 114
USSR 7, 24, 25, 28, 34

vanilla sex 76
Velorek 46, 47, 68, 69, 70, 78, 79, 85, 87, 116, 161, 162
Veronica Mars 175, 201
villain 8, 61, 63, 66, 67, 71, 72, 87, 112
voice-over 8, 64, 66, 186, 187, 188

warrior 4, 16, 29, 40, 55, 56, 82, 83, 101, 129, 179, 191
Whedon, Joss 74, 89, 164, 175, 201
Winona 94, 164, 166
Wisdom Tradition 7, 41, 42, 43, 48, 53
The Wizard of Oz 16, 124
Wormhole 2, 4, 6, 7, 11, 12, 17, 18, 23, 25, 29, 30, 31, 32, 33, 34, 36, 37, 40, 43, 47, 48, 49, 50, 51, 52, 53, 54n4, 61, 63, 64, 65, 66, 71, 72, 80, 83, 84, 86, 90n6, 100, 113, 115, 118, 128, 162, 186, 187, 188, 191, 193
wormhole device 40, 43, 47, 48, 50

wormhole weapon 29, 30, 31, 32, 33, 36, 37, 48, 49, 50, 84

The X-Files 117, 175

Yoda 146, 151

Zhaan, Pa'u Zotoh 2, 4, 8, 15, 40, 41, 44, 55, 64, 68, 69, 70, 78, 79, 80, 82, 83, 87, 99, 100, 101, 104, 110, 114, 117, 119, 120n4, 120n5, 120n9, 129, 139n1, 142, 147, 152, 191, 192

www.ingramcontent.com/pod-product-compliance
Ingram Content Group UK Ltd.
Pitfield, Milton Keynes, MK11 3LW, UK
UKHW042000140426
5217IPUK00015B/900